Moral Life

VALUES AND PHILOSOPHICAL INQUIRY

General Editor: D. Z. Phillips

Also in this series

ATHEISM AND THE REJECTION OF GOD
Stewart R. Sutherland

RIGHTS AND PERSONS
A. I. Melden

Moral Life

RODGER BEEHLER

Basil Blackwell · Oxford

British Library Cataloguing in Publication Data

Beehler, Rodger
    Moral life. – (Values and philosophical inquiry)
    1. Ethics
    I. Title   II. Series
    170   BJ1012
   ISBN 0–631–19020–1

Phototypeset in V.I.P. Bembo by
Western Printing Services Ltd, Bristol
Printed in Great Britain by
Billing and Sons Ltd,
London, Guildford and Worcester

FOR
MY MOTHER
AND
FATHER

Contents

Acknowledgments

Work by others helped me to see the need for this essay. Two writers who contributed greatly to this recognition are Iris Murdoch and Peter Winch. I have also learned from D. Z. Phillips and H. O. Mounce.

The idea which informs the essay first came to me in the autumn of 1971. A first attempt at an argument was written hurriedly in the summer and fall of the following year, and after put away. I have in the last eighteen months added chapters two, three, nine, the greater part of chapter one, and the introduction; and extensively recast the rest. But the first manuscript was read at the time by several people whom I should like to thank. Kai Nielsen followed that first writing with unflagging disagreement and unfailing patience. Brian Grant, H. J. N. Horsburgh, Plato Mamo, J. J. McIntosh, D. H. Monro, H. O. Mounce, and D. Z. Phillips read the early version, and gave me the benefit of their criticisms, which I have tried to meet. I wish to thank all of these people for their good will to me. This expression of thanks will not, I hope, be taken to suggest their agreement with any of what follows.

A part of the recasting of the essay took place in conditions under which, were it not for Mardelle Behnsen, it could never have been accomplished. Siania Beehler read the earliest of the newly added pages as they were written, and encouraged me to think them worth the travail. Support of this last kind was also given, in a less immediate way, by H. J. N. Horsburgh, who together with my wife, for five years sustained me in the belief that I had something to offer of value. Catherine Classen made the work lighter in the final weeks of writing through her friendship and regard. I am glad to be able to express my gratitude to these four for these, and greater, kind-nesses.

The Pacific coast   R. B.
Early summer 1977

I wish to acknowledge permission to reproduce material from the follow-ing works: Basil Blackwell Ltd., for Kai Nielson, 'On Moral Truth', APQ Monograph 1 1968, and John Plamenatz, *The English Utilitarians*; Cam-bridge University Press, for D. H. Monro, *Empiricism and Ethics*; Grove Press Inc., for Hubert Selby, *Last Exit to Brooklyn*; Harper & Row, Inc., for Soren Kierkegaard, *Purity of Heart*, James Rachels, 'Egoism and Moral Scepticism' (from Stephen M. Cahn ©, a *New Introduction to Philosophy*), and Kai Nielsen, *Reason and Practice*; Hutchinson Publishing Group Limited, for *The Moral Law: Kant's Groundwork of the Metaphysic of Morals*, translated by H. J. Paton; Methuen & Company Ltd., for G. J. Warnock, *The Object of Morality*; Penguin Books Ltd., for Fyodor Dostoyevsky, *The Idiot*, trans-lated by David Magarshack, © David Magarshack; Random House, Inc., for Loren Eiseley, *The Immense Journey*, © Loren Eiseley; Routledge & Kegan Paul Ltd., for Josephine Klein, *Samples of English Cultures*, and D. Z. Phillips and H. O. Mounce, *Moral Practices*; Simon and Schuster Ltd., for Jean-Jacques Rousseau, *Discourse on the Origin of Inequality*, translated by Lester G. Crocker.

Note to the Reader

In this book themes introduced in one chapter reappear in others, and things said in one place sometimes bear importantly on issues treated at a later (or earlier) stage of the discussion. Thus the consideration of egoism in chapter two finds support from a further discussion in chapter five; and ·the relation of moral judgments to social agreement, first encountered in the introduction, is engaged with at length in chapters one *and* three. In one or two places where it has seemed important or helpful to do so I have signalled if the issue under consideration is returned to at some other moment of the essay. But ordinarily I have not done this, since at every point the particular discussion mounted is complete and self-contained.

I would *like* to think that what explains this recurring/interlocking pattern is: '. . . the very nature of the investigation. For this compels us to travel over a wide field of thought criss-cross in every direction.—'[1]

NOTES

[1] Ludwig Wittgenstein, *Philosophical Investigations* (Oxford: Blackwell, 1968) p. ix. (Transl.: G. E. M. Anscombe.)

How will you know the pitch of that great bell
Too large for you to stir? Let but a flute
Play 'neath the fine-mixed metal: listen close
Till the right note flows forth, a silvery rill:
Then shall the huge bell tremble—then the mass
With myriad waves concurrent shall respond
In low soft unison.

GEORGE ELIOT

. . . yet one can write only one word at a time, and if these seem
lists and inventories merely, things dead unto themselves, devoid
of mutual magnetisms, and if they sink, lose impetus, meter,
intension, then bear in mind at least my wish, and perceive in
them and restore them what strength you can of yourself: for I
must say to you, this is not a work of art or of entertainment, nor
will I assume the obligations of the artists or entertainer, but is a
human effort which must require human co-operation.

JAMES AGEE

Introduction

What has to be accepted, the given, is—so one could say—forms of life.

WITTGENSTEIN

In this essay I shall seek to establish that if human beings did not care about one another there could not be what we speak of as morality, for the reason that morality is a manifestation of that caring. This will lead me to oppose a number of contemporary theses concerning morality, of which one is that the peculiar force which moral statements have derives from social agreement, and another is that there are no limits to what may be considered a moral point of view. But older ideas, such as that moral understanding is something which persons can be taught to possess, will also be examined, including the perennial view that there are moral truths. I shall seek to show that the belief, which many philosophers profess, that we can give people a reason to live rightly must be adjudged mistaken; as must the claim that morality is a system of social control. At the end I shall take up briefly the relation of God to human morality, and the seeming exclusion from moral concern of the non-human animal world.

I shall begin by considering a recent disagreement in moral philosophy, which may form the point of departure for my own remarks. The disagreement I refer to concerns the relation of statements of fact to statements expressing moral evaluation.

I

David Hume once observed that in every system of morality he had met with, the author passed unannounced from sentences formed by expressions joined by an 'is' or an 'is not', to sentences formed by expressions joined by an 'ought' or 'ought not', without explaining the transition. Yet this transition, Hume remarked, is "of the last consequence".

For as this *ought*, or *ought not*, expresses some new relation or affirmation, it is necessary that it should be observed and explained; and at the same time, that a reason should be given, for what seems altogether inconceivable, how this new relation can be a deduction from others, which are entirely different from it.[1]

In brief, how solely from the fact that certain states of affairs, or relations, obtain can one conclude that persons ought, or ought not, to act in certain ways? How from the fact that a cyclist has been struck by a car and lies writhing on the road, or the fact that my being without money may have the consequence that I starve, can anyone conclude that somebody ought, or ought not, to do anything?

Contemporary moral philosophy has for a generation consisted in the taking of positions respecting this question. One group of writers affirm that it is not possible to deduce from the facts of a situation any conclusion of a moral kind; whenever such a deduction appears to have been accomplished it is only because a prescriptive, non-factual premise has covertly been appealed to. A second group of writers argue that unless evaluative conclusions can be licensed from factual premises there is no avoiding the judgment that morality is not an affair of reason; moral discourse is a disguised contest of wills.

The disagreement I wish to examine is not between these two groups themselves, but between the first group, who assert a logical chasm between fact and moral assertions, and a third group, who hold that this position of the first group is mistaken, but who repudiate the account given by the second group as well. The writers in this third group whose view I shall focus upon are D. Z. Phillips and H. O. Mounce. The theorist against whom they argue, as being representative of the first position noted above, is R. M. Hare.

In their book *Moral Practices* Phillips and Mounce represent Hare's position, and the mistake they deem that position to involve, as follows:

On Hare's account . . . particular value judgements proceed from general principles that the individual has decided upon himself. One decides oneself that Xing is in general wrong, one adopts the general principle that one ought never to perform an act of Xing, and from this, by syllogistic reasoning, one can deduce the conclusion that a particular act, which falls under the principle, ought not to be performed.

Now it should be noticed that the premiss, Xing is wrong, in the above argument is a prescriptive judgement. Thus a prescriptive conclusion has been deduced from a prescriptive premiss, so that the appeal is from one prescriptive judgement to another. In opposition to this, we shall argue that a prescriptive judgement is justified *only by appealing to something that is not itself prescriptive.*[2]

This 'something that is not itself prescriptive' is, according to Phillips and Mounce, a social rule. Their argument to this conclusion is best given in their own words.

It is important to distinguish between prescriptive judgements and mere commands. What distinguishes the one from the other is that a prescriptive judgement carries with it an appeal to authority, most commonly in the form of an established rule. Thus during a game of soccer one player might say to another, 'Stand back! You are off-side'. This utterance, though it takes the form of a command, is really to be distinguished from commands, for the utterance has the implication that the man to whom it is addressed already has a reason for carrying out what is says. The man who says 'Stand back! You are off-side', is not simply commanding the other to do what he wants him to do. He is as much pointing something out which, if the man himself had recognised it, would have led him to perform the prescribed action. We can see that this is so if we consider the statement, 'You are off-side'. Within association football there is a rule which says that a player will be called off-side and penalised if he received the ball or is deemed to be interfering with play when there is no member of the opposing side between himself and the opposing goalkeeper. It is this rule that gives the order 'Stand back!' its prescriptive force and distinguishes it from a mere command. The order carries with it an appeal to a rule that the man in the off-side position recognizes himself. What makes a judgement prescriptive is the appeal to a rule that is accepted or could be accepted by the man to whom the judgement is addressed. Without this rule, the judgement becomes a mere command, the mere attempt by one man to force another to do what he wants.[3]

The disagreement then concerns what it is that enables one person justifiably to assert that another person *ought* to observe a certain course of conduct. On Hare's account it is the individual's adoption of a principle that entitles him to declare that others should conduct themselves according to that rule. On Mounce and Phillips' account the entitlement to prescribe what others should do rests not on a principle to which the individual unilaterally subscribes, but on an established social rule which, as a member of that community, he accepts.

It is at this point that I wish to enter the discussion. I shall try to show that the position Mounce and Phillips propose, while an advance upon that of Hare, carries within it certain difficulties. Exposure of these difficulties will prepare the way for my own account of moral life.

II

One advantage of Mounce and Phillips' account over Hare's is that it seems to square better with the fact that when we tell someone to their face that the way they treat others is wrong we do not see ourselves as having decided that acts of this kind are evil. We have no sense of having 'made it the case' that to act this way is wrong. On Hare's account, however, it does appear that each individual decides what is right, and what wrong, by establishing as a rule of action *for everyone* a principle which *he* or *she* has decided to adopt. Mounce and Phillips' linking of prescriptive judgments to established social rules is more respecting of our sense that, in matters of morality at least, we are appealing to standards which no one has at any point decided shall be the standards of right and wrong. Rather, these standards confront us as calling for observance, *whatever anyone decides*.

A second apparent advantage of Mounce and Phillips' account over Hare's is that they appear able to explain how the addressing of an 'ought'-statement by one person to another can (conceivably) *accomplish* something. If all that is required to entitle one to address 'ought'-statements to others is one's own unilateral subscription to a principle of discrimination, the question arises why such statements should ever have any effect. For even if we allow (what is by no means obvious) that the fact that you subscribe to a principle does make it the case that everyone else ought to act as the principle requires, why, so long as the others do not subscribe to the principle, should one expect them to appreciate and heed this fact? If sub-scription is necessary for *you* to acknowledge that you ought to act as the principle requires, must subscription not be necessary for others to acknowledge this as well? But then until they do subscribe to the principle, your (or anyone's) addressing them in the form 'you ought to . . .' will surely have no effect. Yet these forms of language are found in every human society of which we have knowledge, and there often do have the effect of altering the behaviour, or intentions. of the persons to whom they are addressed.

The explanation given by Phillips and Mounce of 'ought'-statements would seem able to account for this effect. For according to them, what distinguishes a prescriptive judgment from a mere command is the fact the "the utterance has the implication that the [person] to whom it is addressed already has a reason for carrying out what it says". That reason is: that there is an established social rule that persons shall conduct themselves in this way. Thus "stand back!" uttered in a football match is a prescriptive judgment rather than an arbitrary expression of will because the person addressed has a reason for doing what the utterance prescribes; the reason being that it is a rule of Association Football that persons shall not position themselves as this person is positioned during play.

Unfortunately Phillips and Mounce are not as specific about this requirement as one would like. This lack of specificity comes to notice if we ask why, from the fact that there is an established social rule, we can conclude that a person to whom a judgment appealing to that rule is addressed has a reason to do what the rule (and judgment) calls for. Surely the person to whom the judgment is addressed must be in some particular relation to the rule in question before it can be true that he or she has a reason to observe it?

In the long passage quoted above Phillips and Mounce use two expressions which do attribute a relation between the person addressed by the words 'Stand back!' and the rule respecting players' positions. They say that the words "appeal to a rule that the man in the off-side position *recognizes* himself". They also say that the words "appeal to a rule that is accepted or could be accepted by the man to whom the judgement is addressed". The first of these—"a rule that the man recognizes . . . himself"—is ambiguous between (a) a rule that he accepts, and (b) a rule which he recognizes to be an established rule. If Phillips and Mounce intend the first (that appeal is to a rule which the man *accepts*) this does make it the case that the man already has reason to observe the rule. But this achievement is got at the expense of a certain difficulty. The difficulty is that, on this account, one can only address a moral judgment to a person who is himself a moral striver. This is the implication of claiming that what is required for the words "Stand back!" to be prescriptive is *acceptance* by the person to whom they are addressed of the rule the words appeal to. At one point Phillips and Mounce remark:

The man who says 'Stand back! You are off-side' is not simply commanding the other to do what he wants him to do. He is as much pointing out something which, *if the man himself had recognized it, would have led him to perform the prescribed action.* (My emphasis.)[4]

If what would have led him to perform it is his acceptance of the rule, then this makes the prescriptive force of the imperative expression (its being a prescriptive judgment) depend on the person to whom it is addressed being someone *who would not deliberately* stand off-side. Transposed to morals, the effect is to make the prescriptive force of a moral utterance (its being a genuine moral 'ought'-statement) depend on the person addressed being someone who would not willingly do evil. ('The man who says "Stay your hand! You will kill him" is not simply commanding the other to do what he wants him to do. He is as much pointing out something which, *if the man himself had recognized it, would have led him . . .*' etc.) This is an odd result, since it is the vicious, as much as the inattentive man, whom we wish to address moral judgments to.

If, on the other hand, Phillips and Mounce mean that prescriptive judgments appeal to a rule which is recognized by the person addressed to be an established rule, we have a different difficulty. For if all that is true of the man is that he recognizes that there indeed is this established rule, how does this make it the case that he has a reason to do what the rule (and the judgment) calls for?

It may be thought that the second of the remarks noted above clearly indicates that Phillips and Mounce mean by "a rule that the man recognizes" a rule that he *accepts*. For they explicitly state: "What makes a judgment prescriptive is the appeal to a rule that is accepted or could be accepted by the man to whom the judgment is addressed". In fact the remark cannot be used to settle the question in this way. In declaring that a judgment is made prescriptive by appeal to a rule that *could* be accepted by the person to whom the judgment is addressed, what do Phillips and Mounce mean by 'could be accepted'? That it is logically possible that the man should accept the rule? That it is psychologically possible for him to accept it? That were he to be acquainted with the rule he would accept it? But more immediately, whichever of these constructions they intend, if the man to whom the judgment is addressed *does not* in fact (even though he 'could') accept the rule to which the judgment appeals, is it then true that he "already has a reason for carrying out what it says"? I do not see how it can be true unless we introduce some fact or facts other than that there is this established rule of the society, which he recognizes to be a rule, and which he could accept (but does not); such a fact as, for example, that non-observance will incur sanctions of some kind.

What Phillips and Mounce say then, in the passage quoted, concerning the relation of the person addressed by a prescriptive judgment to the rule the judgment appeals to is unsatisfactory. If we interpret them as saying that the person addressed accepts the rule which the judgment appeals to, this does enable them to avoid any suggestion that the person addressing the prescriptive judgment is merely attempting to force the other to do what he (the prescriptor) wants. They avoid it by representing the situation as one in which the person addressing the prescriptive judgment urges upon the other what *he* (the other) wants. But this benefit has the unacceptable result that only the good-intentioned can be morally addressed. Yet unless we interpret Phillips and Mounce as saying that the person addressed by a prescriptive judgment accepts the rule that the judgment appeals to, the reason they allege the person has for acting as the judgment prescribes appears to evaporate.

III

There is however a further passage in which Phillips and Mounce attribute a relation between the person addressed by a prescriptive judgment and the rule the judgment appeals to. This passage follows directly the long passage quoted above.

Having seen that a prescriptive judgement is related to a rule, we must now consider the precise nature of this relation. A prescriptive judgement can never *establish* a rule, but rather, a rule must already be accepted in order for the prescriptive judgement to be possible. Thus the statement of a rule is not itself prescriptive. If one says, 'Within association football there is a rule that no player, etc.' then one is not advocating anything, but simply stating what is the case within association football. Given that a person follows this rule, then on a particular occasion one can make a prescriptive judgement on the basis of it; one can tell a man that he ought to stand back if he does not wish to be off-side. It is to be noticed, however, that one is here advocating a particular act, where one can take for granted that the man one is addressing is following a particular rule. One is not advocating obedience to the rule itself. Once again, it is only where one can take *for granted* that a man is following a rule that one can offer him a prescriptive judgement.[5]

The second sentence of this passage insists upon acceptance of the rule; but it fails to specify by whom the rule must be accepted. It admits of three different readings.

(A) A rule must be accepted by a person before a prescriptive judgment appealing to the rule can be addressed *to* him by another.

(B) A rule must be accepted by a person before a prescriptive judgment appealing to the rule can be addressed *by* him to another.

(C) A rule must be accepted by *both* persons before a prescriptive judgment appealing to the rule can be addressed by one to the other.

The closing remarks of the passage may seem to indicate that Phillips and Mounce are to be understood as stating (A)—with the resulting difficulty already noted above. They declare that only where we can take for granted that a person *is following* a rule can *we* address *to him* a prescriptive judgment. Unfortunately, people can follow rules they do not accept. Thus where we can take for granted that a man is following a rule we cannot take for granted that he accepts the rule. This difference is important and more will be said about it in later chapters. But there is something else troubling in this passage. The fourth sentence in it represents two quite different claims as one and the same. The remark I refer to is:

Given that a person follows this rule, then on a particular occasion one can make a prescriptive judgment on the basis of it; one can tell a man that he ought to stand back if he does not wish to be off-side.

The first half of this remark asserts

(1)   Given that a person follows a rule one can make (and address to him) a prescriptive judgment on the basis of the rule.

The second half asserts

(2)   Given that a person follows a rule one can tell him that he ought to stand back if he does not wish to be off-side.

Now (2), notice, is not

(2A)   Given that a person wishes (for whatever reason) not to be off-side, you can tell him "You ought to stand back (because you are off-side)".

It is rather the quite different

(2B)   Given that a person follows a rule respecting off-side you can tell him "You ought to stand back *if you do not wish to be off-side.*"

It is clear that (2B) is *not* a more specific form of (1). For the words "You ought to stand back if you do not wish to be off-side" *are not a prescriptive judgment at all.* They assert, rather, a logical relation. They are not even of the type "You ought to hurry if you do not wish to be late". They are of the type "You ought to move your rook thus and so if you do not wish to play illegally".

Nor must someone follow the rule respecting the position of players before one can say to him "You ought to stand back if you do not wish to be off-side". One can address these words to him, and *be justified in what one says*, whether he follows the rule (or wishes to follow the rule) or not. For what entitles us to say this to him is not some relation of his practice, or attitudes, to the rule, but a relation of his physical position to the rule. If he is indeed positioned on the field such that he is correctly to be described, according to the Rules of Association Football, as 'off-side', then indeed: he ought to stand back if he does not wish to be off-side. If, however, he *does* wish to be off-side—well, then, he ought to stay where he is.

This outcome is fateful for Mounce and Phillips' account of moral judgment. What we find them asserting here respecting statements in football we in the end find them asserting respecting statements in morals. But before turning to their arguments to establish this I want first briefly to note that there is no analogue to (2B) in moral judgment. Coming upon a man assaulting his neighbour we do not say "You ought to stop if you do not wish to be in the wrong". We say: "You ought to stop—whether you wish to or not." That is to say: in making a prescriptive judgment one is, *pace* Phillips and Mounce, "advocating obedience to the rule itself".

IV

The most effective way to show that the above difficulty does in fact attach to Mounce and Phillips' account of moral statements is to consider a hypothetical society which they use to represent their view.

Let us consider a people who have the practice of promise keeping, and let us suppose that it is their sole moral practice. These people use the word 'ought' in what we should call a moral sense only in connection with the keeping of promises. Thus children are taught to do whatever they have undertaken to do, and sometimes to remind people who have not kept their word that they ought to do so. Their use of 'ought' is confined to this kind of circumstance. This practice of promise keeping is therefore comparable with our own, except that we are to imagine it as being self-contained, as being isolated from any other moral practice.

Now it is evident, we believe, that there can be no question of these people deciding that promises ought or ought not to be kept. Their moral judgements cannot be derived from a principle that they have arrived at by means of a decision. For by what procedure could they arrive at such a decision? It would have to consist in their asking themselves the question, 'Ought promises to be kept?' Yet within this society that question would be meaningless. These people are taught the use of 'ought' in its moral sense only with regard to keeping promises. The fact that a man has undertaken to do an action is their criterion for saying that the action ought to be done. To ask whether a man ought to keep his promises, that is, to ask whether a man ought to do what he has undertaken to do, is therefore, in this society, to involve oneself in a piece of nonsense, as if one were to ask, 'Ought one to do what one ought to do?' Of course, we can suppose these people to possess, as we do, a second sense of 'ought', of the kind that appears in the statement, 'You ought to keep your matches dry because it will pay you to do so'. On this conditional use of 'ought', it will be possible to ask whether promises ought to be kept, because it will then be equivalent to asking whether it pays one to keep them. This use of 'ought', however, is distinct from its moral use . . .[since one] can continue to tell a person that he ought (in a moral sense) to perform a certain act even if it has been shown that it will not pay him to perform it. In terms of the moral use, therefore, it is evident that within this society it makes no sense even to ask, 'Ought promises to be kept?'[6]

The first thing to note about this passage is that a distinction is being drawn between a *moral* and a *non*-moral use of 'ought'. The basis of the distinction is said to be that the second is a conditional use of 'ought', while the first is not. In fact I shall later argue that the so-called "moral 'ought' " is, when used (as Mounce and Phillips here use it) in respect of a human action, every bit as conditional as the other. But here I wish to attend only to why Phillips and Mounce believe the "moral 'ought' " is not conditional. The reason they give involves the example "You ought to keep your matches dry". This they say is a conditional, and so not a moral, use of 'ought', because whether you ought to keep your matches dry depends upon whether this practice will be to your advantage; whereas that you ought to keep your promises does not depend upon its being to your advantage.

On what then does it depend? The answer Phillips and Mounce wish to give is that it does not *depend* on anything. Or more precisely, however things actually go in the world, whatever states of affairs in fact obtain, or come into being, one ought to keep one's promises. This is because it is a *necessary truth* that promises ought to be kept.

[W]e should think of phrases such as 'Lying is bad' or 'Lying is wrong' [or 'Promises ought to be kept'] not as expressions of a moral position, but as setting out one of the conditions under which a moral position can be expressed. They may be compared in this respect with a necessary proposition such as 'Red is a colour'. . . .[A] person might say 'Red is a colour, in order to teach someone the meaning of the word 'colour'. We are suggesting that the phrase 'Lying is wrong' is also a necessary statement which, if it tells us anything at all, tells us about the meaning of 'morally wrong'. In saying that lying is wrong we are saying that what the term 'lying' describes is for us necessarily wrong.[7]

What makes it necessarily true that breaking promises is wrong—that promises ought to be kept—is the meaning of these words. Just as in the football example you are necessarily (i.e. it is a logical truth that you are) off–side, if you in fact are in the position to which the word 'off–side' refers, so in the promising example you necessarily (i.e. it is a logical truth that you) are in the wrong, if in fact you are acting in relation to another in the manner to which the words 'breaking your promise' refer. If you go on to ask *why* you are in the wrong, this is just to ask: what justifies us in saying you are in the wrong? And what justifies us is: the rule respecting the use of these words.

These people are taught the use of 'ought' in its moral sense only with regard to keeping promises. The fact that a man has undertaken to do an action is their *criterion* for saying that the action ought to be done.

[Compare: These people are taught the use of 'ought' in its prescriptive sense only with regard to playing football. The fact that a man has taken up position such–and–such is their *criterion* for saying he ought to stand back.]

What we have here in each case is the application of a rule.* In order to decide whether a particular player is off–side you look to see what the rule for applying the term 'off–side' is. In order to decide whether a particular action ought to be done, or is wrong, you look to see what the rule for applying the words 'ought' and 'wrong' is. This last rule is: if he promised, then the act ought to be done; and once he has promised, refusal to do the act is wrong.

Now whoever asks "Ought promises to be kept?" appears to be asking for justification of this rule itself. This, on Mounce and Phillips' account, cannot be given. For if the words "Ought promises to be kept?" are intended to ask "(Morally) ought promises to be kept?", one is attempting the logically impossible. One is trying to ask a moral question about that which makes moral questions (*sc.* "Ought I to give him the money?") possible. It is as if one were to try to get outside morality to ask whether morality is morally all right. ("Ought I to do what I ought to do?") The words "Ought I to give him the money?" do ask, however, a moral question; and the criterion for answering it is: did you promise? If you promised this *means*: you ought to give the money. This is because "you promised" and

---

* This is something which Phillips and Mounce apparently wish to deny; since a few pages before they remark that it is not their view "that particular [moral] decisions must be viewed as the application of general rules".[8]

"you ought to" are literally synonyms. (Hence the nonsense of "Ought I to do what I promised?")

If on the other hand the words "Ought promises to be kept?" are intended as "(*Prudentially*) ought promises to be kept?" one is asking a genuine question. But one is not, by these words, asking a *moral* question. And this is all that was claimed. You cannot raise the question "(Morally) ought promises to be kept?" That they ought to be kept is—unquestionable.

V

The consequence of this view is to empty moral practices of life. They become literally unintelligible. For until we appreciate, for example, why people judge the breaking of promises to be wrong, how can what they say make any sense to us? The question "Ought promises to be kept" must be in order from the start. Phillips and Mounce, in their determination to resist the view that people have decided that promises ought to be kept, end up representing moral language as activity which has no justification; it just is. ("This language game is played!")

The step which first leads them toward this position begins on the sixth page of their book:

If [Hare's] view were correct . . . it would be possible to adopt any principle whatsoever as a [rule of action], and derive genuine prescriptive judgements from it. Thus, one should be able to turn the utterance, 'You ought to wear a hat on Wednesdays' into a prescriptive judgement simply by deciding that all men ought to wear hats on Wednesdays. As we have seen, however, this is precisely what cannot be done. In order to make a prescriptive judgement, one must be able to appeal to something that does not itself need to be prescribed, and the principle that all men ought to wear hats on Wednesdays is not such a principle. But how do we know this? What right have we to rule this principle out in this context? In order to answer these questions we need to consider what within our society does serve to justify our particular value judgements.

It can be shown, we believe, that when we wish to justify our moral judgements or render them intelligible, we make use of such concepts as honesty, truthfulness, generosity, etc. These concepts have in consequence a special rôle in our society. It is extremely difficult to be clear about the character of this special rôle, however, because of the use philosophers sometimes make of such phrases as, 'Honesty is good', 'Lying is bad', 'Generosity is right', phrases that are rarely found in actual discourse. By their use of such phrases, philosophers give the impression that honesty, truthfulness and generosity are themselves the subjects of prescriptive judgements. They imply that in our society we need to arrive at a moral position in relation to these things. Now we can and do speak of adopting a moral position towards, say, capital punishment or pacifism, because these are both things about which people disagree, and we can imagine ourselves being asked to state our opinion about them, to say, for example, whether we consider capital punishment right or wrong. But it would be difficult to imagine ourselves being asked to give an opinion on truth telling or generosity. Someone confronted with a choice between telling the truth and helping a friend might ask whether or not a lie is justified *on this occasion*. Yet such a question could hardly arise were it not taken as a matter of course that a lie is normally to be condemned. It is therefore difficult to imagine the kind of situation in which a person would utter an expression like 'Truth telling is good'. It might be said in the course of instructing a young child about how he should behave. But such an utterance could hardly raise an *issue*, for it would be difficult to know what someone who disagreed with it could mean.[9]

It would be difficult to know what someone who disagreed with it—who asserted that lying is good—could *mean*. This concluding remark is oddly discordant with what goes before. The burden of the passage is the claim that "it would be difficult to imagine ourselves *being asked* to give an opinion on truth telling or generosity". But this is because "it is taken as a matter of course [by everyone] that a lie is normally to be condemned". It is not because the words "Ought one not to lie?" would have no sense. Indeed Phillips and Mounce themselves give an example using these very words: "Ought one not to lie—even where it would help a friend?" How then do they arrive at the view that the words "Ought one not to lie?" (or, "Ought one not to break a promise?") are nonsense? The move which delivers them to this position has already been cited:

What is being urged is that we should think of phrases such as 'Lying is bad' or 'Lying is wrong' not as expressions of a moral position, but as setting out one of the conditions under which a moral position can be expressed.

Recall Mounce and Phillips' claim that in our society it is taken as a matter of course that a lie is to be condemned. Surely this is to say: it is taken as a matter of course that lying is wrong? Furthermore the words "it is taken as a matter of course by us that lying is wrong" just mean: we no longer *deliberate*, in each instance, whether a lie is to be condemned. We condemn lies, as a matter of course. But this is because *knowledge*, once acquired, replaces the need for continued investigation. Having learned that lies are ordinarily a cause, or instrument, of harm to persons, and caring that that harm not be done, we no longer wait upon further intelligence. We condemn lies, simply upon detecting their commission.*

Nevertheless that condemnation is the product of (and its sense may continually need to be reawakened by) deliberation and judgment. Which is just to say: truthfulness *is* something in relation to which we have *arrived at* a moral position. Phillips and Mounce urge against this the view that expressions such as 'Lying is wrong' do not express a moral position, but tell us about the meaning of the words 'morally wrong':

[A] person might say 'Red is a colour' in order to teach someone the meaning of the word 'colour'. We are suggesting that the phrase 'Lying is wrong' is also a necessary statement which, if it tells us anything at all, tells us about the meaning of 'morally wrong'.
Lying is the kind of thing we apply the word 'wrong' to.[10]

But how (for example) does this last remark give us the meaning of 'morally wrong'? A child (or an adult) could be taught to use the word in this way (always understanding when someone is spoken of as having done wrong that a lie, or a broken promise, is involved) and still not know what people mean in condemning lying as morally wrong. This is because learning about moral wrong is *not* like learning about colours. To state two obvious reasons for this: one is that the moral wrong in the act of lying is not there to be perceived as the colour red is there on the chart. (I cannot help seeing the red. Can I not help seeing the moral wrong?) Another is that colour judgments are not prescriptive. Making colour judgments just is a matter of applying colour terms correctly, according to their rule of application. But is making moral judgments simply a matter of applying moral terms correctly, according to their rule of application ('wrong'

---

* Which condemnation can be overturned, or forestalled, where extenuating circumstances, or over-riding considerations, are apparent or come to notice.

to lying, 'good' to generosity, and so on)? Mounce and Phillips declare that

Someone who did not apply the term ['wrong'] in this way would have difficulty in understanding what we mean when we call something wrong.[11]

What needs to be said is that even if he does apply the term in this way he does not, *eo ipso*, understand what we mean when we call something morally wrong. This is because uttering words according to a rule of language is not *expressing a moral position*.

VI

However if you do view moral discrimination in this way you will of course be inclined to view our moral valuations as logically unquestionable. (". . . we are saying that what the term 'lying' describes is for us *necessarily* wrong.") And of course what is logically necessary (and so unquestionable) is the exact opposite of what depends upon individual decision. Once more the quarry is Hare. Phillips and Mounce want something as a basis for moral judgment which the individual does not himself decide shall be the standard of right and wrong. They look for this in something which is *socially established*. What they fix upon are rules of language. Being *established*, they are not brought before the court of decision. Indeed they are what make deciding possible. Being *social*, they are not the result of any individual's judgment and will. The standard for judgment is there, unquestioned, nay unquestionable.

In the pages that follow I shall give reasons for repudiating this view. I shall argue that people have in fact decided that lies are wrong, that generosity is a virtue, that promises ought to be kept. Nevertheless Phillips and Mounce are right in believing that at the foundation of morals there is something which people have not decided. There is. What people have not decided is that *it shall matter to them* that lies are not told, or meanness practised, or promises neglected. To this subject I now turn. But it may help to put my argument thus far in perspective to remark that where Phillips and Mounce go wrong is to seek the given in rules of language. The given is: *forms of life*. And the form of life which is the foundation of morality is: caring about others. The answer to the one who asks why lies ought not to be told, or promises broken, is not—'This language game is played'. The answer is, because pain will be given.

NOTES

[1] David Hume, *Treatise of Human Nature*, Book III.
[2] D. Z. Phillips and H. O. Mounce, *Moral Practices* (London: Routledge & Kegan Paul, 1970) p. 4.
[3] Ibid., pp. 4–5.
[4] Ibid., p. 5.
[5] Ibid., pp. 5–6.
[6] Ibid., pp. 11–12.
[7] Ibid., p. 9.
[8] Ibid., p. 8.
[9] Ibid., pp. 6–9.
[10] Ibid., p. 9.
[11] Ibid.

I

Moral Concern

I shall not surely be contradicted in granting to man the only natural virtue which the most passionate detractor of human virtues could not deny him, I mean that of pity, a disposition suitable to creatures weak as we are, and liable to so many evils; a virtue so much the more universal, and withal useful to man, as it takes place in him before all manner of reflection; and so natural that the beasts themselves sometimes give evident signs of it.

ROUSSEAU

[R]emember that it is a primitive reaction to tend, to treat, the part that hurts when someone else is in pain . . .

But what is the word 'primitive' meant to say here? Presumably that this sort of behaviour is pre-linguistic: *that a language game is based* on it. . .

WITTGENSTEIN

I wish to return to a question asked several pages back. How, until we appreciate *why* people judge breaking promises to be wrong, can what they say in claiming they are wrong make any sense to us? It seems to me, that, until we do, it cannot, and the search for this appreciation is what I propose to embark upon in this chapter. For heuristic reasons I shall shift from a consideration of promising to an instance of brutal assault. The reason for this is that violence is more economically (and compellingly) prosecuted in moral philosophy as much as in law.

I.i

One need not look outside one's own city or village for examples of physical assault. I shall take my example from a work of fiction, because this will enable me later to connect the discussion of this chapter to a consideration of moral understanding. This cannot, I think, be judged in any way to affect the validity of the discussion; for in these matters truth is at least as terrible as fiction.* Consider, then, from Hubert Selby's *Last Exit to Brooklyn*, the following human encounter:

They got in a cab and drove to a downtown hotel. He bought a bottle of whiskey and they sat and drank and he talked. She kept filling his glass. He kept talking.

[Tralala] kept pouring but he wouldnt pass out. The bastard. He said he just wanted to be near her for a while. . . .She had been there over an hour.

The hell with it. She hit him over the head with the bottle. She emptied his pockets and left. She took the money out of his wallet and threw the wallet away. She counted it on the subway. 50 bucks.

They were sitting at the counter when the [soldier] came in. He was holding a bloodied handkerchief to his head and blood had caked on his wrist and cheek. He grabbed Tralala by the arm and pulled her from the stool. Give me my wallet you goddamn whore. She spit in his face [and] kicked him. . . .He grabbed her again. He was crying and bent over struggling to breathe from the pain of the kick. If I dont have the pass I cant get in the Base. I have to get back. Theyre going to fly me home tomorrow. . . .Ive been all shot up. Please, PLEASE. Just the wallet. . . .The tears streaked the caked blood and he hung on Tonys and Als grip and Tralala swung at his face, spitting, cursing and kicking. . .
Tony grabbed the doggie around the neck and Al shoved the bloodied handkerchief in his mouth and they dragged him outside in a darkened doorway. He was still crying and begging for his ID card when Tony pulled his head up by the hair and Al punched him a few times in the stomach and then in the face, then held him up while Tony hit him a few times; but they soon stopped, not afraid that the cops might come, but they knew he didnt have any money and they were tired from hitting the seaman they had

* Four years ago in a North American city two robberies were performed, one on a Saturday night, the other the following Sunday evening. The first was from a grocery store, the second from a garage. In both cases a small amount of money was taken. In both cases the eyes of the store-keeper and garage-attendant were put out to prevent their identifying the robber. From the reports of the victims, and examination of their wounds, authorities concluded that no weapon was used to accomplish this. The eyes of these men were put out by the bare hands of their assailant.

lushed earlier, so they dropped him and he fell to the ground on his back.
Before they left Tralala stomped on his face until both eyes were bleeding
and his nose was split and broken then kicked him [.][1]

The acts of these young people against this soldier are a brutal
instance of what it is morally wrong to do. What we are to seek to
appreciate is what you, and I, and others, *are saying* when we say that
these acts are morally wrong.

I take it we are saying: they ought not to be done. This obviously
does not get us very far. But it is a beginning, since it identifies the
crucial expression to be (as Hume saw) 'ought', rather than 'wrong'.
Any act is wrong to do which is what you ought not to do. It is
wrong *in being* what you ought not to do. If, for example, you are
trying to fill the radiator of your automobile with water, what you
are doing is wrong to do if you are pouring the water into the oil-fill
pipe. It is wrong, because it is not what you ought to do to accomplish what you intend. (Thus when, as a young boy, I lean, watercan
poised, under the hood, trying to recall the previous lesson, and
touch hesitantly with my free hand first the generator cap, then the
carburettor hood, then the oil-fill pipe, my watching father calls out
at my elbow: 'Wrong . . . Wrong . . . Wrong . . .') Only if you wish
to fill the engine with water is what you are doing the right
thing—the thing you *ought*—to do. It is the same way in moral
matters. That act is (morally) wrong to do which is what you ought
not to do. It is the sense in which you, and I, and these young people,
ought not to do what they are doing that we are after.

I.ii

Imagine that you are walking along a wilderness forestry road, with
trees and brush growing densely up to the edge of the narrow gravel
roadbed. As you walk along in the hot still air suddenly you hear, and
then see, a logging truck approaching you from a short distance at
high speed. Startled, you quickly climb through the brush to stand
well out of the way. *Ought* you to have moved out of the way?

Your answer comes back that of course you ought to have. But
suppose you are asked *why* you ought to have: what now will be
your answer? Because you would have been killed if you hadn't?
This fact may explain *to you* why you ought to have moved. But why

is the fact that you would have been killed supposed to explain *to others* why you ought to have moved out of the way? (For it is others, notice, who are directing this question to you.)

Perhaps you will be inclined to answer by asking in turn: Had your questioners been in the same place, would they not have moved? Each replies that, indeed, he would have And would they not admit that, in such a situation, they *ought* to move? They do admit this. But then must they not appreciate that in the same situation *you* ought to move? The reply comes back that, must or not, they fail to appreciate it.

Your questioners are right of course. What you have established may be stated simply thus:

(a) You appreciate that (in the situation imagined) you ought to move.

(b) They appreciate that (in the same situation) they ought to move.

But it doesn't follow

(c) That they appreciate that you (in the imagined situation) ought to move.

However a further argument may now occur to you. Your questioners, you inquire, will accept it as true that you wish to live? They will. But then in order to continue living it was necessary for you to move from the path of the truck? They accept this. But then what you did you *ought* to have done, *if* you were to avoid death? This too they accept. But they go on directly to point out that when they questioned why you ought to have moved they had this appreciation in mind all along. They were not asking, ought you to have moved (or jumped high in the air, or lain down in the roadbed, or whatever) if you were to avoid the truck. They were asking, *ought* you to have avoided death—however you did it. How are you to get them to appreciate that you ought to have?

Voltaire has recorded the reply of the Comte D'Argenson to a man who protested, when rebuked by the Comte for the lowliness of his profession: "My Lord, I must live." The Comte's reply was: "I do not see the necessity".[2] Rousseau has (rightly) described this remark of the Comte as *cold* (". . . lui repartit froidement . . ."³). By 'cold' is meant: without feeling, indifferent, uncaring.* The Comte's words (taken at face value) express complete indifference as to the man's life or death. They also express the logical consequence of this indifference or unconcern: inability to appreciate that the man must do something to support his life. For why *must* he live?

It will not do to reply: because his life is dear to him. For the point is, it is *not* dear to the Comte. And it is this which makes all the difference. Until the man's life is dear—for whatever reason—to the Comte, until it *matters* to the Comte that the man lives, the Comte will never see any 'necessity' for the man to live. However once the man's continuing to live is something the Comte desires (is something he *cares* should be so) the Comte will accept that that ought to be done, by the man himself, or whomever, which will have the effect that the man continues to live. (And so as the estate doctors work upon the man's broken body, dragged from beneath the wheels of an overturned carriage, we hear the Comte's shouts ring hysterically from the next chamber: 'He *can't* die! Not just when everything is literally within hours of being concluded. *Don't bungle this one you toads!* Or I swear it will be the gutter for you all! He MUST live!')

The same holds true for your questioners. If it is a matter of indifference to them whether you live or die, then you will never be able to get them to regard your avoiding death as something that *ought* to be achieved. For their being indifferent—their not caring—logically entails that your avoiding death cannot have the status for them of *what ought to be achieved.* Undeniably, your avoiding death is for you (on your own testimony) of the greatest importance. That you ought to move out of the road of the truck is therefore, for you, unquestionable. (Nor do you at the time ask yourself any questions. *You move!*) Yet it is just this moving that your interrogators question. They do not deny that if you didn't move out of the path of the truck you would be killed. They admit that you must, and so ought to, move, *if* you are not to be struck. Still they refuse to acknowledge that your avoiding the truck—your not being struck—is something that *ought* to happen. They grant

(A) That you ought to move, if you are not to be struck.

* The metaphor is linked to 'heartless', i.e. 'without blood', i.e. without life/warmth, i.e. without feeling, or pity (as a dead man to others).

Yet they do not grant

(B) That you ought not to be struck. (That you ought *in fact* to move.)

How is this possible?

It is possible because in (A) the word 'ought' expresses a relation between *an act* (your moving) and a fact (your not being struck by the truck), whereas in (B) the word 'ought' expresses a relation between YOU and a fact (your not being struck); or as I should prefer to say, it expresses *your relation to* that fact— and so to the act which brings about the fact. It is therefore possible for your questioners to accept (A), i.e. to accept that the relation expressed by (A) holds, and yet refuse to accept (to endorse) (B). For all they are doing in refusing to accept (B) is refusing—rightly—to subscribe to words which accurately express *your* relation to not being struck (which relation is—your caring that you are not struck), but which do not express their relation to that fact. They (apparently) don't care a damn whether or not you are struck; in which case they can hardly regard your not being struck as something that *ought* to be realized. Hence that you ought to move they 'don't see the necessity' of at all.

II

Let me return to the soldier being brutally beaten by the young people. Suppose I ask, straight out, what explains these acts *being* what ought not to be done? The only answer I can see to give is: their being the inflicting of harm and suffering. But why should the fact that they are acts of this kind matter? Why should inflicting harm and suffering on the soldier be something that *ought not* to be done?

Now someone has to answer these questions. And as I have tried to show in section I the answer you are able to give will depend ultimately upon your relation to the person against whom these acts are directed. If you are uncaring of whether the soldier is brutally beaten and injured, then the acts of these young people will not—cannot—be regarded by you as mattering. If on the other hand you do care that the soldier is not in pain and terror, or maimed, your response to these acts will be to care that they are not done. This caring that they are not done is what is expressed by the words "these things ought not to be done".

But we are not through yet, for everything will depend on *why* you care whether your concern that these acts not be done is a *moral concern* or not. In the words which (with philosophic license) I put into the Comte D'Argenson's mouth I deliberately gave an example of a concern that a man lives which is a completely self-interested concern. Similarly, if your concern that these acts not be done to this soldier proceeds from some use you have for him (from your desire, say, to pry out of him information about the war-zone he has just left), then as you watch from a window above the street and exclaim "They oughtn't to do that—they'll ruin everything!", your concern that these acts not be done is not a moral concern. You do not express with the words "They oughtn't to do that" that sense in which the young people's acts ought not to be done that we are seeking.

What sort of concern must inform these words for them to express that sense? A wonderfully ordinary example of the concern we are seeking is given in the following remembrance.

It happened in Calgary some thirty years ago. I was rushing along the street to catch a train when a little girl walking in front of me dropped the bottle of milk she'd been sent to buy. The bottle broke, the milk spilled, the child started to weep. I went past and got my train. I have never forgotten that incident, never forgiven myself for my failure to stop and give the kid the price of another bottle. I should have known then what I know now: that there's always another train.[4]

What is remembered here is a moment when a man did not do what he should have done. The man did not stop to help the child, and I believe he would agree that he was wrong not to. The man now regrets his failure to stop. Why? Because the child was unhappy and afraid, and he did not help when he could have. He cannot for-give—or forget—his hurrying by. What this man's regret and shame reveal is a concern about the child, a caring that she was unhappy, and a wish to have helped her in her trouble. If the man could go back now and stop and help, he would do it, for the child. He would go back and give her the money because this would make a difference in her life which he wishes had been made, could be made, by him, or anyone, if this were possible. This regard for the child's happiness and suffering, this concern for how she is, is a paradigm of what we speak of as moral sensibility, moral concern. What does such concern or sensibility involve?

The man sees the milk fall and the child begin to weep. He responds to these things, and appreciates them, even as he hurries by. (For there is nothing in the remembrance as reported to suggest that it is only later that he begins to feel remorse at what he has done. As the train pulls out of the station his regret may begin to form, and his sense of having done the wrong thing start to erode his peace of mind.) Why does this that he sees make this difference—where a crate of bottles standing idly on the sidewalk does not? Why is he affected by what he sees? This man himself knows what it is to break something that is wanted. He also knows something of the life of families, and the place of money there, and so of the possibilities there of exasperation and want. If the child were one of a family where money did not matter, would the broken bottle throw her into tears? It might, if it nevertheless mattered to her to perform this errand well. But to see this possibility requires an understanding of the importance to a person, even as a child, of achievement; of doing something well, or of being able to help someone who is loved and has given one a task to accomplish. Perhaps as likely, what now awaits the child at home (what may have awaited her before) or perhaps what she mistakenly fears awaits her, is anger and resentment, a return to the store, with fear of dropping the milk again. Perhaps it is simply that now she will be late for school. It may be any one, or more, of these things which accounts for her sorrow. None of these possibilities needs to 'go through the mind' of this man. We learn early that behind tears and fear and broken vessels there lies a human story. A child crying in the street over spilt milk is something we understand. Such distress and fear are appreciated from within an understanding of human concerns and relations and ways of living; from within a knowledge of how things are with people, and what makes us unhappy and afraid. This understanding is not something contingently connected to moral life, something which, while not necessary for, yet, if it exists, makes us 'better at', morality. Understanding of the kind I have sketched here is logically implied by the expressions 'moral concern', 'moral life'. But it is not alone sufficient for moral concern, for moral life. It must be accompanied by just that relation to the child which I have described as *caring* about the child. In the chapters which follow I shall seek to establish further that this is so. For the remainder of this chapter I want to consider the implications of this view for an appreciation of the young people's acts against the soldier.

On the view I am proposing, *morally* to appreciate that the acts of these young people ought not to be done involves caring about the soldier against whom they are directed. This *caring about*, or *regard for*, another person is what in the eighteenth century was spoken of as 'natural affection', but which I shall prefer to characterize as a form of love. It is ultimately this regard, or caring, for other persons which gives our moral language its sense—contrary to the account given by Phillips and Mounce. At one point in their book *Moral Practices* Phillips and Mounce remark of Protagoras' claim that 'man is the measure of all things' that

Precisely what Protagoras meant by this statement may be impossible to determine with certainty, but two interpretations seem plausible. According to the first interpretation, man is the measure of all things in the sense that each individual man, just in so far as he holds an opinion on morality or any other matter, is necessarily correct. Man is the measure of all things, on this interpretation, because each man's opinion is the measure of truth and goodness. According to the second interpretation, however, truth and goodness are determined, not by the opinions of individual men, but by the conventions which they create . . . [T]he standards of truth and goodness lie not in the opinions of any particular man but in conventions; and yet man remains the measure of all things, for these conventions are nothing but a reflection of what the majority of men have decided to call bad or false.

The first interpretation of Protagoras differs in obvious ways from the view we are presenting, for, in our view, it is not the individual who is the measure of what is morally right or wrong, but rather the individual's judgements on these matters derive their sense from the moral practice to which he belongs.[5]

Exactly what Phillips and Mounce mean by the last sentence in this passage is not altogether clear. It is clear that they reject the view that whatever each individual judges to be the case is the standard of truth or goodness. They assert that nevertheless *the sense* of each individual's judgment derives from—depends on—the human social practice to which he belongs. Do they mean by this that the *words* each individual uses *to express* his judgment derive their sense from social agreement—so that the word 'ought', say, like the word 'bottle', has the sense it has because of the precise use human beings have given to (their 'practice' with) this mark or sound? Or do Phillips and Mounce mean that the very *judgment* the individual expresses—WHAT he judges—derives its content (its meaning in *that* sense) from the social practice to which he belongs—so that it is the social practice which determines that something is morally right or wrong? These two are not the same and the second view is almost certainly false. A simple proof of this is the fact that I may use words (which have the meaning they do as a result of human agreement in their use) to say something which no one has ever said before. *What I* say, *what* I judge, *what* I express, by means of language, cannot therefore be determined by human agreement—by "a [social] practice to which [I] belong. . .". If it were, I should never be able to speak *for myself*.

Phillips and Mounce leave no room for doubt as to which of these two possible interpretations they mean. They go on directly to express their view as "it is the practice and not the individual which determines what is right or wrong"[6] (i.e., determines that such and such is right, such and such is wrong). In support of their view they invoke Wittgenstein, quoting a remark from the *Investigations* at I:242:

If language is to be a means of communication there must be agreement not only in definitions but also (queer as this may sound) in judgements.

Now this remark will (as Wittgenstein knew) sound queer, only if one thinks that all "judgment" *involves* using language. Mounce and Phillips' moral philosophy reveals an inclination to think exactly this. Their gloss on Wittgenstein's remark at I:242 reveals this inclination, and explains their own position.

On Wittgenstein's view, we judge the truth of a statement by the criteria for verifying that statement. Whether it is true, for example, that an object is red, will depend on whether that object satisfies the criterion by which an object in given circumstances is judged to be red. If people did not agree in their application of this criterion, it would be meaningless to speak of such a criterion, and meaningless, therefore, to speak of judging whether an object is red.[7]

Meaningless, because, on their view, without such a criterion —whose existence requires that "people agree in their application of [it]"—there can be no "judging whether an object is red." But Wittgenstein's point is not that "If people did not agree in their application of the criterion, it would be meaningless to speak of such a criterion, and meaningless, therefore, to speak of judging whether an object is red." His point is that if people did not agree *in judging* the object to be red we could not *have* such a (public) criterion. If you and I and the next person did not agree *in what we see* when we regard the object, then indeed it would be meaningless—because impossible—to speak of "the criterion by which an object in given circumstances is judged to be red". For that criterion is: its looking red. How could I assess the truth or falsity of your judgment (and report) that the object is red, by appeal to "the criterion etc . . .", if we did not *agree* in our "(queer as this may sound) [colour] *judgments*"?

It is what human beings *say* that is true or false, and they agree in the *language* they use. That is not agreement in opinions but in *form of life*. [Lebensform][8]

We do ordinarily agree in the language we use to describe the colour of objects. But it is human agreement in what *is seen* that makes possible our (public) colour concepts such as 'red'—i.e. this *word*, this *bit of language*. Because we see the object to be red, we can agree in the language we use to describe its colour. Where we do not agree in the language we use (where you indifferently use 'blue' or 'green' of what I describe as 'red') this signals a difference in our primitive apprehension—"judgment"—of the colour. This agreement in seeing, which makes possible our colour vocabulary, and our mutual confirmation or disconfirmation of each other's colour ascriptions, is not "agreement in opinions" but agreement in primitive biological a-perception: in "form of life". Agreement in opinions is agreement in what we judge or believe—what we "want to say"—about something. But for there to be the possibility of agreement in our opinions, and the confirmation of these as true or false, there must first be agreement in form of life. Mounce and Phillips' talk of people agreeing in their application of the criterion by which an object in given circumstances is judged to be red obscures Wittgenstein's point, and delivers us to their own position. For the words "agree in their application" suggest that the criterion exists prior to each individual's "application" of it; and the word "application" itself suggests the consulting and following of a rule—the rule for the application of the word 'red', say. Now it is true that the criterion for the application of the word 'red' exists prior to each individual's application of it. The object is red before people see, and say, that it is. This is true even at the level of the origination of 'red' as the English word for this colour. (The initial stage of "definition".) But in another, and crucial sense, the criterion does not exist prior to each individual's "application" of it, since, as Wittgenstein is trying to show in these remarks, for the object's being red *to be* a criterion for *us* of the truth or falsity of what we each *say* about it, there must be agreement in our perceptual apprehension—"judgments"—of the world. This is not agreement in (i.e., not at the level of) *"definitions"*, but in *"form of life"*—i.e. *experience*. (This is one reason why, as Wittgenstein remarks, "If a lion could talk, *we* [my emphasis] could not understand him."*) Mounce and Phillips' talk of "application" misleads, for it suggests that first there is the criterion, *and then* there is each individual's *application* of the criterion—all of which applications must for some (unexplained) reason agree for it to be possible to speak of such a criterion in the first place. Whereas it is our *agreeing*—in what we see—that constitutes (creates) the criterion in the first place. For a *criterion*, remember, is something that can function as a *public* test. There is a public criterion, which "people" can appeal to, here, by virtue of the fact that we agree in what we see.

Consider now the situation in morals. Phillips and Mounce are admiring of a remark by J. L. Stocks in which Stocks calls attention to some words by Browning:

The moral attitude is essentially a concern for the rightness of action . . . morality requires that all means shall be justified in some other way and by some other standard than their value for this or any end: that however magnificent is the prospect opened out by the proposed course of action, and however incontestable the power of the means chosen to bring this prospect nearer, there is still always another question to be asked: not a question whether in achieving this you will not perhaps diminish your chances of achieving something still more important; but a question of another kind. 'There is a decency required,' as Browning said, and this demand of decency is prepared to sacrifice, in the given case, any purpose whatever.[9]

Now this requirement of decency of which Browning speaks is a function, surely, of agreement in *attitude*, not in practice. This is true for two reasons. The first is that the decency Browning speaks of is itself a kind of attitude. The second is that whatever requirement a social practice could make of one could at best be a logical, and at worst, a physical (i.e. coercive), requirement. I shall try to illustrate

---

* Whether Wittgenstein is right about this does not greatly matter; the point of the remark is what is important.

what I mean here by recalling the example of the man who did not stop to help the child.

Consider a man to whom a similar incident occurred, and who now remembers it with regret, but with this difference. He regrets not doing then what he knows would have been the right thing to do, not because he is now, or was then, touched by the plight of the child, which might in fact mean nothing to him, but because he sees that here was a case where he did not do what (as society judges) it was right to do, and the awareness of this 'moral' failure is irksome to him. Now the man whose remembrance I quoted above also regrets his failure to stop. He is ashamed, and does not forgive himself, because the child was unhappy and afraid, and he did not help when he could have. This first man's remembrance reaches out to the child. The second man's remembrance reaches out to that *incident*, and then only, as it were, to return to himself. He regrets that he did not do what it was right to do (which he identifies by appeal to society's moral norms, and which it matters to him always to observe). But from this it does not follow that the man regrets the child's suffering and fear. Perhaps *these* things do not matter to him at all. (Perhaps he even resents the child, for being the occasion of his moral fault.) There is a kind of concern about one's actions which might be characterized as pharisaism. This is a concern always to do what it is right to do, because one wishes to be someone who does right, but where the importance one attaches to one's right actions is, so to speak, that one has done them. That is, it is possible to attach importance to doing what it is right to do, and yet to be indifferent to human suffering or happiness and so to be indifferent to what *is* done. As I remarked before—if the first man could go back now and stop and help, he would do it, for the child. But were the pharisee able to return, he would do so, not on the child's account, to restore her to untroubledness, but to perfect his record of uprightness. His act would be done, not for the child, but, as it were, for himself. This, I wish to claim, whatever it is, is not what Browning means by "decency", but something which one might want morally to condemn.

What I hope to have shown here are two things. First, that the expression "concern for the rightness of action" must include the pharisee as well as the good man, and therefore any attempt to characterize moral action, that is, action from moral considerations, must require more than this or similar expressions to do it.—Unless, of course, action from moral considerations includes the pharisee's action; and this is a question about which one might wish to get clear. I have said enough to make plain that my own view is that where an action is called for by moral considerations, and the action called for is help or consideration of some sort to others, then any attempt to elucidate the *moral character* of this action cannot appeal solely to one's personal concern about some 'moral state' of oneself, for if this is the case it will be hard to see the connection between one's action and the persons with whom one is involved. These persons must seem to be simply occasions for 'moral' action, and the 'moral' concern must appear here to be a concern about the person who acts, rather than a concern about those toward whom one's actions are supposedly directed. I shall later try to show that the point of departure of moral action in such cases cannot *solely* be a concern to be a certain sort of person, since *this* concern can itself only be a *moral* concern if concern for other persons is at its heart. Because one is concerned about others one is concerned not to be someone who treats them in certain ways.

Secondly: shame, remorse, and regret, are features of the moral life, and (for example) regret at not doing what one should have done for another, where this regret is a moral 'act', seems to involve a concern for or a caring about that other, rather than about oneself or some feature of oneself.

Now this last cannot itself proceed from a social practice. The only 'requirement' in respect of decency which society's "moral practices" can make of you (*qua* requirement) is either the logical requirement that you must do such and such if you are to be described as acting rightly, or the coercive requirement that you must do such and such (what it is right to do) on pain of some discomfort if you fail to. Neither of these is what Browning refers to when he speaks of decency as being "required". These words "There is a decency *required*" are an expression of the claim upon Browning of his *regard for* other human beings, or, if you prefer, of his attitude toward human relationships. That attitude is what explains our "moral practices", not *vice versa*.

In brief, Wittgenstein's remarks do not support Mounce and Phillips' view that the individual's moral judgment derives its sense from the moral practice to which he belongs. On the contrary, it is the "moral (social) practice" which derives its sense from individual "judgments". Or to put it less cryptically, it is agreement in that form of life I have called 'caring' which makes possible, and gives sense to, "moral practices". Just as in the case of colour discrimination there is a public criterion of 'red' which we can appeal to by virtue of the fact that we agree in what we see, so too in the case of moral discrimination there is a moral concept (and specific criteria) of "decency" to which we can appeal by virtue of the fact (and to the extent) that we agree in caring about one another. The agreement here is not agreement in practice but agreement in attitude. It is not social but *psychological* agreement. Each responds as the others (not: each "applies" the 'socially dictated' response). Where there *is* among people a caring about one another there will arise—and there can be agreement in—moral judgments. You, and I, and another can see what these young people do, and agree that they ought not to do it. Failure of an individual to share in this "form of life" will have as its consequence the non-intelligibility of the moral.

NOTES

[1] Hubert Selby, *Last Exit to Brooklyn* (New York: Grove Press, 1965) pp. 97–99.

[2] Francois-Marie Arouet de Voltaire, *Alzire, Discours Preliminaire*. (see *Oeuvres complètes*, ed. L. Moland, 52 vols., Paris 1877–5.)

[3] *Emile*, Book III.

[4] R. J. Needham, *A Writer's Notebook* (Toronto: MacMillan, 1969) p. 9.

[5] Op. cit., pp. 61–2.

[6] Ibid., p. 62.

[7] Ibid., p. 63.

[8] Ludwig Wittgenstein, *Philosophical Investigations*, Part I, s.241.

[9] J. L. Stocks, *Morality and Purpose* (Routledge & Kegan Paul, 1969) p. 27. (Ed. D. Z. Phillips.) See *Moral Practices*, p. 39.

II

Moral Considerations

Take any action allowed to be vicious; wilful murder for instance.
Examine it in all lights, and see if you can find that matter of fact, or
real existence, which you call vice. In whichever way you take it,
you find only certain passions, motives, volitions, and thoughts.
There is no other matter of fact in the case. The vice entirely escapes
you, as long as you consider the object . . .

Reason . . . can never be the source of so active a principle as con-
science, or a sense of morals.

HUME

In the previous chapter I have argued that an understanding of what
is wrought in human life by human acts is not sufficient for a moral
appreciation of these acts. Yet such an understanding, I have claimed,
is necessary for moral appreciation. In this chapter I shall seek to
explore further the relation between these two features of moral life.
In particular, I shall address the fact that not every act or judgment
can be described as undertaken or grounded on *moral* considerations.
What exactly is it about an act or judgment which makes it an
instance of "moral life"?

I

I propose to begin by examining an account of morality to be found
in a recent work by G. J. Warnock, to which he has given the title *The*
Object of Morality. It is Warnock's intent in this work to depart from
what he considers to be the two prevailing modes of contemporary
inquiry in ethics. These he describes as "a certain kind of general
theorizing about moral judgment or moral discourse as a whole, and
[a] comparatively restricted, detailed scrutiny of particular moral

concepts or particular limited issues."[1] Warnock wishes "to identify
and understand the subject-matter of moral discourse, and to take up
the old question . . . 'concerning the foundation of morality'."[2] This
puts his work (as he realises) into the first category, but with an
important difference. Most other contemporary works of this kind
have taken the form "of attempts to analyse or characterize moral
concepts and moral judgment only so far as that could be done
without mentioning the application of the former, or any grounds of
the latter."[3] It seems to Warnock that "if one is to understand any
kind or class of evaluative judgments" this must involve seeing
"what must and what might be appropriate or relevant standards for
[that] species of evaluation." To do this, Warnock believes, "it is
essential to try to see what that species of evaluation is done *for*, or, as
one might put it, what the *interest* is in doing it" (Warnock's
emphasis).[4] Moral judgment, Warnock remarks,

. . . is a practical matter; it is supposed to make, and often does make, a
practical difference. So: what difference is it supposed to make? And how?
And why is there a *need* for just that sort of difference to be made?[5]

It is this which gives the title to Warnock's essay. He wishes to
inquire after the *object* of morality, the point or rationale of this
species of evaluation. Warnock believes that the answer to the questions he has put must lie in certain features of people and of the
circumstances in which they live; features which, if the 'moral law' is
not to be variable and unstable, must be present and unchanging
throughout human communities.

Warnock's position concerning the nature of morality is sketched,
in his own words, as follows:

It is obvious that human beings have, in general, an *interest* in the course of
events in which they are involved: for, though they may indeed want some
things which they would not be at all better for having, they do have many
entirely harmless and proper and reasonable wants: and they also have
interests and actual needs, satisfaction of which may be absolutely necessary
for their well-being. But the course of events is not at all likely, without their
intervention, to go in a way at all satisfactory to them; and even with
intervention, there is still so much that may go wrong. Resources are
limited; knowledge, skills, information, and intelligence are limited; people
are often not rational, either in the management of their own affairs or in the
adjustment of their own affairs in relation to others. Then, finally, they are

vulnerable to others, and dependent on others, and yet inevitably often in competition with others; and, human sympathies being limited, they may often neither get nor give help that is needed, may not manage to co-operate for common ends, and may be constantly liable to frustration or positive injury from directly hostile interference by other persons. Thus it comes about that—as Hobbes of course most memorably insisted—there is in what may be called the human predicament a certain 'natural' tendency for things to go very badly; meaning thereby not, of course, in this connection, *morally* badly, but badly merely in the sense that, given the above mentioned wholly indisputable facts about people and the circumstances in which they exist, there is the very evident possibility of very great difficulty in securing, for all or possibly even any of them, much that they want, much that it would be in their interest to have, even much that they need. And the facts that make this so are facts about the *human* predicament; there is probably no great interest in speculating about possible circumstances of other conceivable species of rational beings, but still it is worth bearing in mind that the facts we have so summarily surveyed are contingent facts. It is easy enough to see in general terms how very different the situation would be if the beings concerned were less vulnerable, less aggressive, less egotistical, less irrational, more intelligent, more self-sufficient, and more favoured by material circumstances.

Now, the general suggestion that (guardedly) I wish to put up for consideration is this: that the 'general object' of morality, appreciation of which may enable us to *understand* the basis of moral evaluation, is to contribute to the betterment—or non-deterioration—of the human predicament, primarily and essentially by seeking to countervail 'limited sympathies' and their potentially most damaging effects. It is the proper business of morality, and the general object of moral evaluation, not of course to add to our available resources, nor—directly anyway—to our knowledge of how to make advantageous use of them, nor—again, not directly—to make us more rational in the judicious pursuit of our interests and ends; its proper business is to expand our sympathies, or, better, to reduce the liability to damage inherent in their natural tendency to be narrowly restricted.[6]

In the first sentence of these passages Warnock distinguishes between things which men would be the better for not having, and their harmless, proper and reasonable wants. Is this a moral distinction? He also speaks of the interest "they" have in the course of events. Has he in mind individuals here, each of whom has a personal interest (but who are not interested in what happens to others), or has he in mind an interest which each has in the way events affect them all, that is, one another?

Since Warnock is intent upon an a-moral characterization of the human predicament, a characterization of the human condition *without* morality and in which no appeal is made to moral considerations, the notion of harmless, proper and reasonable wants is intended to make no moral distinction between wants. It is a distinction based upon the effects of acting on (i.e. in response to) certain wants. For example, men have certain needs, a failure to satisfy which will mean death to them. They also have needs which, if they are satisfied, men will be better off than before. Thus a man needs a minimum of food if he is to stay alive, but he needs even more if he is to be strong and healthy and able to resist disease. A proper and reasonable want would certainly include, then, wanting what was necessary for strength and health. Is this also a harmless want? If there is only enough for one and there are two of us is my desire for what there is that will keep me strong and healthy a harmless want so far as you are concerned? Warnock does not ask, or answer, this question, but it seems that he assumes that there are resources enough to feed everyone if men would only use them wisely and humanely—though this last word is of course out of place here. In any case some wants he does conceive as harmful, because involving harm to others. But he also means by "harmful wants" (he has to, since he wishes to justify the importance of this distinction in an a-moral situation), wants which ultimately harm the one who acts on them. This gives the answer to the question about whom 'they' refers to. It refers to individuals. And individuals have harmful wants in so far as their acting on them should directly, or indirectly, bring about harm to themselves. (Indirectly harming oneself would be, for example, harming someone on whom one depended for something, or harming someone where this led to harm to others whom one wished not harmed, and so on). Harmful wants would include then wants which, if acted upon, would harm oneself, by deteriorating, or standing in the way of, arrangements or states of affairs within which one is, or would be, much better placed to satisfy one's needs and best able to engage in projects eminently compatible with one's interests and nature.

Warnock conceives of this set of arrangements as existing (though in a form capable of a very great increase in perfection). He does not in these passages depict a 'state of nature', from which escape is to be got by the institution of society. He marks out in the first of these passages features of society, of social life, and the ways in which that social life goes badly. The object of morality, remember, is to be discerned through contemplation of the features of people, and the circumstances in which they live. And of course people live in society. A man, then, who wants what is not consonant with the continuation or improvement of the social conditions in which his interests are, or would be, most effectively realised is, if he acts upon this want, unreasonable (perhaps we should ordinarily say irrational), for he is unreasonable—if one might put it this way—with himself. He 'calls on himself' to perform an action (to satisfy this unreasonable want) which he himself, in his more rational appreciation of his interests, must condemn. What he wants is an 'unreasonable' demand of himself, not just of others.

The notions, then, in Warnock's account, of harmless, proper, and reasonable wants, are not moral notions. Warnock himself wishes to emphasize that things go badly, but not *morally* badly, without morality. It is the purpose *of morality* to countervail this tendency. It sometimes looks however as though Warnock does have a certain conception of what is going on in the human condition which is (despite himself) morally influenced. Thus *he* looks upon the limitations of resources, intelligence, sympathy, and so on *as limitations*, and also as *evils*. He apparently does this because he sees these things in terms of the provision to all persons of what they need and what it would be in their interests to have. But do these persons whose conditions of life he is describing see it this way? Does each want enough for all, or only enough for himself and perhaps a few others? On Warnock's own account this limitedly-sympathetic desire is what each has. But then their conception of these limitations may not be Warnock's. Some of them at least may look upon these things as advantages, since, if nature is mean, yet hunger makes men vulnerable to threats or cajolment; if men care only for themselves or at best a small circle of others then they will not interest themselves too greatly in what happens to others (may even agree to help take what they have) and so on. The conception of *what limits what* is, I agree, given by the facts. But it is only given once we know *what* is being attempted or aimed at. And this last can be read off from the facts only if the facts *include* here people's wants; what *they* are attempting or aiming at. But I do not wish to pursue this aspect of the matter further. I wish only to bring out the 'empirical' and 'rational' character of Warnock's 'derivation' of morality. He considers a society with morality as rationally preferable to one without morality, because it is a society in which each individual is most favoured by circumstances and better able to satisfy his needs and wants, among which is the need not to be interfered with by others or deprived of what he needs. The conception of what is rationally preferable is an appeal to the facts, and to what best serves the interests of persons. It is open (Warnock admits this) for someone to dispute the facts, and claim that morality does not favour *him*; or even to seek to make the situation other than it is. But Warnock believes that on the first count the man would be wrong, and (I think) he believes the second is not really possible.

I should like to look more closely at the notion of morality's having an *object*, and specifically at Warnock's conception of what that object is. Warnock isolates "four sorts of general *desiderata*" which he considers are necessary to keep human affairs from going quite so badly as they might:

—knowledge, so that what is in fact amelioratively practicable is brought within the scope of feasibility by human action; organization, so that the doings of many people and of groups of people can be brought into directed, co-operative, non-conflicting channels; coercion, so that at least to some extent people may be made to behave in desirable ways, and stopped from behaving otherwise; and 'good dispositions', that is, some degree of readiness voluntarily to act desirably, and to abstain from behaving otherwise.

But it seems to me reasonable to insist that, among all these ramified and mutually interacting *desiderata*, a certain absolute priority must be seen as attaching to human dispositions. We have already found, in an earlier chapter, some reason for thinking that, of the limitations which constitute (in a sense) the human predicament, the most important are those that might be called most 'internal' to human beings—that is, limitations of rationality and sympathy. It may now seem to be the case that, essentially for just the same reasons, what is crucial for betterment is the promotion of 'good dispositions'. All the other things—acquiring, disseminating, preserving, and transmitting knowledge, setting up and maintaining organizations and institutions, devising and operating means of making people do things—all of these things are things that people do: so that everything in the end depends on their readiness to do them, and to do them at least some of the time without being compelled to do so.[7]

Warnock then observes that among the different "good [human] dispositions" one can distinguish between those which make a man a more effective agent, whatever his purposes are, and those which tend to determine to what purposes he will bring his efforts and capacities to bear. Hence industry or courage may be features of evil as well as good actions, but certain other virtues, which are alone to be called *moral* virtues, tend "directly to countervail the limitation of human sympathies, and [their] exercise accordingly is essentially —though indeed not, by itself, necessarily effectively—good *for* persons other than the agent himself."[8] These, the moral virtues, are fundamentally (there are others) four in number: "the disposition to abstain from (deliberate, unjustified) maleficence", "the disposition towards positive beneficence", the disposition to be fair, and the dispostion to not-deceive.[9]

After these remarks about what are the moral virtues there then follows a paragraph which, as it is important to Warnock's account, I shall (as with the earlier summary) quote it, or a part of it, at length.

. . . If it were agreed that we have here, in these 'good dispositions', four moral virtues, it could scarcely be contentious to derive from this the proposition that we have here, by the same token, four fundamental moral *standards*, or moral *principles*. To have and to display, say, the moral virtue of non-deception could be said to be to regulate one's conduct in conformity to a *principle* of non-deception, or to refer to that as to a standard in one's practical decisions. But such a principle would be a principle of judgement as well as of decision. That is, if I accept a principle of non-deception, I may judge others to be morally condemnable in so far as (without excuse) their acts constitute breaches of it, or morally praiseworthy in so far so they (laudably) comply with it in practice. And thus we can say what a 'moral reason' is. Namely, it is a consideration, about some person, or some person's character, or some specimen of actual or possible conduct, which tends to establish in the subject concerned conformity or conflict with a moral principle. That your act would inflict wanton damage on some other person would be a 'moral reason' for judging that—at least 'from the moral point of view'—you ought not so to act, since it tends to establish that your act would be in conflict with the moral principle of non-maleficence, or, to put just the same point in a different way, would be inconsistent with exercise of the moral virtue of non-maleficence.[10]

Warnock has earlier in his book distinguished acting for a reason from complying with a rule. To act for a reason is not to comply with a rule since of any compliance with a rule one can always ask whether one had a reason to comply with it. Thus if someone complies with a rule 'Do not practice abortion' one can always ask what the reason is for complying. If on the other hand someone does

not practise abortion, because he considers it wrong to do so, this is
not a case of following a rule but of acting (or not acting) for a reason:
because it is wrong to abort. What people have called 'moral rules'
cannot be any more than the moral *views* people have. "If I believe
that, say, contraception is morally wrong, I am not in a position to
characterize it in any *new* way if I suppose it to be a breach of a 'moral
rule'; for that is, if anything, just to say again that it is morally
wrong." This part of Warnock's discussion (which I think is excellent) may help us to make out the above passage. In his discussion of
rules Warnock notes that rules are a useful device for the regulation
of conduct. If one wishes to regulate the actions or affairs of people
according to a certain desired pattern then to get them to observe
rules in what they do may achieve this. Now Warnock says that a
man who does not deceive other persons may be said to regulate his
conduct in conformity to a principle of non-deception. This looks
unhappily like a reintroduction of the notion of regulation by a rule.
Is it?

Certainly one thing needs to be said. Not anyone who does not
deceive others *should* be said to be regulating his conduct in conformity to a principle. From the fact that a man does not deceive
others it does not follow that he *regulates* his conduct at all. All that
could be said of everyone who does not in fact deceive others is that it
is as if he regulated his conduct according to a principle of non-
deception. (Just as when I converse, though I may not use a rule or
rules to speak, yet I speak as if there were a rule or rules I were
following, for I always use certain words in roughly similar ways
and a rule might be formulated which, if I followed it, would
produce the same result as before). Anyone, then, whose life is free of
deception could be said to act *as if* he regulated his conduct according
to a principle of non-deception. Certainly if one examines this man's
conduct in the light of this principle it will be found not to contradict
it. Warnock appears to have in mind persons who deliberately keep
from deceiving others, and for purposes of the discussion I shall
assume that everyone is of this sort. Everyone who does not deceive
deliberately conforms to a principle of non-deception. By a moral
principle Warnock means, I think, something like a reason. The man
who acts on a moral principle acts as he does for a reason. Thus the
man who does not deceive on principle does not deceive for a reason.
(It is important to see that principles *could* operate like rules, in that
there could be reasons for holding these principles; but someone may

only be aware that there are these principles of action, 'Act always so as not to deceive', and so on, and so he keeps to them 'blindly' as it were. Warnock does not have such a situation in mind. Perhaps he would wish to say that this is not principled action at all). If a man regulated his conduct in conformity to a principle, then it is not by a rule that he regulates his actions (a rule the reason for which is still to be found or given) but by a reason. He is a rational and reason-heeding man, and he acts as he does because he has *considered* the matter and decided that he has reason to act this way. That this is the correct account of Warnock's meaning (which others may have had no difficulty with at all!) might be thought to be borne out by the expression which follows the one I have glossed: "or to refer to that as to a standard in one's practical decisions." The notion of a standard is the notion of something to which one is committed, presumably because one sees some reason to commit oneself that way, some reason to *make* that one's standard of behaviour. This does, I think, support my rendering of Warnock's remark. The trouble is that a slight unclarity attaches to the expression "to refer to that as a standard." To what does the 'that' refer here? If one looks back to the entire passage it appears that that to which one refers as a standard is either the principle of non-deception or the virtue of non-deception. The most likely of these candidates is the principle, since a plausible account of having the virtue would be being someone who refers to the principle as a standard. If (having) the virtue were one's standard we could go on to ask, why that standard? But if the principle is one's standard in deciding, this looks like another way of saying that in deciding one will attach importance to the question whether one would be deceiving others, because one appreciates the sort of importance non-deception (this good disposition) has. We arrive, then, at this. According to Warnock, if you are someone who does not deceive others, then, where you are also someone who is aware of the considerations which count against deceiving others, we may say of you that you act according to a moral principle of action, the principle of not deceiving others. This is one of your standards of morally acceptable behaviour according to which you fashion your practice.

It follows then that you can apply this standard to the behaviour of other persons. You can judge other persons according to whether or not they deceive others. "And thus", concludes Warnock, "we can say what a moral reason is. Namely, it is a consideration, about some person, or some person's character, or some specimen of actual or possible conduct, which tends to establish in the subject concerned conformity or conflict with a moral principle." Now the moral reason which Warnock uncovers here is a reason for your judging that others (or others judging that you) ought not to act in a certain way. There is reason for judging that they (or you) ought not so to act, wherever their (or your) action is in conflict with a moral principle; that is, wherever to act that way would not be in accord with the principle, were the principle applied. But what about the reason *for acting* on the moral principle? Is that a *moral* reason too? On Warnock's account that reason is the tendency of action in conformity with that principle to make the human predicament less grim than it is. And it is clear that on Warnock's account this reason is not a moral reason.

On Warnock's account, what distinguishes morality is its object (to expand our sympathies) and its method (the evaluation of human actions according to certain principles). Morality is something which is justified by the very good reasons we have for it. But it is not a *moral* appreciation of human affairs which brings this home to us, but simply a patient attention to the facts. Things go badly here (but not 'morally' badly) and so on. It seems incontrovertible then that the reasons we have not *to* deceive or act malevolently etc. are not describable as moral reasons. It is the good effects of not doing these things and the even better effects of being positively beneficent etc. that impel Warnock to single them out, on rational grounds, as good dispositions. But these good effects, which are the reasons we have to encourage and display these dispositions, are not moral reasons. They are just very good reasons. Moral reasons are reasons we have for judging that actions are not in conformity with a moral principle.

But now I want to ask how these *principles* got to be moral. The short answer is, of course: because they are appealed to in moral judgment. Warnock has not departed as far from the contemporary beaten path in ethics as he believes, for he ends up identifying morality with evaluation. It will be asked what difference this makes so long as Warnock also insists that morality is evaluation upon certain grounds (viz. the 'moral principles' he isolates). The difference is that there is a very old tradition, expressed in the language and reflections of ordinary, unphilosophical men, according to which what decides whether a man acts morally or not is the *sort* of consideration on which his decision turns. Not any judgment or decision is a moral decision or judgment, and what will show whether a man has judged morally or not will be the sort of considerations that determines his judgment. A judgment becomes a moral judgment by being made on *moral* grounds.

If this is true, Warnock can never get morality started. He begins, remember, from an a-moral consideration of the human condition. He uncovers there certain beneficial features, or possibilities (it does not matter which), and he then proceeds to identify these as moral standards or principles. But his justification, on his own theory, for doing so cannot be that they are *themselves* moral in any sense, but rather that they provide standards for a species of evaluation which is to be called 'moral'. That is, these good dispositions are not morally good, not moral standards in *that sense*. They are moral standards in being the standards one uses in doing what is called morally judging, morally evaluating. But in the ancient tradition one wants first something moral in order to *get a moral judgment*, since this last is just a judgment like any other except that it appeals to a *moral* consideration. One might say: if the moral is to lie anywhere it must lie, not in my judgment, but in the considerations (the grounds) on which I judge, since if the considerations are not moral any judgment according to them will not be moral either. But Warnock's considerations are not moral—they cannot be (on his account) since they are the *rational* considerations which we appreciate will *justify* morality, will make reasonable the 'introduction' of this practice. But then how do his moral judgments ever arise?

Well, they just arise, and he calls them 'moral'. He sees the use of the sort of discrimination between actions he describes, and he accords this evaluation and judgment the epithet 'moral'. But I wish to ask why he does this, since no new *consideration* or *reason* has been brought forward into the picture, only this new technique, this practice (with its promised effects). Warnock of course sometimes speaks as though morality ('the moral') were not just this species of evaluation: as though this evaluation had a *basis* which *was* morality. Thus on page 26 he begins:

Now, the general suggestion that (guardedly) I wish to put up for consideration is this: that the 'general object' of morality, appreciation of which may enable us to *understand* the basis of moral evaluation, is to contribute to betterment—or non-deterioration—of the human predicament, primarily and essentially by seeking to countervail 'limited sympathies' and their potentially most damaging effects. It is the proper business of morality, and the general object of moral evaluation, . . . etc., etc. [see above]

These remarks suggest something (morality) which, if we knew what *it* was, we would see the basis, the point, of moral *evaluation* (evaluation according to 'the moral'). But one looks in vain for what this (moral) basis is. The basis of course is the *effect* of the evaluation (the *rationally preferable* effect of acting as the practice of 'moral' evaluation enjoins). In other places Warnock speaks more frankly of an 'exercise'[12] and 'apparatus'.[13]

It may be claimed that Warnock identifies this (moral) basis with *the concern to evaluate* morally. I do not think this suggestion will stand a reading of the book. But in any case, if Warnock were to claim this I should want to ask how he explains this passage on pages 150–151.

. . . Moral *agents*, we have said, are rational beings; if we now say that the beneficiaries, so to speak, of moral principles are, unrestrictedly, persons, should we take 'person' here to mean 'rational being'? There is plain reason, I believe, to hold that we should not so take it—to hold, indeed, that 'person' is itself too restrictive a term here. Notice, first, that we do not in fact place this limitation upon the class of beneficiaries of moral principle. We do not regard infants and imbeciles as moral agents, as liable to judgement for their conduct on moral principles, since we take them not to possess those rational capacities which are a condition of being capable of moral thought and decision; but we do not for that reason regard them as morally insignificant, as having, that is, no moral claims upon rational beings. Why is this? Is it that they are in some sense, though not actual, yet potential rational beings, members, so to speak of a potentially rational species? I do not think so. Infants no doubt could be said to be potentially rational; but is it for that reason that they are not to be, say, physically maltreated? Not all imbeciles, I dare say, *are* potentially rational; but does it follow that, if they are reasonably judged to be incurable, they are then reasonably to be taken to have no moral claims? No: the basis of moral claims seems to me to be quite different. We may put it thus: just as liability to be judged as a moral agent follows from one's general capability of alleviating, by moral action, the ills of the predicament, and is for that reason confined to rational beings, so the condition of being a proper 'beneficiary' of moral action is the capability of *suffering* the ills of the predicament—and for that reason is *not* confined to rational beings, nor even to potential members of that class. *Things go badly, in general, if creatures suffer*, better if they do not; to come within the ambit, then, of the ameliorative object of moral principles is, not to be capable of contributing to such amelioration, but to be capable of suffering by its absence—that is, capable of suffering. [The last italics are mine].

The basis of one's claim to be treated in accordance with the 'moral principles' Warnock has isolated is that one's suffering contributes to the tendency of things to go badly. This is a concern about what the suffering of persons leads to, not their suffering as such; a concern about the fact, not *that* persons suffer, but that their suffering has certain effects. Yet this is the place, if any, where the moral might have been thought to enter in the form of a kind of concern. Warnock speaks of 'badly' and 'better' here, but these are (as before) intended as a-moral, aseptic terms, referring to the *interest* each has in the amelioration of the suffering of others. To be capable of suffering is to be one of the class of moral patients (Warnock's term), not because one suffers *tout court*, but because of the implications of one's suffering. Warnock does not (nor would he, I expect) disclaim that someone might be concerned to eliminate or lessen suffering just because he wishes that others should not suffer. Warnock simply does not mention any such concern. But whoever did this would not be acting under the aegis of morality. Or rather, to be correct, he would be achieving the object of morality (since in lessening suffering he would supposedly lessen the tendency of things to go badly) but he would be, as they say nowadays, over-determined. It is enough to appreciate morality, and to practise it, on Warnock's account, to realize that the suffering of others is inconvenient, because tending always to be troublesome.

II

It may, I think, help at this point to consider a detailed example of human inter-relationships, and to contrast our moral appreciation of the example (and my account of the moral appreciation in the example) with the account of morality Warnock gives. The example I have chosen is from Dostoevsky's novel *The Idiot*. In the early part of the novel the central figure Prince Myshkin relates the experience of a young woman who lived in a village to which the prince had been sent for medical treatment.

Her mother was an old woman. One of the two windows of their ramshackle little house was set apart by permission of the village authorities, and from it the old woman was allowed to sell laces, thread, tobacco, and soap, all for a pittance, and that was what they lived on. She was an invalid; her legs were all swollen, so that she always stayed in the same place. Marie was her daughter, a girl of twenty, weak and thin; she had contracted consumption long before, but she kept going from house to house doing heavy work as a daily—scrubbing floors, doing the washing, sweeping out yards, looking after the cattle. A French commercial traveller, who was passing through the village, seduced her and took her away, but a week later he deserted her and went off, leaving her stranded. She returned home, begging on the way, all bespattered and in rags, with her shoes all in holes. She had walked for a week, had spent the nights in the fields, and caught a bad cold. Her feet were covered in sores, her hands were chapped and swollen. But then she had never been a beauty before; only her eyes were gentle, kind, and innocent. She was terribly taciturn. One day—it happened long before—she suddenly burst into song when she was at work, and I remember how surprised everyone was and how they all laughed: "Marie was singing! What did you say? Marie was singing!" She was terribly put out and was silent for ever after. In those days people were still very kind to her, but when she came back ill and bedraggled, no one felt any pity for her! How cruel people are in a case like that! What distressing ideas they have! Her mother was the first to welcome her spitefully and with contempt: "You have disgraced me now!" She was the first to expose her to public contumely: when the news of Marie's return spread through the village, everyone ran to have a look at her, and almost the whole village gathered in the old woman's cottage—old men, children, women, girls, all—a scrambling, eager crowd. Marie was lying on the ground at the old woman's feet, hungry and in rags, and she was crying. When they all crowded into the cottage, she buried her face in her dishevelled hair and lay huddled up face downwards on the floor. They all looked at her as if she had been something too vile to be regarded with anything but profound disgust. The old men blamed and scolded her, the young people laughed, the women scolded her, blamed her, looked upon her with contempt as though she had been some loathsome spider. Her mother allowed it all, sitting there nodding her head and approving. The mother was very ill at the time and almost dying, and yet up to the very day of her death she made no attempt to be reconciled to her daughter. She did not speak to her, she turned her out to sleep in the passage, and gave her hardly anything to eat. She had to bathe her bad legs in hot water, and Marie bathed her legs every day and nursed her. She accepted all her services in silence and never said a kind word to her. . . . When the old woman took to her bed at last, the old women of the village took turns in nursing her, as is their custom. Then they stopped giving food to Marie altogether, and in the village everyone drove her away and no one would even give her work as before. They all seemed to spit on her, and the men no longer looked on her as a woman, and they all said such horrible things to her. Sometimes, though very rarely, when the men got drunk on a Sunday, they amused themselves by throwing coppers on the ground for her to pick up. Marie picked them up without uttering a word. She had begun to cough and spit blood by that time. As last her rags became so tattered and torn that she was ashamed to show herself in the village. She had gone barefoot ever since she came back. It was just then that the children in particular, the whole gang of them—there were over forty schoolchildren—began teasing her and even pelting her with mud.[14]

Is anyone to deny that those who treated this young woman as they did were wrong in doing so? Perhaps someone will wish to say that she deserved to be treated in this way, because of what she did. I realize that this appreciation is a possible one, though I think it is a deeply ignorant and mistaken one. But I shall ignore it, since the appeal to desert (which is a moral concept) gives at least this much of what I want, an appreciation that if Marie *had* not deserved this treatment they would have been wrong to treat her so. For the purposes of the discussion I shall proceed on the assumption that I have found a second example which we are agreed is an example of moral wrong.

I wish first to discuss the mother's treatment of Marie. I want first to say that the mother is not only wrong in what she does, she is ignorant. Or perhaps it would be better to say, she acts as though she were ignorant. She acts as though certain features of what happened to her daughter and what her daughter did were not known to her. Her daughter was for a long time ill. She was also crushingly poor, and forced to perform the most unpleasant and humiliating kinds of work. She was not physically attractive. She was, accordingly, deeply vulnerable to any show of attention to her. When it was shown, she was drawn into a response which enabled this person to use her. (Does anyone believe that a person with the daughter's life and experience would be knowledgeable about people, or able, when thrown into confusion by an unaccustomed attention to her, to weigh the character and motive of this attention?)

The mother condemns her daughter. I want to condemn what the mother does. Nevertheless I do not find it hard to see how it is that the mother acts as she does. What is hard is *to say* how it is that she comes to act as she does.

There are two possibilities. In the first, the mother cares about no one except herself. She cares not even for her daughter. This case is the easiest to explain. Because she does not care, because she has no love for others, it does not matter to her that her daughter suffers, or that she contributes to that suffering. What matters to her is only what she herself feels or suffers. And she suffers a social disgrace. That is reason enough for her to treat her daughter as she does, since the daughter has thwarted her will and abused her self-importance.

I do not think, however, that this is the situation as Dostoevsky draws it. I believe we are to regard the mother as caring *something* for her daughter. This is the second possibility spoken of above. —Though I think it is clear from what happens how much she cares for her daughter, and how much she cares for herself. Nevertheless the mother is, I believe, capable of morally appreciating what she does. Yet she treats her daughter as we are told. How is it that she does? My short answer is, she is selfish, which keeps her from appreciating what she does.

Perhaps I can bring out what I want to say in this way: the mother has lost sight of her daughter *as her daughter is*. Her daughter is a woman, like herself, who has known the life she has known. Perhaps the mother has even known a better life, at a time before her poverty. Her daughter is a creature with feelings and a certain conception of herself and of others. She needs and wants to be cared about, to be an object of love and respect on the part of someone. She desires to be understood and accounted significant. She is a creature such that what her mother does in treating her this way cannot but cause her the most annihilating pain. For her mother is the only person on whom she can with any reason depend for understanding and compassion.

All of this the mother knows. Certainly she has no reason not to know it. I want to say that she does know some at least of these things about her daughter. Yet she treats her as she does. How does she do this? She does it because she is selfishly attending to what she accounts the injury her daughter has done her. Her concern with her daughter's actions and what they have brought about is centred upon certain consequences to her, the mother; specifically, she is concerned with how the daughter's actions have placed her in a position of social disgrace. It is with her own pain and discomfort that she is preoccupied, and from within that preoccupation she reacts to her daughter as to one who has pained and hurt her.

Philosophers sometimes speak of consciousness as though it were a sort of vision, as though we must always be conscious of what confronts us. They fail to heed the fact that what we are conscious of is deeply affected by what preoccupies us. We need not be conscious of all that is present to us, but only of certain features of it. This is especially apparent once we appreciate that what is present to us depends upon our mode of understanding and attention. Sometimes we are not conscious of anything present to us at all, as when we are distraught—obsessed by some insistent thought or hope or regret. And of course we cannot be conscious of what we do not understand or recognize (except we are conscious of it *as* something we do not understand or recognize). It follows from these facts that someone who is capable of morally appreciating human life will not always do so, or may do so mistakenly. Indeed we are especially *prone* to deceive ourselves about the moral features of our lives and practices; as when, for example, we conceive some action we desire to do as justified by love or compassion, and so ignore the dishonesty or selfishness, and the hurt, it involves. Our moral appreciation is extraordinarily sensitive to our desires and our passions, which should not surprise us since it is not exaggerating very greatly to say that our moral appreciation can only exist in the absence of our selfish desires, in the absence of exclusive love of self. Selfishness, we often say, blinds us to features of our lives or actions.

How far, and for how long, one can escape moral self-appreciation will depend on countless things. The one thing on which it will depend most is how loving, or how selfish, we are.

The mother of Marie hurts her daughter, because her daughter hurt her. But there are at least these differences between the two cases of hurt. Marie's hurt to her mother was not intended. And the daughter's hurt to her mother is not, in a real sense, the daughter's hurt to her at all. The hurt the mother suffers is essentially connected with her concern for herself. Had she a proper appreciation of the situation she would not be hurt, or at least *not as hurt*, in the first place. A person can be hurt by another's action in at least two ways: when the action is itself an injury to them in some way; or when the action realizes some disappointment or vexation to them. An example of the first kind of hurt is where a man prevents the marriage of two persons by ruining one of them financially; an example of the second is where a person is hurt because another has chosen in marriage someone else and not him or her. When is a hurt given a wrong on the part of the person who gave it? Whether a particular action constitutes a moral wrong depends upon considerations which are in part independent of how the person affected *feels about* the particular matter or action. Whether a person *feels* hurt about a certain action is not necessarily enough to make it the case that he is wronged, any more than because a man does not feel anything he is not wronged (for he may not know of the actions which wrong him). Whether an action constitutes a wrong depends on what is done. But what is done is not something which depends simply on how the one to whom it is done feels about it. A man may of course not be troubled by wrongs done him. But in the same way, that one feels wronged does not, *eo ipso*, make one wronged. In certain cases, what it is wrong to do rests upon agreement, in the sense that within a community there is an appreciation of what it is reasonable to demand or expect of others. If a parent demands what it is unreasonable to demand of a daughter or son, the parent may be hurt if the son or daughter does not comply. But that hurt is not something which the son or daughter is necessarily wrong in being responsible for. It may be that the parent is wrong in his or her self-centred demand. Here one wants to say of the hurt: the parent brings it on himself (or herself).

The mother of Marie, if she is aware that she does wrong in treating her daughter as she does, does what she does out of a cruel selfishness. What I believe is more likely the truth is that she to some extent *keeps herself* from seeing the wrong she does, by dwelling always on the hurt to herself, by being possessed by her selfishness and resentment. Selfishness is an insistent concern with what one feels or suffers or desires, and a response to others within the ambience of that concern, such that others confront one as threats or irritations or pleasantnesses, according as they work to retard or realize one's own satisfactions. Selfishness generates a willingness to achieve one's own desires or alleviate one's own discomfort at cost to another. Thus while selfish acts are not always wrong, they are often so, because often the cost to another it is wrong to inflict. Selfishness is tenacious, and fertile. It is a great corrupter. There is an ordinary example of this in Dostoevsky's novel. It concerns Marie.

She had asked the cowherd to let her look after his cows, but the cowherd drove her away. Then she began to go away with the herd for the whole day without his permission. As she was very useful to the cowherd and he realized it, he no longer drove her away, and sometimes even gave her the remnants of his dinner, bread and cheese. He thought it a great kindness on his part.[15]

One does not need to look into books to find examples of works of charity which are a celebration of self, and not an instance of love of others. The cowherd is someone who does a good deed 'in order to be good'. He does it to please himself, to reinforce his own good opinion of his nature (perhaps as well to collect the good opinion of others). Though perhaps when confronted with Marie he does experience moments of genuine compassion. Perhaps it is these which wring from him this little kindness. That he sees the kindness as greater than it is is an effect of ignorance, but also of egoism, of selfishness and self-esteem. Selfishness may take even a good impulse and so suffocate it in the tentacles of self that it is no longer able to escape the self, but is become a servant of its glory.

Consider now this part of the story of Marie.

But the children would not let her alone. They teased her more than ever and threw mud at her. When they chased her, she ran away from them; when she, with her weak chest, stopped, panting for breath, they were still after her, shouting and cursing and swearing at her. Once I even had a fight with them. Then I began to talk to them; I talked to them every day as much as I could. Sometimes they stopped and listened to me, though they still abused me. I told them how unhappy Marie was, and soon they stopped abusing me and began to walk away in silence. Little by little, we began talking together. I concealed nothing from them. I told them everything. They listened with great interest and soon they began to feel sorry for Marie. Some of them began greeting her affectionately when they met her. One day two little girls got some food and took it to her. They gave it to her, then came back and told me about it. They told me Marie had burst into tears and that now they loved her very much. Soon all of them began to love her, and at the same time they suddenly began loving me too. . . .I at once told them of the pastor's action [he held Marie up to public shame at her mother's funeral, and said she was the cause of her mother's death] and explained it to them. They were all angry with him, and some of them were so disgusted that they threw stones and broke his windows. I stopped them, for that was wrong. But everyone in the village got to know about it at once, and it was then that they started accusing me of corrupting the children. Soon they got to know that the children loved Marie and they were terribly alarmed; but Marie was happy. The children were forbidden to meet her, but they ran out secretly to the herd, nearly half a mile from the village, to see her. They brought her presents, and some of them simply ran to hug and kiss her and say, '*Je vous aime, Marie!*' and then ran back as fast as they could. By that time she had become very ill and could hardly walk; at last she gave up working for the cowman altogether, but went out with the cattle each morning all the same. She used to sit apart. There was a ledge on one sheer, almost vertical, rock there. She used to sit down on the stone, leaning against the rock, out of sight of everybody, and sit there motionless all day, from early morning till it was time for the cattle to go home. She was already so weakened by consumption that she mostly sat with her eyes closed and head leaning against the rock, dozing and breathing heavily. Her face was as thin as a skeleton's, and the sweat stood out on her brow and temples. That was how I always found her. Sometimes the children came with me. When they did so, they generally stood a little way off to keep guard over us against someone or something, and that pleased them exceedingly. When we went away, Marie was again left alone, sitting motionless as before, with her eyes closed and her head leaning against the rock; perhaps she was dreaming of something. One morning she could no longer go out with the herd and remained at home in her deserted house. The children got to know of it at once, and almost all of them came to see her that day; she lay in bed, all alone. For two days she was nursed by the children, who ran in to her by turns, but afterwards, when it became known in the village that Marie was really dying, the old women went to sit with her and never again left her alone. I believe the villagers had begun to pity Marie, at least they no longer interfered with the children and did not scold them as before. Marie was drowsy all the time, her sleep was restless: she coughed dreadfully. The old women drove the children away, but they kept running under the window, sometimes only for a moment, just to say, '*Bonjour, notre bonne Marie.*' As soon as she caught sight of them or heard them, she grew all animated and, without paying attention to the old women, tried to raise herself on her elbow and nodded to them and thanked them. They brought her presents as before, but she scarcely ate anything. I assure you it was because of them that she died almost happy. Because of them she forgot her bitter troubles; it was as though she had received forgiveness from them, for to the very end she considered herself a great sinner. Like birds, they fluttered their wings against her window, calling to her every morning: '*Nous t'aimons, Marie.*' She died very soon.[16]

The children come to see as wrong the treatment of Marie by the others, a treatment in which they earlier joined. How do they come to that appreciation? It has been claimed to me that they come to see the wrong in having it impressed on them how unhappy Marie is. I do not deny that this account of the matter is correct, so far as it goes. But I want to ask why their appreciation that she is unhappy should make a difference. It seems to me that it makes a difference because these children are compassionate and caring, and when finally they come to appreciate Marie's hurt and loneliness they see it *as* something which the others should not inflict on her. They now consider it wrong to treat her as the others do and as they too treated her before, because they now appreciate that it gives her pain and distress to be treated in this way. They want her treated better because they care how she is treated. They want the ridicule and ostracism to stop, because of what it does to Marie (not because what is done to her is, or could be, done to themselves).

I have called attention to the children's relation to Marie in order to show more clearly the connnection between moral wrong and human appreciation: that to appreciate wrong one must not merely be capable of caring for persons, one must care for them in fact. The children did care for persons before they befriended Marie. What shows that they did is that when they are brought by the prince to appreciate her situation and suffering they respond, not just by ceasing to torment her; they respond with sorrow, and with generosity. In time they come to love Marie. But from the first, when 'their eyes are now opened', they care that Marie is unhappy, and seek to be kind and friendly toward her. The children would, I expect, wish to say that they came to see that the way they had treated Marie before was wrong. It might be thought that this is something that cannot be said on my account, since an action's being wrong is at bottom a matter of people caring, for the sake of the one to whom it would be done, that it not be done. On this account, until the children in fact care that they and others treat Marie differently, surely it is not yet wrong for them to treat her as they then were doing? Surely the wrong only arises at the time they begin to care that it not be done? But then before that they did not (so far as they are concerned) wrong her, and what sense is there in the claim that they come to appreciate that what they did before *was wrong* to do? They can at best come to appreciate that it *is* (now) wrong to do; or perhaps, that others before considered it wrong.

This objection rests upon a misunderstanding. A person may in fact care about others, and yet sometimes hurt people. He may even *love* some particular person, and yet bring the loved one hurt or suffering. If he does this there may be one of several explanations of it. The explanation may be that he not merely loves but also hates. He loves some feature of the person but hates others; or he loves the person but resents the claims this love makes on him, perhaps because he loves, or at least desires, other things which are incompatible in certain ways with the claims of this love. His hurting the other may be a manifestation of his resentment or hatred. The man may however love the other person deeply and without reservation, and yet, being also desirous of other things, or in the grip of some insistent need, he may sometimes be caught up by his desires or passions and do what hurts the loved one. Later he may condemn what he did, and regret that he did not do what he should have done, "—But how is it that there *is* something that he should have done then, but which he did not do? Did he not in fact want to do what he did, what brought the hurt?" He did, but at the same time he did not *desire to hurt*. Indeed he wanted not to hurt. He wanted not to hurt because he loved the other. In the case I am imagining what the man most deeply wants is not to hurt this one he loves. But he also sometimes wants other things incompatible with this, and because he is a creature some of whose desires are more insistent than others, and whose resolution depends upon the clarity of attention and consciousness he is able to summon, which last are themselves affected by the play of his desires, he may sometimes do what he "would not" do. If he often does it, or does it without great temptation, we shall perhaps say that he merely *thinks* he wants most not to hurt. But if he very frequently resists small, and sometimes resists even powerful inclinations to do what would hurt the other, would we not be right to say that, despite his occasional lapses, he does love deeply and desires that the other not be hurt? This is the form of the children's relationship to Marie (with the difference that there is no intimacy beforehand). The children are caught up in the general condemnation of Marie. Taught perhaps that those who do wrong deserve to be punished, and not encouraged ever to inquire into the basis of the condemnations which they hear on their parents' and others' lips, they naturally accept, and read off from the overt hostility of the others, that Marie deserves to be derided and harassed. There is no physical attractiveness or vitality to raise in them a natural obstacle to accepting this condemnation. There is only weakness, and also the sheer animal delight of hooting, running, throwing and generally being audacious and yet also approved. These things work against the play of sympathy or the awakening of recognition. And yet I want to say that the children care about persons even as they do this. If they did not, how is one to explain the fact that when it is impressed upon them the state Marie is in, they respond with pity, with sorrow? How can one sorrow except one cares?

A slightly different objection would be to admit that to sorrow is to care, but yet to urge that the children's compassion is not there all along, in the form of a caring about persons, but is at best a disposition to respond in the appropriate situation, in the way we call 'compassionately'. This, it might be thought, removes again the possibility that they should see what they did in the past as a *wrong* they have done. This argument too, I think is a mistake. Even if we were to accept this account of the children's caring about Marie and how she is treated, as something which just arises in the appropriate recognition of her state, and does not presuppose some prior state which is their caring about others (which account I believe is false), even then it does not follow that the children (and others) cannot now see as wrong what they did in the past. For again, we must avoid insinuating the notion that there is some wrong there in the past which exists independent of their (or others') *attitudes* toward what they do. If, before their appreciation of their actions as wrong, we say that they wrong Marie but do not know that they do, we are saying that we account wrong what they do. If later they agree with our judgment this is because they now consider it wrong as well. To say that they now know to be wrong what they did in the past is just to say that they now condemn what they did then, and, had they then the appreciation they have now of what they did, they would have condemned it then (in the past).

III

What this example reveals in relation to Warnock's account of morality is two things. The first is that while Warnock rightly seizes upon the question of the appropriate or relevant standards for moral evaluation as central, and rightly fixes upon considerations of harm and suffering in seeking to answer this question, he misrepresents that relation of persons to these considerations which constitutes *moral* judgment and action. He represents each individual as having a stake in whatever lessens or increases the tendency of things to go badly in society, and casts the difference which moral action is supposed to make in terms of sustaining or strengthening the delicate ecology of human interrelationship and mutual progress. This egocentric axis of his story leads him effectively to misdescribe what are the considerations appropriate to moral action, since it leaves out of account the defining parameter of moral sensibility: concern for persons other than oneself. A second thing the example points up respecting Warnock's position is the intuitive implausibility of any account of morals which represents moral reasoning, judgment and sensitivity as a species of economic rationalism. The developing undertanding and response of the children in Dostoevsky's story to Marie's "predicament" is not easily caught in a net of prudent forbearance and far-seeing calculation. This second aspect I shall return to in chapter eight. But I should like to say something further here about the issue of egocentrism and morals.

People have seriously argued that egocentrism and morality are not in any opposition, logical, or psychological, but that in fact egoism is itself a perfectly viable—indeed the only viable—moral stance. This is so-called 'ethical egoism', according to which one ought (morally) always to do what is in one's own interest, regardless of the effect of doing so on other persons. A greater number of writers have taken up the more modest position of arguing that, repugnant as 'ethical egoism' may be when morally considered (i.e. when considered from the point of view of the critic's morality) it cannot be denied the description 'ethical'. It is *a* genuinely moral position.

Now a consequence of this more modest position is that virtually anything can be described as a moral consideration, provided only that it holds a certain place in the deliberations of the person whose morality it forms an element of. D. H. Monro is one of several moral philosophers who hold this view. Monro writes:

We are presumably trying to define 'moral' in the sense in which the word is contrasted with 'unmoral' or 'non-moral', not in the sense in which it is contrasted with 'immoral'. We are concerned, that is, with the descriptive and not the evaluative use of 'moral'. In saying that some principles are not moral ones, we are not trying to condemn them. We are not ourselves trying to make a moral judgement, but merely to get straight what kind of thing a moral judgement is.

A parallel may be illuminating here. If we say that Bacon's essays are not poetry, but prose, we are not evaluating'; but if we say that what Patience Strong writes is not poetry, but verse, or perhaps doggerel, we are evaluating. We are making an aesthetic judgement, which may well be a sound one. As an aesthetic judgement, it needs to be supported by reasons, and the reasons will not be merely linguistic ones. It will not do to say 'We just don't happen to use the word "poetry" of this kind of thing'. This would invite an answer, 'But it may be just as well worth reading, for all that'. If someone were to give us this answer to the statement that Bacon's essays are not poetry, we would say 'That is not in dispute. I didn't mean to imply anything about the literary value of the essays.' But we cannot say that about Patience Strong. For, in this use of 'poetry', to say that something is 'not poetry' *is* to imply something about its literary value. Consequently the remark needs to be supported by an aesthetic theory; it cannot be passed off as a neutral investigation into usage.

In the same way, to say that a given principle is not a moral one may mean that it is immoral, and so to be avoided; or it may mean that it is one about which moral questions just do not arise. If the first, it needs to be backed by reasons which are not merely linguistic reasons. The criterion by which we distinguish between the moral and the immoral will itself be a moral principle, and as such open to attack and defence. The criterion by which we distinguish between the moral and the non-moral, on the other hand, must not itself be a moral principle. An immoral principle is, indeed, a moral one in the other sense of 'moral', that is, it is not non-moral, not outside the sphere of morality. For this reason we may be suspicious of the view that the egoist's principle is not, in this sense, a moral one; for many people would regard it as an immoral principle.

It may be objected that we condemn the egoist, not because he adopts this principle, but because he allows it to usurp the place of moral principles. This objection, however, merely brings out another implication of the word 'moral'. We expect a moral principle to take precedence over others: in the terminology we have been using, it has 'authority'. It can hardly be denied, however, that the egoist's principle has authority *for him*. When it is said that he allows it to usurp the place of a moral principle, what is meant is that he gives it authority when it *ought not* to have authority. It is presupposed that only moral principles ought to have authority. But, if this is so, then to say that a given principle is not a moral one is to say that it is not the kind of principle that ought to take precedence over others. This is clearly not a morally neutral remark.[17]

Monro, if I understand him, decides what principles are moral principles by finding out whether they have authority with a man or not. Their having authority with a man (again if I understand Monro) is their being the principles on which he does in fact decide.

If he doesn't always decide on them at least they are what he wishes always to decide on, though sometimes he may slip up. (Al Capone, say, now and then departs from his deliberately ruthless pursuit of power because of a soft spot for a pal. He may condemn this afterwards as stupid (and dangerous).)

Is this how we in fact decide whether a man's principles are moral principles or not? I thought we decided by looking to see *what* his principles were? And this looking to see need not be a moral act. We can imagine Al Capone requiring each new candidate for his gang to go to confession beforehand. The man is told to turn up at the cathedral at a certain hour. Capone disguises himself as a priest, waits in the confessional, and hears the confession. After he says: "This guy won't do. He's got too much conscience." And notice, when we say to someone "Consider the claims of morality" we do not mean, "Consider what you want most." We may know what you want most. That's why we are trying to get you to consider the claims of morality!

Monro's position is that to describe a principle as immoral is to condemn it from the point of view of one's own morality, while to describe a principle as non-moral is to identify it as one about which moral questions do not arise. I would prefer to say it is to identify it as a principle which is not grounded on moral considerations. Thus (to recall an example of Mounce and Phillips') the principle "Always keep your matches dry" would not ordinarily be thought to be a moral principle of action, though in fact moral questions can quite easily arise in relation to this principle. Thus a scoutmaster who takes a group of young boys into the desert or mountains and irresponsibly pays no attention to the need to keep matches dry, water enough for the return, etc., may be judged to be acting morally badly. The reason the principle "Always keep your matches dry" would not ordinarily be identified as a moral principle is because it is considerations of practicality and convenience that people usually have in mind when they urge this principle on individuals. But in certain (easily imaginable) circumstances the considerations they would appeal to (sc. the need to be able to provide light and warmth for feverish, or otherwise distressed, children) would make it wicked to neglect this ordinarily 'merely practical' injunction.

Monro's parallel with poetry I find especially unhappy. The parallel he draws is

| (a) Bacon's essays are not poetry. | (a') Principle X is a non-moral principle. |
| (b) What Patience Strong writes is not poetry. | (b') Principle Y is an immoral principle. |

What I find unsatisfying in this parallel is that while (b), as Monro suggests, can be taken to say that Patience Strong's stuff is not *good* poetry (i.e. (b) is an aesthetically engaged pronouncement upon the merit of the work before one, where (a) is not) nevertheless (b) entails that what Patience writes *is* poetry (however awful)—or else (b) collapses into (a). That is, either Patience succeeds in writing poetry, though pretty bad poetry (hence the point of (b)), or, she fails to write even awful poetry, in which case there is no difference between (b) and (a). But (b'), notice, does not entail that Y is still a moral principle, although a bad one, on pain of collapsing into (a'). For a principle can be non-moral—i.e. not appeal to moral considerations—and also be *im*moral, precisely for that reason. (The principle "Always exploit the weak" is such a principle).

This asymmetry is important, for Monro remarks that "we should be suspicious of the view that the egoist's principle is not . . . a moral one; for many people would regard it as an immoral principle." But why should this give rise to suspicion? The fact that many would regard it as immoral does not *eo ipso* rule out their being able to show it to be amoral—non-moral. To do this they have only to point to the consideration that informs the egoists' principle, which is exclusive self-regard. (The exclusiveness is important here, for regard for one's own needs and entitlements is, like regard for those of others, a perfectly respectable moral consideration. What makes the egoist's principle amoral, and immoral, is this *restriction* of the criteria of judgement to one's own wants—i.e. the disregard of the needs and wants of others). This discrimination of the considerations to which the egoist's principle makes appeal is not itself a moral condemnation of the principle, any more than the appreciation that someone has reasoned mistakenly from what are undeniably moral considerations is a moral discrimination. Discrimination of the considerations to which any principle makes appeal is logically distinct from, and prior to, moral condemnation of the principle. One can reason morally but do it badly (commit a fallacy, say), and appreciation of this error of reasoning is logical discrimination. So too one can reason successfully, but not from moral considerations, and the appreciation of this too is a case of logical (category) discrimination.

I do not see how the question of whether a man has a morality or not can be settled other than by looking to see what considerations he lives by. A Hindu, say, may be recognized to have a morality, though differing perhaps in some ways from ours. Still we recognize it as a morality. "—Exactly!" the egoist will cry. "And my morality is just *more* different from yours. But it's what I live by! And so—it's a morality!" But isn't this rather like saying: *Your* painting (which is exceptionally impressive) is what you attach importance to. *His* different achievement at painting (which is just as talented and impressive) is what he attaches importance to. Therefore *my* painting, which I attach importance to, is also an impressive achievement? But whether my, or your painting *is* an achievement within that human activity we call art is not to be determined by whether you or I attach importance to it or not. I may attach all the importance to it I like, and say, "Oh, it's nothing." Those who are informed about art may say: It *is* nothing.

It seems to me that this is the case with morality. Only *some kinds* of reason, only *some kinds* of considerations are moral reasons, moral considerations. Of course, if one doesn't find these reasons compelling, well, one doesn't. But that does not make the reasons one does find compelling, *moral* reasons—by default, as it were. Of course one can say they are moral. One can *say* anything. But whether they are or not will depend on what sort of reasons they are, and one wants first to look at them to see.

Monro gives the following example in support of his claim that egoism is a moral practice:

We can speak quite intelligibly of the morality of Satan; meaning thereby the principles which Satan consistently follows as his over-riding ones, even though in content these principles would presumably differ quite drastically from our own. It is true that Satan's principles must, at least, have the same subject-matter as our own: that is to say, they would be concerned with the pleasure and pain of sentient beings. They might, however, be completely selfish. And I think that, if we did discover someone who felt guilt and remorse about matters which seemed to us to have nothing to do with morality at all, we would still have to regard his attitudes on these subjects as moral attitudes.
It it true, of course, that there is another sense of the word 'morality' in

which we would say that the code of conduct followed by Satan was not a morality at all, but rather the negation of all morality. We might also say of the thorough-going egoist, not that his morality was a purely selfish one, but that he followed self-interest to the exclusion of all morality. I do not want to say that one of these uses is correct and the other incorrect. The meaning of a word is what it is generally used to mean; and both these uses are standard in English. The point is that normally when we use the word 'morality' we have both these uses in mind and do not distinguish between them. That is to say, we normally think of a man's moral principles as both having authority over him, and as having a certain content.[18]

"We normally think of a man's moral principles as both having authority over him, and as having a certain content." That is true, but that does not mean that we can separate one of these off and speak of what simply has authority over a man as a morality. Or better: if the man *has principles*, they *have* authority over him; but to think of his *moral* principles is to think of a certain *sort* of principle which has authority over him.

On the score of Satan's morality, if, before I had read Monro's passage, someone had said to me that Satan had a morality I should have found that claim intelligible. But I would not have thought this a reason for accepting it as true. Satan, certainly the Christian Satan (however incongruous this may seem given his alleged beginnings) is without morality. (Milton's Satan may be another matter). Once however the speaker tells me that he means by morality what Monro means by it ('that which has authority over one') then I am untroubled. I must confess I am also uninterested. If ethical egoism just means: the egoist always puts himself first, and so has a morality, because there is some consideration which always counts with him (his own interest), well, I am now apprised of this definition.

IV

The view that ethical egoism is the *only* (or the only viable) moral position is more difficult to deal with, partly because it is not at all clear what this claim amounts to. My guess is that some of what is meant is that only ethical egoism addresses to each moral agent reasons for acting rightly which he will willingly admit the force of and so heed in his action. This will be so, since what it is right for each to do is (on this 'morality') what will benefit him or her, and each individual must therefore in every case admit the rationality of acting morally. (This is the philosophical equivalent of making a desert and calling it peace). The whole question of reasons and rationality in morals I shall treat more fully in chapter 6. But something needs to be said concerning it here.

Let us put the question "Ought one always to do what is in one's interest?" I want directly to inquire who is being asked this question. If I am being asked it I shall answer, no, and this will be a moral reply. A man ought not always to do what it is in his interest to do (assuming that to do so will sometimes involve harm or injustice to others): this is my position. My questioner (or the so-called 'ethical' egoist) will answer, "Why oughtn't he to? Surely he ought to do just that. That is what it is in his *interest* to do." Now I do not see any difference between the 'oughts' in any of these statements. Where I do see a difference is in the presence in one case, and the absence in another, of a reason. The reason is that other people will (almost certainly) be harmed if someone acts this way. This fact is reason enough for me to say that one ought not to live that way. But it is not a reason, or reason enough, for the other man to say that. He insists that he ought always to do what is in *his* interest, even if others suffer as a result, or even if it means deliberately making them suffer or harming them. The fact that these others will be harmed is not disputed by him. But it is not a reason for him to keep from acting that way because what he wants most is what is in his interest, and he does not care what it costs others if he gets it. Now if this *is* what he wants most, and acting on the rule 'act always from self-interest' is the most certain way for him to get what is in his interest, then to act on that rule is undeniably (judged from his point of view) what he ought to do. When *I* say he ought not to act in this way I am appealing to facts to which he is indifferent. These facts are a reason for me not to act that way. They are a reason, because I care that others should not be harmed or unjustly deprived of what they have. But these facts are also a reason for anyone not to act that way. This may seem paradoxical, and puzzling, since I have just said that these facts are not a reason for the other man.

What I mean is this. These facts are a reason for *anyone* just in the sense that, in the case of any man, if he acts solely from self-interest others will almost certainly be harmed by him, even wilfully harmed (since he will be prepared always to pursue his interest at the expense of their good, or even their lives, if he can expect to get away with it). But then if, in the case of any man, were he to act this way, others would almost certainly be harmed, there is reason for any man not to act this way. This just means: I accept that there is good reason, not just for me, but for anyone, not to act this way. It is not just that I judge that *I* ought not to act this way. *Everyone* ought not to act this way. "But I thought we had decided that the other man *ought* to act this way?"

We had: *on his terms*. On his terms, of course he ought to act this way. If what he wants is E and S will get him E, and E is *all* he wants, then S is the practice he ought to follow. If I say he ought not to follow S I am not claiming that he acknowledges that he ought not to follow S. Nor am I saying that he has a moral obligation not to, if this is to mean something like 'There is some realm of value (or divine command) which binds him whatever he thinks, or wishes'. For to say this seems to me manifestly unhelpful. I shall accept that he has a moral obligation not to follow S if this means: *no* one should follow S (and so of course he shouldn't). In short, when I condemn an exclusive attention to self-interest, because I care that what must be the cost to others not come about, I condemn *any* exclusively self-interested 'ethic'. I condemn *any*, because the cost in each case will almost certainly be the same: others will be harmed. So naturally if, in my view, one ought never exclusively to pursue one's self-interest then in the case of the man above, he ought not to either.

Of course he does not accept that view. But I do not claim that he does. All I say is: he ought not to do what he does. And what I mean here I have just explained.

Briefly, what divides him and me is not the gap between a 'moral' ought and a 'non-moral' ought. What divides us is that something that is a reason for me is not a reason for him. And what accounts for that is that I care that certain things not happen, and he doesn't care. What he cares is that he should get what he wants, so long as it is in his interest to get it. Now if someone wants to insist that what divides us *is* the difference between the 'moral' and 'non-moral' *ought* I shall not try to refute this claim. I shall ask what it means. If it means that my 'he ought not to' appeals to the good of others and the egoist's 'I ought not to' appeals to his own good (his own interest) that is something I am perfectly content to accept (though I do not see how 'ought' functions differently in the two cases). I accept it, because it appears to me to be just another way of saying that the reason *I* have *he* doesn't have.

Once more, what determines whether a man has (and heeds) morality or not is the kind of *considerations* he appeals to and is moved by. D. H. Monro has the idea that if you decide that the considerations or principles a man lives by are not moral considerations by appealing to the content of these considerations or principles, this is itself a morally engaged action. I think (as I have tried to show with the Capone example) that this idea is mistaken. Monro fixes upon the factor of over-ridingness as constitutive of morality. But if you show that morality is (as we have seen Stocks stress) a commitment which is over-riding, you haven't shown that any over-riding commitment is morality. Morality is 'commitment' to certain *sorts* of things. It just is a fact that only some kinds of principle or consideration are describable as *moral* principles and considerations. Within the range of considerations which are moral considerations, there is no self-declaring weight which each of them carries: thus disagreement (not necessarily irreconcilable) between people, each of whom is deciding on moral grounds, is possible, because each may give more weight to one consideration than to another. But it is not the case (as Monro, and R. W. Beardsmore,[19] among others, aver) that *whatever* a man attaches most weight or importance to is morality. The considerations which are moral are not any considerations a man is committed to putting first.

True, I spoke above of the "self-interested 'ethic' ". Does this mean that I do accept after all that there is such a thing as 'ethical egoism'—a *moral* position according to which one ought to do whatever will further one's own interest at whatever cost to others? We nowadays speak of the egalitarian ethic, the liberal ethic, the military ethic, the professional ethic, and so on, and we certainly do not mean to imply that these are all *moral* principles or goals or conceptions of what is important. If, then, someone claims there is an egoistic 'ethic' I shall be properly signalled what he means, and shall assent.

NOTES

[1] G. J. Warnock, *The Object of Morality* (London: Methuen & Co. Ltd, 1971) p. vii.

[2] Ibid., p. viii.

[3] Ibid.

[4] Ibid., p. 9.

[5] Ibid.

[6] Ibid., pp. 22–3, 26.

[7] Ibid., pp. 76–7.

[8] Ibid., pp. 79–80.

[9] Ibid., p. 86.

[10] Ibid., p. 86.

[11] Ibid., Chapter 4, especially pages 40–1.

[12] Ibid., p. 71.

[13] Ibid.

[14] Fyodor Dostoevsky, *The Idiot* (Harmondsworth: Penguin Books, 1970) pp. 95–7. (Transl.: D. Magarshack.)

[15] Ibid., p. 97.

[16] Ibid., pp. 98–101.

[17] D. H. Monro, *Empiricism and Ethics* (Cambridge: The University Press, 1967) pp. 141–2.

[18] Ibid., p. 129.

[19] R. W. Beardsmore, *Moral Reasoning* (London: Routledge & Kegan Paul, 1969). More accurately, Beardsmore's position is that whatever a community, or "way of life", attaches most importance to is morality. This is an important difference between Monro (and Hare) and Beardsmore (whose view here is shared by Stuart Hampshire). For a criticism of this second view see R. Beehler and A. R. Drengson (eds.), *The Philosophy of Society* (London: Methuen, 1978) pp. 6–7; and R. Beehler, "Moral Delusion" (forthcoming).

III

Moral Truth I

It is impossible to conceive of anything at all in the world, or even out of it, which can be taken as good without qualification, except a good will.

KANT

An objection which is almost certain to be directed at my account of moral life is that, on my understanding of morality, we cannot *know* whether (or what) things are right or wrong, since on my account there is no possibility of moral truth, and so no possibility of knowing (in morals) anything. Whether this objection is telling or not depends, of course, on whether, and in what sense, there are moral truths.

Those who assert that moral judgments must be separable into the true or the false may divide between them only two possibilities: moral judgments which are true are contingently true, or moral judgments which are true are necessarily true. I shall begin by considering in this chapter the second of these positions: True moral judgments are *necessarily* true.

I

The allegation 'Necessarily true' will recall the remark of Phillips and Mounce quoted in the Introduction that

In saying lying is wrong we are saying that what the term 'lying' describes is for us *necessarily* wrong.[1]

Now in that introductory chapter I observe that one advantage of Mounce and Phillips' account of moral utterances over that of Hare is that their account seems to square better with the fact that when we tell someone to their face that the way they treat others is wrong we do not see ourselves as having *decided* that acts of this kind are evil. Mounce and Phillips' linking of moral judgments to established social rules is more respecting of our sense that, in matters of morality, we are appealing to standards which no one has at any point decided shall be the standards of right and wrong. Rather, these standards confront us as calling for observance, *whatever anyone decides*. It may be thought that precisely what explains this sense of the non-dependence of moral standards upon anyone's decision *is* their necessary truth. I shall try to show that both this sense of non-dependence, and the allegation of necessity, are confusions.

Let me begin by focusing upon something I also called attention to earlier: Mounce and Phillips' position concerning what they term "the moral sense" of 'ought'. They invite us, you will remember, to consider

a people who have the practice of promise keeping, and [to] suppose that it is their sole moral practice. These people use the word 'ought' in what we should call a moral sense only in connection with the keeping of promises. . . .[2]

They then go on to remark that

Of course, we can suppose these people to possess, as we do, a second sense of 'ought', of the kind that appears in the statement, 'You ought to keep your matches dry because it will pay you to do so' . . . [T]his conditional use of 'ought', . . . however, is distinct from its moral use.[3]

It is this distinction drawn by Phillips and Mounce between a moral and a non-moral use of 'ought' that I wish first to attend to. This distinction reoccurs throughout their book, and on each of five later occasions when they explicitly invoke the distinction they explain it in terms of the difference between appealing to moral considerations and appealing to prudential considerations. The moral use of 'ought' expresses the heeding of moral considerations; the non-moral use of 'ought' expresses the claims of prudence. This explanation, when set beside the remarks just quoted, gives rise to a question. For while the example given by Phillips and Mounce, in this passage, of a non-moral use of 'ought' is undeniably an appeal to one's appreciation of what it is prudent to do, Phillips and Mounce do not refer to the 'ought' in this example as 'prudential'; they refer to it as 'conditional'. Are we to take it then that these two are the same? By "a conditional use of 'ought' " they mean "prudential use of 'ought' "? There is evidence to suggest that Phillips and Mounce do mean this. One piece of evidence is the passage I have quoted, where the example they give of a conditional use of 'ought' is an appeal to self-interest. Another is a remark they make directly following this, where, in underlining the difference between the moral and non-moral 'ought', they observe that

We can continue to tell a person that he ought (in a moral sense) to perform a certain act even if it has been shown that it will *not* pay him to perform it.[4]

A third piece of evidence is their account of Socrates' teaching in the *Gorgias*:

In the Gorgias [Socrates] is concerned to distinguish between the kind of role played by moral considerations in action and the kind of role played by prudential considerations. This distinction is extremely important.

Socrates . . . in the *Gorgias* . . . says . . . that the good man cannot be harmed. If one takes this to be a straightforward factual claim it is false. We know of scoundrels who flourish, and of good men who are plunged into distress. Socrates is not denying these facts. . . . Socrates says that the good man cannot be harmed [because] He refuses to call anything which results from a pursuit of the good harmful. It is not the world which is to determine what is harmful. On the contrary, harm, for Socrates, is to be measured by the extent of a man's deviation from the good.

We can [now] . . . see something . . . of what Socrates meant by saying that the good man has good done to him. He is not suggesting that the pursuit of goodness is a conditional policy. . . .[H]e is saying that goodness is its own reward. . . .[T]he good man . . . cannot be at a loss if the regard for goodness remains with him. *He* does not feature prominently, if at all, in this regard. It is a regard for goodness not for himself.[5]

"[T]*he pursuit of goodness is* [not] *a conditional policy*"; i.e., that one ought to live (and thus act) rightly is not conditional upon it being to one's advantage, prudentially considered, to do so. The pursuit of worldly advantage, on the other hand, does give rise in every case to a conditional policy. Whether one ought to do something will always be conditional upon its benefiting one prudentially. These three passages suggest, then, that when Phillips and Mounce refer to the non-moral use of 'ought' as conditional they do mean nothing more than that it is prudential.

But if this is the correct account of Mounce and Phillips' meaning, a further question arises. The question concerns the implication in the passage with which I began that, if the non-moral 'ought' is conditional, the moral 'ought' is *un*conditional. This is not expressly stated by Phillips and Mounce in *Moral Practices*, but it is directly implied by the passage quoted, which draws a contrast between the moral and non-moral 'ought' and marks the difference between them by identifying the latter as 'conditional'. This straight-forwardly invites the conclusion that the moral 'ought' is 'unconditional'. This conclusion we find confirmed by D. Z. Phillips himself a year later. In his exchange with Ilham Dilman published as *Sense and Delusion* Phillips argues that judgments about the meaningless of a person's life are often moral judgments, and

moral judgments of meaninglessness are unconditional judgments: they do not wait on what the [person whose life is being judged] wants or happens to think worthwhile.[6]

That is, Phillips' position is that:

1. Some judgments of the meaninglessness of a person's life are moral judgments.

2. Moral judgments are unconditional.

3. Therefore some judgments of the meaninglessness of a person's life (those that are *moral* judgments of meaninglessness) are unconditional judgments.

Phillips remarks of Tolstoy's *The Death of Ivan Illych* that

Ivan's realization on his death-bed of the meaninglessness of his life would not have the force it does were it not for the fact that it involves an unconditional judgment of value. Ivan does not deny that [in the past] he had thought his life was meaningful. Now, however, he sees that given the limits of that life, from a certain moral and religious perspective, it cannot be seen as other than meaningless.[7]

Now it can, I think, be shown that when Phillips speaks in this later book of moral judgments as unconditional he is working with a slightly different concept of 'unconditionality' from that of the earlier book. When in *Sense and Delusion* Phillips speaks of moral judgments as unconditional judgments of value he means that they are not conditional upon the person whose life is being judged *assenting* to the values which are the ground of the judgment. Thus long before Ivan's deathbed conversion someone else can judge Ivan's life to be, morally considered, a wasted life, because that judgment does not have to attend upon what Ivan wants or thinks worthwhile. Whatever he thinks or lives for, *morally considered*, his life is a wasted life. Now this judgment is also appreciated by Phillips and Mounce to be unconditional in the *Moral Practices* sense, in that it does not rest upon prudential considerations.* But this first kind of unconditionality is not equivalent to the latter. On the *Moral Practices* concept of unconditionality, the judgment that P (morally) ought to do X is unconditional in not being conditional upon X being in P's interest. In the *Sense and Delusion* concept of unconditionality, the judgment that P (morally) ought to do X is unconditional in not being conditional upon P's subscribing to the moral values appealed to in this judgment. It is clear that these two are not the same. The first relates to the kind of considerations on which we base our moral judgments; the second relates to the kind of agreement required for moral judgments to be in order. Phillips' view of the second of these I have remarked upon already. What I wish to ask here is whether there is not a *third* sense of 'unconditional' being attributed to the moral 'ought'; that is, whether the claim that moral judgments are *unconditional* is not just a way of saying that they are not prudential, or do not depend upon the assent of the person or persons whose acts are being judged, but is intended to say something *more*. The evidence that this may be the case is also to be found in the book *Sense and Delusion*. That book arose out of a disagreement between Ilham Dilman and D. Z. Phillips concerning the proper account of judgments of the meaninglessness of individual lives. Nevertheless in that book Dilman reveals a thorough going subscription to the moral philosophy developed by Mounce and Phillips in *Moral Prac-*

---

* This comes out, for example, in Phillips' own characterization in *Sense and Delusion* of the conditionality of "moral judgments of meaninglessness": such judgments do not wait upon what the person judged "*wants*, or happens to think worthwhile".

tices (which effectively dates from 1965—see note on page 73 below).

Now in the opening chapter of the book *Sense and Delusion* Dilman at one point declares that

> . . . the request for reasons why one should pay attention or attach weight to moral considerations [i.e. why one ought or ought not, to do what these considerations are considerations *in favour* of doing or avoiding] at least partly comes from confusion, [similar to that which leads people to seek] to justify induction, to prove the validity of mathematics, to demonstrate the existence of the material world. In the case of moral judgments and decisions, *any reason that one may give for the beliefs in terms of which the judgments and decisions are reached would turn moral considerations into considerations of prudence or expediency.*[8] [My emphasis.]

The 'beliefs' Dilman refers to here are "our beliefs in justice, decency, honesty, and courage", etc. And the most plausible way to interpret what he is saying here—which Phillips at no point in their exchange in the book repudiates, or even calls attention to—is this. Any attempt to explain why one believes in justice, honesty, or decency, could only take the form of seeking to show that our reasons for believing in these things (for having these 'practices') are prudent or expedient reasons. That is: while one can explain why one judges a *particular* act to be wrong—*by pointing out that it is unjust or dishonest*—one cannot explain *why the fact that it is* unjust or dishonest makes it something that (morally) ought not to be done. For this would be to seek to 'turn' (i.e. justify) our moral beliefs, "in terms of which [our particular] judgments and decisions are reached", into prudential or expedient—i.e. *conditional* practices. But our moral beliefs, or practices, are not prudential or expedient.—They are unconditional beliefs or practices.

But then what reason *can* one give, one wants to ask, for the moral beliefs in terms of which our particular moral judgments and decisions are reached? The only straightforward way to interpret these philosophers as answering is: one cannot give a reason.

> One can imagine oneself asking whether a particular lie is justified, but if one asks whether lying in general is right, one finds oneself at a loss, not simply to answer the question, but to imagine the kind of consideration that would lead one to answer it. This is because one is no longer asking oneself a genuine question.[9]

Now—finally—there are two ways to interpret this position. The first is:

(1) Moral beliefs, moral practices, cannot be explained—cannot be given a reason for—because the search for such a reason is *senseless*.(". . . one is no longer asking oneself a genuine question.")

The second is:

(2) Moral beliefs, moral practices, cannot be explained—cannot be given a reason for—because this would be to turn them into prudential or expediential considerations—i.e. into *conditional* considerations. But while particular moral judgments may be admitted to be conditional upon the presence or absence of moral considerations, these moral considerations *being* considerations which give rise to the rightness or wrongness of actions *is not conditional upon anything*. Injustice, dishonesty, indecency—lying—are for us *necessarily* wrong.

I shall consider the second of these first.

II

The attribution of 'unconditional' to the "the moral 'ought' " is, as we have seen, the result of an attempt to drive a wedge between moral and non-moral judgments. To accomplish this, non-moral judgments are identified with prudential judgments; and this leads on to the assertion that non-moral judgments are therefore 'conditional', the implication being that moral judgments are not. *Moral* judgments are '*un*conditional'. But behind this move is the implicit assumption, or at least, suggestion, that, just as to establish the prudentiality of the non-moral 'ought' is to establish its conditionality, to establish the *non*-prudentiality of the moral 'ought' is to establish its *un*conditionality. This move is logically unwarranted. 'Prudential' entails 'conditional'. But 'not prudential' does not entail 'not conditional'. This is because the class of the conditional includes but is not exhausted by the class of the prudential. It is entirely conceivable that there are considerations other than prudential considerations, appeal

to which nevertheless constitutes a conditional use of 'ought'. I shall in
fact argue that there are such considerations; that they are precisely of
the kind Phillips and Mounce would accept are moral considerations;
and that therefore the moral use of 'ought' is in one important and
crucial respect every bit as conditional as its non-moral use.

The *locus classicus* for Mounce and Phillips' distinction between a
moral and a non-moral use of 'ought' is Plato's *Gorgias*. There, in the
discussion with Polus, Socrates elucidates the distinction between
prudential and moral regard. But what Phillips and Mounce draw
from this dialogue in *Moral Practices* is (as I have said) expressed in
only one instance in their book (the first passage quoted above) in
terms of 'conditionality'. And this ascription is in reference only to
prudential judgments. There is no *express* ascription to moral judgments of the epithet 'unconditional'. What brings about a difference
in this regard, such that this later becomes the characteristic way for
the Swansea group of philosophers to express the nature of the
moral, is Wittgenstein's 'Lecture on Ethics'.*

At the very beginning of that lecture, after certain preliminary
explanations as to why he has chosen to speak on ethics, Wittgenstein undertakes to elucidate the subject of his talk—i.e. the ethical. In
the course of seeking to do so he offers a number of different
characterizations of the ethical ('what is good', 'what is valuable',
'what is really important', 'what makes life worth living', 'what is
the right way of living'), and he goes on to declare that each of these
expressions

is actually used in two very different senses. I will call them the trivial or
relative sense on the one hand and the ethical or absolute sense on the other.[10]

Wittgenstein then proceeds to give an example of these two different
uses.

Supposing that I could play tennis and one of you saw me playing and said
"Well, you play pretty badly" and suppose I answered "I know, I'm playing
badly but I don't want to play any better", all the other man could say would

---

* This may seem an odd suggestion to make, since Wittgenstein's lecture
appeared in 1965, and Mounce and Phillips' book in 1970. But the explanation of this is easy. The central chapters (3, 4, 5 and 6) of *Moral Practices*
reproduce two papers by Phillips and Mounce written prior to, and published in, 1965. These earlier, pre-"Lecture on Ethics", discussions control
the argument and idiom of the entire book.

be "Ah then that's all right". But suppose I had told one of you a pre-posterous lie and he came up to me and said "You're behaving like a beast" and then I were to say "I know I behave badly, but then I don't want to behave any better", could he then say "Ah, then that's all right"? Certainly not; he would say "Well, you *ought* to want to behave better." Here you have an absolute judgment of value, whereas the first instance was one of a relative judgment.[11]

What Wittgenstein calls an absolute judgment of value is Mounce and Phillips' unconditional judgment of morals. It is a moral judg-ment of value, and Phillips and Mounce understand Wittgenstein to be saying that the judgment *is* absolute, rather than relative, in *being* unconditional: that is, in not being conditional upon what the person whose acts are being judged wishes to achieve. Judgments about a man's efforts at tennis must (ordinarily) be sensitive to that man's engagement with the game. They are in order, or misplaced, relative to his wishes or purposes in playing. But judgments about his wilful lying (where no extenuating circumstances justify the lie) are not sensitive to his personal commitments or lack of desire. Whatever he wants, or does not want, he *ought* to want to behave better.

Now Wittgenstein, having illustrated by means of these two examples the two different uses of 'good' 'right' 'important', etc., goes on directly to say that

The essence of this difference seems to be obviously this: Every judgment of relative value is a mere statement of facts and can therefore be put in such a form that it loses all the appearance of a judgment of value: Instead of saying "This is the right way to Granchester", I could equally well have said, "This is the right way you have to go if you want to get to Granchester in the shortest time"; "This man is a good runner" simply means that he runs a certain number of miles in a certain number of minutes, etc. Now what I wish to contend is that, although all judgments of relative value can be shown to be mere statements of facts, no statement of fact can ever be, or imply, a judgment of absolute value.[12]

It may seem for a moment that all Wittgenstein is doing here is restating Hume. But clearly he is not. For Hume distinguishes sharply between statements of fact and judgments of value; he does not claim that judgments of relative value can be shown to be statements of fact. Nor does he say that no statement of fact can ever be, or imply, a judgment of absolute value; he says that no statement of fact can even be, or imply, a judgment of any kind of value, relative or absolute. Indeed, while he does not say so, it is, I think, possible that Hume would deny that there are such things as judgments of absolute value. Or more carefully, that he would assert that all judgments of 'absolute value' are either in fact judgments of relative value, or else they are not judgments of value, or of anything, at all.

This position of Wittgenstein's concerning ethical judgments occurs side by side in the lecture with arguments that reveal his continued subscription in 1929 to the *Tractatus* doctrine about how language refers, and to the conception he took in that book of the human will. These ontological and metaphysical underpinings of Wittgenstein's lecture I do not intend to explore here.* My reason for not doing so is that these Tractarian elements are logically separable from his already quoted statements, and it is not necessary to go further than these to show that his stress upon the difference between absolute and relative judgments is important and revelatory, though his *characterization* of that difference is not satisfactory.

Consider again what Wittgenstein identifies as the essence of this difference: that relative judgments of value are mere statements of facts, while absolute judgments are not; and note specifically the two examples he gives of a relative judgment, and his transformation of these into statements of fact:

Instead of saying "This is the right way to Granchester," I could equally well have said, "This is the right way to go if you want to get to Granchester in the shortest time"; "This man is a good runner" simply means that he runs a certain number of miles in a certain number of minutes, etc.

To bring out more clearly what is both important, but also unsatisfactory, in Wittgenstein's argument let me modify slightly his version of the tennis example. Instead of "Well, you play pretty badly" being (as Wittgenstein intends) a comment upon Wittgenstein's skill at playing, let it refer to the fact that Wittgenstein cheats when he has an opportunity to, and constantly badgers his opponents in the course of playing. The words "Well, you play pretty badly" now express an ethical (and so on Wittgenstein's account, an absolute) judgment of value. Let us further suppose, to make things easier, that we express this ethical judgment, not as "You play pretty badly",

---

* But I shall treat of them briefly in Chapter IX.

but as "That is not the right way to play". Now it might be urged
that this ethical judgment ("That is not the right way to play") can be
transformed exactly in the manner of the relative judgment "This is
the right way to Granchester". There the transformation was "This
is the right way to go if you want to get to Granchester in the shortest
time". Here the transformation is: "That is not the right way to play
if you want to play the game courteously and fairly". That is, this
ethical judgment does *not* differ from the 'right road' relative judgment on Wittgenstein's criterion of transformability. Each "can . . .
be put in such a form that it loses all appearance of a judgment of
value".

This claim is, I think, correct. (Thus we can imagine the aristo-
cratic wastrel in the film *Nothing But The Best* observing his young
working-class protégé play tennis, and after remarking approvingly:
"Well done jocko! Almost found myself envying such vitality. But
that is not the right way to play if you want to play courteously and
fairly—which your absurd betters attach importance to.") Now for a
time it seemed to me that there is, nevertheless, a difference between
these two transforms, and that it was (perhaps) this difference that
Wittgenstein had in mind as holding between absolute and relative
judgments of value, but failed to express successfully. The idea I had
was this. In the Granchester example, "This is the right way, etc."
asserts a relation which *contingently* holds between a certain course of
action (going this way), and the achievement of a particular desire
(getting to Granchester as directly as one can); but in the tennis
example "That is not the right way to play, etc." asserts a relation
which *tautologically* holds between a certain course of action (playing
in that manner) and the achievement of a particular desire (playing
fairly and courteously). It is possible to imagine circumstances in
which this road would not be the way to Granchester (if the road
were, for example, as the result of the damming of a river, now
beneath a lake; or if the town, as a result of volcanic activity, were
moved from its present location). But it is not possible to imagine
circumstances in which that way of playing tennis would be the way
to play fairly and courteously. If, for some reason—a match, say,
between a human being and some extra-terrestrial being of enormous strength and agility—it were to be considered fair for the human
to play in the way Wittgenstein does, this could only mean that the
rules of the game have changed (i.e. this game is not, properly
speaking, tennis); for 'fair to play in this way' *means* 'acceptable

according to the rules'. Nor would it make a difference to suggest that one might consider it fair for the human *secretly* to play as Wittgenstein does, i.e. to cheat, because of the superior advantage of the extra-terrestrial being, and of what hangs on the game—their leaving earth uninvaded, say. For this would only be to urge that, in this case, for the human to play unfairly—i.e. depart from the rules—is *justified* by the unequal strength of the players and the enormity of the outcome. It could never be fair to play tennis in this way, unless the reference of the word 'tennis' is changed. But this would be a change in language not just in 'circumstances'.

I no longer think this difference can be made out. For one thing, the "change in language" referred to would be itself (as admitted above) also a change in circumstances. 'Circumstances' are now such that tennis—the game—has changed. But also: if the town of Granchester, because of volcanic activity, or the damming of a river (which floods the valley the town lies in, say) is moved to a different location, doesn't this mean that "the reference of the word ['Granchester'] is changed"? If so, isn't this too "a change in language, not just in circumstances"?

In any case, whatever Wittgenstein might have had in mind, there is nothing very convincing in his *statement* of the difference between absolute and relative judgments of value. Still, there is, I think, something important to be quarried here. Consider for a start the appellation *relative* judgments of value. Relative *to what*? I think what Wittgenstein wishes to point to by this nomenclature becomes clear when we consider his assertion that every judgment of relative value "is a mere statement of facts". That is, it is a statement of the relation between what some person wants *and* a particular object or course of action. It is at bottom the judgment: *this* is what you want. It is this fact about such judgments which is the reason for describing them as 'relative'. They are relative because in each case the judgment is 'this' is 'the right way', or 'a good chair', or 'the most important thing to do', *given your wants and purposes.*

Let us next shift from the stated difference between Wittgenstein's 'absolute and relative' judgments of value to his four illustrations of the difference between these two kinds of judgments. Recall that in the tennis example (as Wittgenstein presents it) the relative judgment "You play pretty badly" differs from the absolute judgment "You're behaving like a beast" in that the first is sensitive to what Wittgenstein wants in playing, while the second is not sensitive to what he wants in lying. It is Wittgenstein's declaration *"I don't want* to play any better" which provokes withdrawal, not of the judgment upon his skill (for it is still true that Wittgenstein plays badly), but of any hint of admonition that these words may carry. This withdrawal is signalled by "Ah then that's all right". Now if we compare these two examples with those of the right way and the good runner, in the example of the right way to Granchester, notice, our judgment is also controlled by what the person wants. (This is the right way *if you want* to get to Granchester in the shortest time.) But in the example of the good runner it is not. That is, while the road's being the right way is conditional upon what the person wants, the man's being a good runner is not conditional upon what he wants (any more then Wittgenstein's being an excellent tennis player is conditional upon what he wants). A man is, or is not, a good runner, conditional upon his capability at running, quite apart from what he wants. This asymmetry between "This is the right way" and "This man is a good runner" is revealed (see p. 74 above) by Wittgenstein's own 'transform' of these judgments. Yet "This man is a good runner" is by Wittgenstein's own declaration a relative judgment of value. (He has chosen it as an example of such.) *But it is relative, notice, not to what the man wants, but to human capacities, the point of a race, the limit of contemporary achievement in running,* and so on. (So that a man who would have been judged a good runner in 1950 might be judged only mediocre today.) It appears, then, that at least one kind of relative judgment is not conditional upon what the person being judged seeks or wants; it is conditional upon something else.

Is it possible that ethical judgments are of this kind?

III

Recall the acts of the young people in Selby's story against the soldier. Now our moral judgment upon what the young people do here—our judgment that they *ought not* to do it—is not conditional upon their not wanting to do it. Nor is it conditional upon what they do want. Our moral judgment is in order, and sustained, whatever these young people want in violating the soldier. It may be thought that this is not true, in that it is possible to imagine a change in the situation such that by the young people wanting something different

from what they do, what they do would no longer be wrong. If the
soldier, for example, were an enemy assassin, and the injuries
inflicted in the assault were to prevent his killing important persons
in the American war effort, then, if the young people know this, and
assault him in order to prevent it, what they do is no longer wrong.
This suggestion is, I think, a mistake. For quite apart from the fact
that by changing the character of the young people's acts—i.e. *what
they are doing*—it changes the very object of our judgment (and it was
those acts whose wrong was claimed to be not conditional upon what
they want), it is equally important to see that even in the revised
circumstances it is not that the young people want to prevent the
assassin killing which (allegedly) justifies their act. It is that the man
is an assassin, that he will, if given the opportunity, kill, that these
killings will have such-and-such effect, and so on. Even here, what
the young people are in fact doing (killing an assassin, or making a
terrible mistake) is not conditional upon what they are wanting to
do; and whether what they do ought or ought not to be done is not
conditional upon their wanting to do it. In each case it is conditional
upon the man being in fact an assassin, on their act being therefore an
act that works to prevent murder, human harm, treason, and so on.

This relation of the morality of an act to human wanting comes
out in a way that is especially instructive in Wittgenstein's tennis
example already discussed. There the suggestion that Wittgenstein
ought to try to play better is sensitive to his not wanting to play
better. But this is because there were apparent no other, *moral* considerations bearing on the issue. If, however, Wittgenstein has a heart
condition, and should be exercising vigorously and regularly, then
when we see him playing the game in a lackadaisical and completely
neglectful manner, that he doesn't want to play any better does not
matter: he ought to try to play better, because his health requires it.

In sum, then, moral judgments upon a person's acts are, as
Mounce and Phillips claim, not conditional upon what the person
being judged wants. But they are conditional upon the acts in question having certain effects. *That some acts ought (morally) not to be done
is conditional upon the world being a certain way*. We have seen Phillips
and Mounce remark that "We can continue to tell a person that he
ought (in a moral sense) to perform a certain act even if it has been
shown that it will not pay him to perform it." This is true. But can
we continue to tell him that it ought not to be done if it will pay *no one*
if he performs it? Would the acts of the young people against the

soldier in Selby's story continue to be wrong if the soldier were not
hurt by them? If their blows and kicks had no effect on him would
what they do still be wrong to do?

It will not do to say that we should still judge the young people's
blows to be wrong even if they had no effect on the soldier since even
if they have no effect on him blows of this kind do have effects on
others, and so the young people's behaviour is condemnable for
what it contributes to: the increase of their taste for viciousness,
which threatens others. For the question is not, 'Are these blows and
kicks morally to be condemned if this particular man is not affected
by them?', but 'Are blows and kicks of this kind to be morally
condemned if no person can be affected by them?' I shall offer two
different arguments which seek to show that if human beings *were
not* vulnerable to hurt or injury, the sense we should continue to find
in moral condemnation would be radically altered.

(1) A moment ago I asked "Would the acts of the young people
against the soldier in Selby's story continue to be wrong if the soldier
were not hurt by them?" I then shifted to the formulation "If their
blows and kicks had no effect would what they do be wrong to do?"
There was a reason for this. The reason is that "Would the acts of the
young people . . ." etc. is, in one sense, tautologically true. For 'the
acts' spoken of here *are*: the bringing about of certain physical and
emotional states of the soldier. Blows and kicks may, or may not,
have effect. But *these acts* cannot, logically, have no effect, for *they are*:
the crushing and tearing of skin and tissue and bone, the causing of
pain and desperation and terror. Consequently if (per absurdum)
these acts did not hurt the soldier it would follow, tautologically,
that they could not continue to be morally condemned; for they
would no longer *be* what we do condemn. Our very conception of
what is condemnable in these acts is logically inseparable from 'their
physical and emotional effects' upon the soldier. We cannot, strictly,
even distinguish between 'the young people's acts' and 'the effects of
their acts' on the soldier. For once more, 'their acts' are: the causing
this pain, the injuring physically in this way. (Hence if someone were
to speak of 'the *effects* of their acts on the soldier', this would ordinarily be taken to refer to such things as the soldier's being dis-
charged from the service because of his injuries, his being plunged
into despair at now being blind, his now hating the young people of
every city. And a more specific reference to 'the *physical* and *emotional*
effects of their acts on the soldier' would be taken to refer to such

things as the collapse of his health as a result of being left to lie in the doorway until morning, his becoming increasingly timid of strangers after nightfall, his no longer being able to see.)

(2) A second way to bring out what I am urging is to imagine a future time in which there is no longer any appreciation of good and evil. There is nothing of what we should call moral understanding. Will acts which are wrong now still be wrong then? If we wish to answer 'yes', is this not because of an unstated supposition that, while no one then living appreciates that these acts are evil, *the world in other respects* remains the same? But if the world were such that men were no longer vulnerable to hurt or injury, then what?* Can we say that acts which it is wrong for us to do are wrong for them to do? For the point is that the conditions in which *these acts* are possible no longer obtain. What logical space could remain in such a world for the judgment "such and such ought (morally) not to be done"?

Consider a situation somewhere between the world as it is now and a world in which human beings are not vulnerable to hurt or injury. A sadistic murderer confined in prison is allowed each month brutally to 'violate' and 'kill' what he takes to be helpless human beings, but what are in fact humanoid artifacts of exceptional sophistication. These 'creatures' perfectly resemble human beings in every way that the violator could possibly investigate. They speak, they cower, they struggle to resist, they scream, they bleed, they appear wholly murderable. Only the violator does not know that what confronts him are not human beings; and we shall suppose that he will never find out differently. Suppose further that it will never be possible for this man to escape, or to assault a real human being. In short no one else will ever be affected (or influenced) by his actions. Can we *morally* condemn what goes on here?

The answer, I believe, is that we can morally condemn what is going on here; but that what we can (and should) condemn is not *what the man does*, but (if I may so express it) *what he sees himself* as doing. What he does is: break up machinery. What he sees himself as doing is: maiming and killing. Or if you prefer, it is not 'what he does' *qua* breaking machinery that makes us condemn his actions, it is 'what he does' *qua* what he wants to be doing that makes us condemn his actions. That is: we condemn what he does *as an*

---

* I shall throughout put aside the question whether the supposition of such a world is logically warranted: whether intelligent and emotional beings who are not (therefore) vulnerable to some kind of hurt are conceivable.

expression of the desire to maim and kill. And what this shows is that it is this desire, this wanting to maim and kill, that we are morally condemning. Strictly speaking, what he does is not wrong; for, once more, what he does is to break machinery. *It is what he wants that is wrong.* For what he wants is: to maim and kill.

Recall at this point Wittgenstein's example of an absolute judgment of value.

. . . suppose I had told one of you a preposterous lie and he came up to me and said "You're behaving like a beast" and then I were to say "I know I behave badly, but then I don't want to behave any better", could he then say "Ah, then, that's all right"? Certainly not; he would say "Well, you *ought* to want to behave better."[13]

Not: "Well, you ought to behave better", but, "Well, you ought *to want* to behave better". These two are different; and in this difference lies the sense in which the moral 'ought' *is* absolute. In the Granchester example, remember, the relative judgment is a statement of the relation between what the man wants and a particular way of going. It is equivalent to: this is what you want. But in the lying example the absolute judgment is a judgment *upon what* Wittgenstein wants. That is, just as in the case of the sadistic murderer it is his wanting to kill and maim which is condemned, so in Wittgenstein's lying example it is his not wanting to behave better which is condemned. And it is this condemnation upon his *wants* that Wittgenstein identifies as an absolute judgment of value.

Now the desire to hurt and injure others could continue even in a world in which hurt or injury could no longer be given. Whether such a desire could be rational, or sane, is another matter. The point is that even though it is not possible to hurt or injure others the wish to be able to is still possible. Such a malevolent will we would, I believe, continue to condemn. This is because our present condemnation of human acts is *the expression* of what I should like to call the compassionate will. Because we care disinterestedly about the well-being of persons, we condemn acts which harm or injure them. The evaporation of the conditions in which such acts can be performed is not the evaporation of that caring. Hence malevolence, however impotent, could still be condemned. Nor can I see any reason for denying that such a condemnation would be a moral condemnation. For it would be condemnation proceeding from a disinterested regard for the well-being of those toward whom this malevolence was directed. Such a regard is the very center of what we call moral concern; and the well-being which is its object is the most generally characterizable paradigm of a *moral* consideration. For again, what distinguishes the "moral" from the "non-moral" use of 'ought' is not that 'ought' somehow functions differently in the first use than in the second; it is that *the considerations* appealed to in the first use differ from those appealed to in the second. In this important sense there is no such thing as 'the moral "ought" '. There are moral, and non-moral, considerations.

That persons *ought not to want* to injure or harm others would appear then to be an absolute ethical judgment, in that it is not conditional upon the world being a certain way. Whatever form or condition persons enjoy, we may wish for their well-being. This moral regard or valuation is not tied to any particular state of affairs. Consequently our condemnation of the malevolent desire to hurt or injure is not tied to any particular state of affairs. It is unconditional in that sense. And this unconditionality is, I believe, the irreducible core of what Wittgenstein means by 'absolute'.

But the ACTS which I ought to do, or keep from doing, vis-a-vis other persons ARE conditionally—i.e. contingently—related to how the world is. In his lecture Wittgenstein identifies 'the ethical' with absolute judgments of value. This is a mistake. (The same mistake one makes in identifying the conditional with the prudential.) The class of ethical judgments is greater than the class of absolute judgments of value. Some ethical judgments—all those which pronounce upon the morality of an act—are relative judgments of value. They are relative in that their justification is conditional upon the effects of the act on human well-being. And it follows from this fact that the position stated as (2) in Section I above is false. For talk of "our belief in justice, honesty, decency, courage" etc. is talk of the importance to us not only of certain states of affairs, but of the importance to us of persons *acting* in certain sorts of ways. Therefore it is false to say that our belief in honesty, say, or in justice, is not conditional upon anything. Our "belief" in the importance of these things, or as I should prefer to say, our regard for acting honestly, justly, courageously, etc. is conditional upon the implications of so acting for human well-being. Dilman declares that "*any* reason" that one might give for the "beliefs" in terms of which our moral judgments and decisions are reached would turn these "beliefs" into considerations of expediency. The error here, of course, is in the words "*any* reason". I can give perfectly intelligible reasons why I regard justice and honesty of the utmost importance. And the existence of these reasons does not turn them into considerations of prudence or expediency. (Dilman seems to be running together the questions: whether you can give reasons here, and whether your reasons must be persuasive to anyone.)

If our commitment to justice, honesty, etc., and our judgment of particular human acts according to whether they are honest, just, etc. were not relative to the relation of these ways of acting to the physical and psychological state of being of persons, there could be nothing of what we call moral *reasoning*. For moral reasoning is logically parasitic upon this contingent conditionality of the relation of particular human acts to human well-being. Mill remarked one hundred and forty years ago that

Whether happiness be or be not the end to which morality should be referred—that it be referred to an end of some sort, and not left in the dominion of vague feeling or inexplicable internal conviction, that it be made a matter or reason and calculation, and *not merely* of sentiment, is essential to the very idea of moral philosophy; is, in fact, what renders argument on moral questions possible.[14] [my emphasis]

I find this insistence altogether right; and in so far as Mill may be taken to be alluding here both to the kind of regard toward other human beings which is the wellspring of moral discrimination, and to the terrestrial condition which is the locus of human *being* (making necessary and possible continuing moral judgment in our lives) these pages may be read as a contribution toward the vindication of such a position.*

---

* Before continuing I should perhaps say something concerning a question which may have been provoked by my supposition of a world in which persons are invulnerable to hurt or injury. I claimed that in such a world the moral condemnation of a malevolent will could continue. Someone may wish to ask whether such a condemnation is conceivable if there is not a history in this community of a time when persons are vulnerable. Would beings whose entire ancestry had never known a state of vulnerability condemn malevolence? (This is connected to, though not the same as, a question I mentioned earlier: whether malevolence would be *intelligible* in such a world.) I am inclined to reply that in so far as these beings are capable of love—of caring about one another, they are capable of condemning the

IV

I wish now to move to a consideration of the first of the two positions sketched at the close of Section I—the position which I believe can incontrovertibly be attributed to Mounce and Phillips. This is the position that our moral beliefs and moral practices cannot be explained because the search for such reasons or justification is *senseless*. ("[O]ne is no longer asking oneself a genuine question.")

I have interpreted Wittgenstein to be saying in the *Lecture on Ethics* that ethical judgments are absolute in not being conditional upon the world being a certain way. This claim, I have argued, is only partly true, in that ethical judgments upon *acts* are conditional upon the world being a certain way. That a certain act (or kind of act) ought or ought not to be done is a conditional, i.e. a *contingent* matter. This is flatly contrary to the view of Phillips and Mounce, according to whom acts such as lying are necessarily wrong.

What is being urged is that we should think of phrases such as 'Lying is bad' or 'Lying is wrong' not as expressions of a moral position, but as setting out one of the conditions under which a moral position can be expressed. They may be compared in this respect with a necessary proposition such as 'Red is a colour'. Someone who uttered this latter statement would not be making an assertion of fact, but stating a necessary truth which, if it conveyed information at all, could do so only about the meaning of the terms involved. Thus a person might say 'Red is a colour' in order to teach someone the meaning of the word 'colour'. We are suggesting that the phrase 'Lying is wrong' is also a necessary statement which, if it tells us anything at all, tells us about the meaning of 'morally wrong'. In saying that lying is wrong we are saying that what the term 'lying' describes is for us necessarily wrong. Lying is the kind of thing we apply the word 'wrong' to.[15]

I have been arguing that to apply the term 'wrong' to lying is to assent that it ought not to be done. I have also claimed that we must

---

lack, or opposite, of this caring. Of course if nothing *can proceed from* the diffidence or hostility of one of them toward the others someone is sure to ask why they should apprehend diffidence or hostility as *condemnable*? And there is the further difficulty in respect of a positive wish to injure, that if these persons have never been able in fact to hurt or injure, how are they to conceive of being able in fact to hurt or injure? But then how could one of them wish to do what none of them can conceive of doing?

To these questions I have no answers.

be able to ask *why* lying—or cheating, or letting crying children go ignored, or brutally beating another human being (the list is endless) ought not to be done. Phillips and Mounce urge the opposite view:

> In order to ask whether something is right or wrong, we must abide by the rules governing the use of these terms. The application of the word 'wrong' to uses of lying is one of our criteria for the [correct] use of that term. When we consider lying in a purely descriptive aspect, then for a moment we step outside these criteria. Having done so, however, we can no longer ask whether a thing is right or wrong. We cannot seriously ask whether lying is wrong because in deciding whether an act is wrong we use lying as one of our criteria. One can convince oneself of this simply by trying to imagine the situation in which one would ask whether or not lying is right. One can imagine oneself asking whether a particular lie is justified, but if one asks whether lying in general is right, one finds oneself at a loss, not simply to answer the question, but to imagine the kind of consideration that would lead one to answer it. This is because one is no longer asking oneself a genuine question.[16]

(It is at this point in the book that we are asked to consider the society who have only the moral practice of promise keeping.) Now I for one have no difficulty at all imagining the kind of consideration that would lead me to answer—negatively—the question whether lying in general is right. It is the kind of consideration I would appeal to to settle whether a particular lie is justified: the effect of doing so on others. And if lying—in general, *or* particular— didn't have these effects, it wouldn't be morally wrong. Of course there is another objection against lying in general (it doesn't hold against lying in particular) which consists in construing 'lying in general' as 'lying *always*'—i.e. *whenever* one utters words—and then pointing to the fact that if people (i.e. all people) were to do this the result would be the collapse of language. Is it possible that this is what Phillips and Mounce have in mind? Something which suggests that they may is their urging that we "think of phrases such as 'Lying is bad' or 'Lying is wrong' not as expressions of a moral position, *but as setting out one of the conditions under which a moral position can be expressed*".

Consider the following 'analogue':

(i)   If people lied 'in general' (i.e. if every time anyone said something he or she said what was false) language would break down.

(ii) If language breaks down, one cannot lie—or *say* anything.

(iii) Therefore "No lying (in general)" sets out one of the conditions under which a moral position (or *any* position) can be expressed.

It is obvious that this 'objection' against lying 'in general' is a logical, not a moral, objection. Lying 'in general' (i.e. in *this* sense) is *logically* not in the cards. Thus to try to imagine a situation in which lying 'in general' was morally right is logically impossible, since lying in general is self-defeating; it defeats the possibility of lying, or telling the truth, or saying anything. Therefore it is a *necessary* truth that there could not be "lying 'in general' ". But *is* it a necessary truth, then, that lying 'in general' is not (cannot be) *morally right*? I do not think so, since we surely must distinguish

(a) Lying 'in general' (i.e. in the above sense) is a logically impossible state of affairs.

(b) Lying 'in general' is a morally wrong state of affairs.

What makes lying 'in general' impossible, and so *necessarily* ruled out, is not what makes it morally wrong—i.e. *morally* ruled out. Lying 'in general' *is* "morally impossible", one might say. But it is morally impossible for logical, not moral, reasons. It is, if one could put it this way, not because one cannot imagine the kind of consideration which would constitute its wrongness; it is because one cannot imagine the 'it' *about which* one wishes to make a moral appreciation.

The only other arguments I can find given by Phillips and Mounce in the passages under consideration are two in number. The first comprises three claims.

(1) In order to ask whether something is right or wrong, we must abide by the rules governing the use of these terms.

This is surely correct. (Just as in order to ask you to give—not to receive—a small fortune I must abide by the rules governing the use of these terms.)

(2) The application of the word 'wrong' to [cases] of lying is one of our criteria for the [correct] use of that term.

It is, I suppose, one of our criteria. But correctly to use the term does not entail that one understands what people mean to say with it. (Thousands of students acquire a reliable competence in the application of all manner of 'sociological' and 'psychological' terms or jargon, without getting anywhere near the actual signification of those expressions. One could even perhaps contrive to have a computer print (or even 'utter' aloud) the word 'wrong', whenever 'confronted' with a case of lying. It does not follow that the computer is engaging here in moral discrimination.)

(3) We cannot seriously ask whether lying is wrong because in deciding whether an act is wrong we use lying as one of our criteria.

Now this is a shift, and an important one. We have just been told (2): application of the word 'wrong' to lying is one of our criteria for the (correct) use of that term. We are now told (3): the presence of lying is one of our criteria for whether an act is wrong. That is, in trying to determine whether what someone does to get what he or she wants involves wrongdoing, we look to see whether he or she lies to get it.

But why does the fact that they *lie* make what they do wrong to do? Or (to render the issue even simpler) suppose the act in question just is an act of lying. (Smith's sister has been waiting all day to speak to her sweetheart who lives across the street, and from whom she has, through a misunderstanding, been estranged. It is approaching the time when the young man can be expected to arrive and she is sitting twisted with anxiety and tension in the next room. Her brother, who has said he will watch and let her know when her friend comes home, sees his car pull up and the young man alight and enter his parent's house. Smith's sister hears the sound from the street and calls out weakly, "Has he come yet, David?" Smith answers, "No", and his sister shudders with disappointment and the tension of waiting.) What now? *Can't* we seriously ask: why is this wrong?

It is at this point in the passage from which I have drawn these three claims that we are given the recipe (already vetted) for convincing oneself that one can't seriously ask the question "Why wrong?" of lying in general. I want to ask this question of this lie in particular. And I do not want simply to be told that "Lying is the kind of thing we apply the word 'wrong' *to*". For my question is, why *do* we apply the word 'wrong' to it?

The outlines of the answer I seek have already been given. If human beings were, for example, 'omnisentient', so that Smith's sister were not vulnerable to what Smith does (which is: to keep from her the knowledge that the person she awaits has returned), then what Smith does could not then be *wrong*-doing, for the reason that it could not then *be done*. *Lying* is now impossible. On the other hand if human beings (and so, Smith's sister) were incapable of any emotional relation to another human being, then what Smith does here could continue to be done; but it would no longer have the effect it has; in which case we would no longer condemn it, *qua* lie—or *qua* expression of malignancy. (For in these altered circumstances it *cannot be* a vehicle of malign intent.) This is just to say: "what 'lying' describes" —the act of saying what is false with the intent to deceive—is not necessarily, but contingently, wrong.

V

There remains the last of the three arguments given by Phillips and Mounce in the two passages being examined. This is the argument which alleges that

> . . . 'Lying is bad' or 'Lying is wrong'. . . may be compared with a necessary proposition such as 'Red is a colour' . . . We are suggesting that the phrase 'Lying is wrong' is also a necessary statement which, if it tells us anything at all, tells us about the meaning of 'morally wrong'.[17]

That is, it tells us (for the last time) that lying "is the kind of thing we apply the word 'wrong' to". Now to take these last words first, it simply is false that telling someone the meaning of 'morally wrong' is telling him or her that lying (for example) is the kind of thing we apply the word 'wrong' to. It would be a perfectly acceptable description of this book to say that it seeks, among other things, to tell you what the meaning of 'morally wrong' is. But could I have accomplished this *simply* be getting you to appreciate that lying (or stealing, or neglecting to help distressed children) is the kind of thing we apply the words 'morally wrong' to? It is also surely false that the phrase 'Lying is wrong' tells us at best (i.e. "if it tells us anything *at all*") the meaning of 'morally wrong'. The simplest answer to this allegation is an example:

Eddie sat wedged against the gunnels in the prow of the shallow rowboat, his knees drawn up to his sunburned nose, and idly dipped his bare muddy toes in the tepid, slippery puddle that thinly covered the wooden planks separating them from the lakewater. He frowned, and at that moment became aware of his father watching him. "What's on your mind, son?" "Oh nothing. I was just thinking about the way Mom acted toward Auntie Carla this morning when she came back to the table from telephoning Mr. Herscovitz. What was she so mad about?" "She was angry because of what your Aunt Carla told Mr. Herscovitz was the reason she couldn't go to the band concert on Sunday." "What did she tell him?" "She told him that she was not fond of military music, and that she would rather spend an afternoon with him on another occasion during her stay with us." "But what's wrong with that?" "What's wrong with it is that your Aunt Carla has no intention whatever of spending an afternoon with Mr. Herscovitz during this, or any other visit." "But why?—Mr. Herscovitz is a *wonderful* man!" "Why?—Because he is not six feet, and doesn't look like Clark Gable is part of the reason. But basically, it's because he's Jewish." "Is that why Mom was so angry at her?" "Because she refuses to have anything to do with Mr. Herscovitz because he's Jewish? That's part of it. But your mother has long since given up speaking to her sister about that. The reason she was angry this morning is because your Aunt Clara pretty directly lied to Mr. Herscovitz. And lying, as your mother and I have always tried to teach you son, is wrong."

I find it incredible to suppose that in this (I hope reasonably realistic) exchange the phrase 'lying . . . is wrong' is supposed to tell Eddie—"if it tells [him] anything at all"—the meaning of the words 'morally wrong'. What it tells him, if it tells him anything (rather than, say, recalls to him what he already appreciates about lies), is that he now needs to think about what his aunt did here, in order that he may come to realize, as his father does, what there is about it which makes it something one oughtn't to do. For that it *is* something one shouldn't do Eddie now knows—on his father's reliable testimony—is so. *That* much he already understands.

This leaves the comparison of 'Lying is wrong' with 'Red is a colour'. I have already said some things about this aspect of Mounce and Phillips' argument in chapter one, and in the introduction. But what I say here will, I hope, complement, rather than reproduce, what I have said earlier. And perhaps before beginning I should directly state that the objections which I shall make are objections to what Mounce and Phillips *say* about moral judgments—how they *express*, at several different places in the book, their position. My argument is of the form: if you say this, you can only be understood to be asserting this; and this is mistaken. Whether the position I shall criticize is the position Mounce and Phillips (and this applies to any other author I engage with in this essay) *mean* to express, they alone can judge of.

VI

Phillips and Mounce declare of 'Red is a colour' three things:

(a) That it is a necessary truth.

(b) That a person might say 'Red is a colour' in order to teach someone the meaning of the word 'colour'.

(c) That 'Red is a colour' may be compared with 'Lying is wrong', as setting out one of the conditions under which a colour judgment can be expressed.

The relevance of (a) to all that has gone before can be brought out by this remark of D. W. Hamlyn:

[By philosophers] necessary truths have generally been understood to be unconditional. They are universally and unconditionally true and thus do not depend upon any argument for their justification. [18]

Though there is one difference; Phillips and Mounce appear not to subscribe to the word 'universally' in this passage. Their view is that "*for us* what lying describes is necessarily wrong". Who exactly the 'us' are here I shall return to.

The (b) claim I have already given reasons for repudiating. To teach someone the meaning of 'colour' is not all that 'Red is a colour' could be used to tell someone. It could, for example, as easily be used to tell someone the meaning of 'red'. ("William, these words here, " I see you are very red".—He means that she has—how do you say—a good education?" "No Wolfgang, you are thinking perhaps of "well read". 'Red' is a colour. He is commenting on the fact that she has got a burn from the sun.") And notice: could 'Lying is wrong' be used to tell someone the meaning of 'lying'? I want to claim it could not. For even if one knew what 'wrong' means, simply to be told that lying is wrong gets you no nearer to knowing what lying is—except of course to tell you that it is *a kind of act*. This fact is, I think, very relevant here. For what it shows is that the analogous phrase to 'Red is a colour' is 'Lying is an act'. To say that lying is an act is to say nothing at all about the relation of human beings to lies. But to say that lying is *wrong* is to identify lying as a type of act which is *judged* a certain way. It is judged to be an act that one ought not to do. And that judgment is a matter of human beings *regarding* lying in a certain way.

Which brings me to (c): the claim that expressions such as 'Red is a colour' and 'Lying is wrong' set out one of the conditions under which colour, or moral, judgments can be *expressed*. Well, *what is* this condition? The condition, Phillips and Mounce reply, is a certain kind of human agreement. Now in respect of colour judgments Phillips and Mounce at one point in their discussion make a promising beginning. Quoting the passages from Wittgenstein at *Investigations* 241–2 they observe that

There would be no concept of colour, for example, and no possibility of making true or false [or any?] statements about colours, if people did not agree in what they take the colour of objects to be.[10]

This is completely right. (See pages 27–29 above.) But unfortunately Phillips and Mounce quickly lose hold of this recognition. The passage in which one can most clearly see this taking place is here:

One does not determine whether a particular object is red by seeing whether the majority agree in thinking it red; until one has judged the colour for oneself one is probably unaware of what colour the majority are likely to think it. But one does assume, if one has judged with care, that the majority of those who have taken similar care will agree with one. This agreement need not hold in all cases. On a *particular* occasion [my emphasis], there is no absurdity in supposing that a single individual is right and the majority wrong. But agreement with the majority is something one relies on for the most part. If one's judgment about colour turned out [continually] to be different from those of the majority one would be thrown into confusion and be unable to use colour concepts.

One may wonder how an agreement which appears in the course of making judgements may nevertheless be taken for granted before a judgement is made. The answer is that no one makes a judgement in the void but in the course of a social life where judgements are already being made by people with whose ways of thinking one is familiar.[20]

That is: "the given is—so one could say—forms of [*social*] life." But this is not Wittgenstein's position. (Though Phillips and Mounce go on directly to assert that "This is the kind of agreement Wittgenstein is referring to when he speaks of the agreement which is necessary for there to be communication.")[21] Nor is it Wittgenstein's answer to the question how an agreement which only appears (i.e. is manifested) in the course of people actually making colour judgments can nevertheless "be taken for granted". Wittgenstein's answer to this question is not that individuals make these judgments in the course of a social life where others with whose ways of thinking they are familiar are already judging colours. His answer is: this agreement may be taken for "*granted*" (i.e. as "*given*") because these creatures ARE *the same form of life*. Consequently, they agree in their *perceptions* ("what they take the colour of objects to be"). Agreeing with others in their ways of thinking is "agreement *in opinions*". But (for the last time)

If language is to be a means of communication [i.e. of INTER-SUBJECTIVE intercourse] there must be . . . not agreement in opinions but in form of life.

Phillips and Mounce (they have a number of forerunners in this) tend continually to think of the form of life Wittgenstein is referring to here as 'form of *social* life'. (This error also infects at certain stages the work of Peter Winch, a writer from whom Phillips and Mounce borrow. But to seek to argue this would require another essay.)*

* A fourth philosopher who (at least at one point) inclines toward the same reading of the relevant passages in the *Investigations* is Iris Murdoch. Phillips and Mounce quote, in the concluding paragraph of their book, some words from an essay by Murdoch in which she herself quotes Wittgenstein's remark about the given, and comments, "For the purpose of analysis moral philosophers should remain at the level of the differences, taking the *moral forms of life* as given, and not try to get behind them to a single form" (my emphasis). The ambiguity of "moral forms of life" in this comment, and the likelihood that it is to be construed as social practices—"*moral* practices"—is, I think, obvious.

Whether Wittgenstein does sometimes—i.e. in relation to certain specific questions—mean 'form of social life' I cannot here go into. (Though I would like to remark that if and whenever he does mean this he means *also* the other.)

Transposing these results to moral judgments, we get the position that "one of the conditions under which a moral position can be expressed" is the existence of an ongoing social practice "where judgments are already being made by people with whose ways of thinking one is familiar". What Phillips and Mounce mean here they never quite spell out explicitly in respect of moral judgments. But they do spell it out very explicitly in respect of colour judgments, the example they repeatedly offer as analogically instructive. Therefore all one needs to do is to make the appropriate insertions:

For Wittgenstein, it is not that people form their opinions in logical privacy and later come together to construct that agreement which he describes as an agreement in form of life. On the contrary, it is the form of life which makes it intelligible to hold particular opinions. One's opinion that an object is red, for example, is the opinion that the word 'red', as it is used, applies to that object. This presupposes that there is already a use of 'red', an agreement in its application, an agreement in the light of which one makes one's particular judgements, and in the absence of which, the notion of judgement would be meaningless.[22]

For Wittgenstein, it is not that people form their opinions in logical privacy and later come together to construct that agreement which he describes as an agreement in form of life. On the contrary, it is the form of life which makes it intelligible to hold particular opinions. One's opinion that an act is wrong, for example, is the opinion that the word 'wrong', as it is used, applies to that action. This presupposes that there is already a use of 'wrong', an agreement in its application, an agreement in the light of which one makes one's particular [moral] judgements, and in the absence of which, the notion of judgement would be meaningless.

But surely my opinion that an act is wrong is not the opinion that the word 'wrong', as it is used in the existing social 'language game', applies to that action? Part of the problem here is the unclarity of the expression 'as it is used'. Are Phillips and Mounce saying

(i)   my opinion that an act is wrong is the opinion that the word 'wrong', *as it is used in our language* (i.e. with the meaning

'ought not to be done'), applies to that action?—That is, I
regard that action as one that ought not to be done.

(In which case one can surely ask why I regard it as something which
ought not to be done.) Or are they saying

(ii) my opinion that an act is wrong is the opinion that the word
'wrong', *as it is used by other individuals in our society* (i.e. to
express their moral judgments), applies to that action?

But then my opinion that an act is wrong is the opinion that: *the
opinion of the others is that it is wrong.* And one can now see why what
one must be able to take for granted to be capable of expressing a
moral judgment is a social life with others, where these others are
already making judgments with which (i.e. with "whose ways of
thinking") one is familiar. For *my* moral position, or opinion, concerning any act or type of acts, *just is* (on this account): the opinion
that the others apply the word 'wrong' to this behaviour. ('The
word, as it is used, applies to that action.') This is, *pace* Phillips and
Mounce, Protagorean relativism with a vengeance. It is also very
un-Wittgensteinian 'Wittgensteinianism', since it in fact *is* Wittgenstein's view that in respect of that form of life which we are considering (i.e. which is "given") here, people do form, not their opinions,
but—"queer as this may sound"—their "judgments", in logical
privacy. Each sees colours, each experiences feelings for others, *on his
own.* It is not social life which makes it "intelligible", i.e. logically
conceivable, for people to see, or to experience moral concern. It is a
social form of life (language) which makes it possible *to express* what
one sees, or feels, or is moved by.

True, language makes possible certain kinds of human awareness,
relationship, and activity which could not exist without language;
and some of these may even be among the conditions necessary for
the development of that kind of regard for others which is the basis
of moral life. (See chapters seven and ten below.) But language
cannot itself 'make possible' what we express in relation to acts such
as Selby's story depicts. *Language* does not 'create' that caring, that
regard. Human intercourse and relatedness nourish, and deepen, that
regard. Though undeniably, those forms of relatedness and intercourse into which language necessarily enters are among the most
important in this respect. It is highly probable, therefore, that the

psychological agreement which underlies our 'moral practices' is
language-dependent in one sense: it may depend upon human beings
being received and related to from birth by other human beings in
ways that require language for their existence and intersubjective
expression. But it is not language-dependent in the way Phillips and
Mounce imply.

There is a difference between

(a) One agrees with the others in using the word 'wrong' of acts
of lying.

(b) One agrees with the others in judging that lying is wrong.

(a) is not equivalent to (and does not entail) (b), for two reasons. In
one sense of 'social practice', Uriah Heep follows practice (a). But
surely the agreement with others necessary to be a moral judger is
something more than applying (as others do) the word 'wrong' to
acts of lying. One has to apply, to use, the word *as expressing moral
condemnation*. As *judging* lying to be wrong. But as we have seen,
according to Phillips and Mounce, one's judgment—"One's opinion"—that an act is wrong

is the opinion that the word ['wrong'], as it is used, applies to that [action].
This presupposes that there is already a use of ['wrong'], an agreement in
its application, an agreement *in the light of which* one makes one's particular
[moral] judgements. . . .

The claim, in other words, is not

(i)' There is necessary (i.e. presupposed) an agreement in the use
of the word 'wrong', in order that the word have the sense it
does (or *any* sense), and in the light of which *I* use *that word* to
express *my judgment* of lying.

It is rather

(ii)' There is necessary (i.e. presupposed) an agreement in applying
the word 'wrong' to lying, in the light of which *I judge* lying
to be wrong.

It is no wonder, then, that Phillips and Mounce insist that one cannot seriously ask whether lying, or any other way behaving, is wrong. For they end up at a position such that each has no reason for his or her opinion that lying is wrong, *except*: the others 'say it is'. That is, apply the word 'wrong' to acts of lying.

("Why is lying wrong, Eddie?—Why son,—this language game is played!")

NOTES

[1] *Moral Practices*, p. 9.
[2] Ibid., p. 11.
[3] Ibid., p. 12.
[4] Ibid.
[5] Ibid., pp. 31, 41–3.
[6] Ilham Dilman and D. Z. Phillips, *Sense and Delusion* (London: Routledge & Kegan Paul, 1971) p. 60.
[7] Ibid., p. 61.
[8] Ibid., pp. 33–4.
[9] *Moral Practices,* p. 11.
[10] Ludwig Wittgenstein, "A Lecture on Ethics", *Philosophical Review,* Vol. LXXIV, 1965, p. 5.
[11] Ibid.
[12] Ibid., pp. 5–6.
[13] Op. cit., p. 12.
[14] "Bentham", *Westminster Review,* Vol. 24, 1838. Reprinted in J. S. Mill, *On Bentham and Coleridge*, F. R. Leavis, ed. (New York, Harper & Row, 1962) p. 92.
[15] Op. cit., p. 9.
[16] Ibid., p. 11.
[17] Ibid., p. 9.
[18] "Contingent and Necessary Statements", in Paul Edwards (ed.), *The Encyclopedia of Philosophy* (New York: Macmillan and Free Press, 1967) Vol. 2, p. 198.
[19] Op. cit., p. 62.
[20] Ibid., pp. 63–4.
[21] Ibid., p. 64.
[22] Ibid., p. 65.

IV
Moral Truth II

My attitude towards him is an attitude towards a soul. I am not of the opinion that he has a soul.

WITTGENSTEIN

According to Professor Kai Nielsen "[t]he concept of truth has application in morals and we have definite ways of determining truth in morality".[1] I wish to examine the arguments Nielsen gives in support of this position.

I

Nielsen introduces his subject in the following way:

> When we reflect philosophically about morality we are very typically concerned with determining whether we can have any knowledge of good and evil, whether any moral claims have an objective rationale; that is to say, in thinking about the foundations of moral belief, we want very much to know whether any ethical code or any moral claim at all can be shown to be objectively justified.[2]

The concern about moral truth then arises from a concern about the 'objectivity', or lack of it, of moral judgments. Nielsen isolates two features which moral judgments must have if they are to be objective.

[1] First, if someone is claiming that the statements "X is good" or "X is wrong" are objective statements, he is claiming, at the very least, that such statements are not reducible to X is *thought* to be good or X is *thought* to be wrong. If our moral claims are objective, they must be something of which we could correctly say that though people *think* so and so is wrong, they are

mistaken, for it is not wrong. There are people who think that the earth is flat but their thinking so does not make the earth flat. Only if we can get beyond "thinking makes it so" can we be justified in claiming that there are objective moral claims.

[2] [Second] is the condition that some moral judgments can be true and others false. To believe in the objectivity of morals is to believe that some moral statements are true. In short, to correctly claim that a certain "course of conduct is objectively right, it must be thought to be right by all rational beings who judge truly of the matter and cannot, without error, be judged to be wrong."[3]

Nielsen wishes to show that the second condition in fact obtains; "that some moral statements are true". For him the objectivity of moral judgments and their being capable of being determined to be true or false are one and the same.* Therefore whoever accepts that moral statements can be true or false is an objectivist in morals.

Let us begin then with Nielsen's demonstration of condition (2)—his account of the truth of moral judgments. Neilsen remarks that

If a statement is acceptable from the moral point of view, it is true; if not, not. Only certain rules of conduct will satisfy these conditions. This means that no moral statement can be true unless it is made in accordance with and acceptable from the point of view of those norms which incapsulate the moral point of view.[4]

Following the account given by Kurt Baier in a book entitled *The Moral Point of View* Nielsen holds that for "the moral point of view" to be present

1. We must adopt rules of conduct not as rules of thumb designed to promote our own individual interests, but as matters of principle. As Baier points out, "this involves conforming to the rules whether or not doing so favours one's own or anyone else's aim."

* In his statement of the second condition Nielsen says only that "To believe in the objectivity of morals is to believe that some moral statements are true"; but I think it is clear (cf. his words quoted in the opening sentence of this chapter) that this is incomplete. He means: ". . .is to believe that some moral statements are, and can be shown (i.e. determined), to be true".

2. A moral agent must adopt rules to which not only he and his friends conform as a matter of principle, but rules to which everyone can conform as a matter of principle. Moral rules are meant for everybody.

3. Moral rules must be rules which are adopted for the good of everyone alike. The principle of impartiality or justice is involved here, since the interests of all people must be furthered, or at least given equal consideration when some moral rule has to be overridden.[5]

Now it is Kurt Baier's view that "Our moral convictions are true if they can be seen to be required or acceptable from the moral point of view". Nielsen holds exactly this view:

When we say that a moral judgment is true we endorse that judgment; we endorse it as a judgment that is rationally warranted; and when the judgment in question is a moral judgment, to say that it is rationally warranted comes to acknowledging it as acceptable from the moral point of view.[6]

The notion of *endorsing* a judgment is introduced here, together with the notion of a judgment being warranted. In order to make clear that this is not simply a minor detail, a mere choice of words, I shall cite an earlier statement by Kai Nielsen of the condition for the truth of a moral statement or judgment:

To assert that a judgment or statement is true is to give a warranted endorsement of that judgment or statement, but what makes the judgment warranted varies according to what we are talking about. To be capable of being true, a statement need not state a fact or assert that certain empirically identifiable characteristics are part of an object or an action. Rather, what is necessary is that the statement in question be publicly warrantable, that is, that it admit of some publicly determinable procedure in virtue of which rational men could come to accept it. If a given statement has a sufficiently powerful warrant to justify our claiming that we are certain of it, then we can properly say it is true. But what and how we warrant what we are talking about depends on *what it is that* we are talking about. We can properly call a statement or judgment in any area objectively true if it would be endorsed without doubt by informed, reasonable, reflective, and careful observers.

Such a publicly determinable judgment, whether true or false, is objective. If, by contrast its acceptability depends on some cultural or individual idiosyncrasy of the person(s) involved, then the statement is subjective and cannot have the kind of truth required for an objective moral judgment.[7]

[Nielsen earlier in this article puts it this way:] "A moral judgment is objective if, and only if, it is either true or false and if its truth or falsity does not depend on the peculiarities of the person who makes the judgment or on the culture to which he belongs, but shall be determinable by any rational agent who is apprised of the relevant facts."[8]

It is, I hope, becoming clear what sort of account of moral truth we have developing before us. It would not be inaccurate to say that (so far) a particular moral statement or judgment will be true if (and only if) it is the judgment, or expresses the judgment, which the moral point of view—i.e. *morality*—calls for. *But of course the question is,* what *does* morality call for? As Nielsen remarks in the essay from which I have just quoted:

In everyday life we are barraged with a variety of moral claims and counter-claims; the moral arguments in support of them are diverse and conflicting. How are we finally to decide among them? Is it really the case that metaethical relativism or some variety of subjectivism is correct? Moralists have traditionally claimed objectivity for their moral principles, and this claim of objectivity seems to be embedded in our everyday moral discourse. But is this claim actually justified? Can we show that there are objectively true moral judgments or that there are sound moral arguments?[9]

At this point I wish to go back to the beginning, to Nielsen's statement of the first condition of the subjectivity of moral judgments.

II

Nielsen declares in that passage that

[A] If our moral claims are objective, they must be something of which we could correctly say that though people *think* so and so is wrong, they are mistaken, for it is not wrong.

Now this declaration Nielsen makes in [A] is, as he expresses it, ambiguous between

(a) If our moral claims are to be objective, they must be something of which we could correctly say that though *some* people think it is wrong, they are mistaken, for it is not wrong.

(b) If our moral claims are to be objective, they must be something of which we could correctly say that though *all* the people living think it is wrong, they are mistaken, for it is not wrong.

(c) If our moral claims are to be objective, they must be something of which we could correctly say that though *all the people who have ever lived* think it is wrong, they are mistaken, for it is not wrong.

Now directly after the remark we are considering Nielsen states

There are people who think that the earth is flat but their thinking so does not make the earth flat.

This makes it reasonable to assume that in [A] Nielsen means by 'people' all the people who have ever lived. [A] is to be understood as (c); since no matter what anyone, living, dead, or to be born, *thinks*, the earth is not flat. Nielsen seeks then to establish that the same is true respecting brutal assault. No matter what anyone, living, dead, or to be born, thinks, brutal assault is wrong.

Only if we can get beyond "thinking makes it so" can we be justified in claiming that there are objective moral claims.

This is so, because

. . . claiming that the statements "X is good" or "X is wrong" are objective statements . . . is claiming, at the very least, that such statements are not reducible to X is *thought* to be good or X is *thought* to be wrong.

Thought to be good or thought to be wrong *by whom*? The next sentence [A] tells us. "People". And this appears to mean: all the people who have ever lived. Such statements *are not reducible* to X is thought (by *someone*) to be good; *X* is thought (by *someone*) to be bad. For this is "thinking makes it so".

Well, what do they reduce to?

III

Let us suppose that some person P thinks that some act X is morally wrong. Does it follow that X is morally wrong? Obviously it does not. How then are we to determine whether what P thinks concerning X is true or not? Baier and Nielsen answer: we appeal to the moral point of view. P's conviction is true if it can be seen to be required or acceptable from the moral point of view. And for P's conviction to be required or acceptable from the moral point of view it must be the result of P's applying to X a rule of conduct R which P has adopted for the good of everyone, which he applies indiscriminately to everyone, and which is not a device to promote his own individual interest, or the interest of some favoured class of persons.

Now remember, the whole idea here is to uncover a 'decision procedure' for morals according to which any candidate moral statement *S* can be determined to be true or false by appeal to criteria whose validity does not depend on what either the utterer of Ŝ, or the assessor of S, *thinks* concerning that act (or whatever) about which S alleges some moral fact.

Consider first the requirement that R be " adopted for the good of everyone alike".[10] Nielsen gives an example which is meant to illustrate, and establish the credentials of, this requirement.

Suppose *A* claims that wives ought not to have lunch alone with men who are not their husbands, and *B* claims that this is absurdly medieval, that it is perfectly all right for a woman to have lunch alone with a man who is not her husband. Now these two judgments are both moral judgments, both satisfy Baier's three conditions and they are logically incompatible. We should want to say that they both can't be true. . . .

We must. . . note that moral judgments are judgments that are ideally made in the light of a full knowledge of the relevant facts and they must, logically must, be made in the light of the facts that it is reasonable to expect the moral agent to have in his possession when he must make his moral decision or render judgment. To take the moral point of view is to reason in this way and it is to use "good" in the relevant contexts with this factual content. Since this is so, it cannot be the case that two logically incompatible moral judgments, like A's and B's about wives dining with men who are not their husbands, could both be acceptable from the moral point of view. They have different consequences for human well-being and, everything being equal, if A's judgment is such that it would, if followed, make for greater general welfare than B's, then only A's judgment is acceptable from the moral point of view; and, if there are no other alternatives acceptable from the moral point of view here, then A's judgment is required from the moral point of view and *a fortiori* true.[11]

One (in my view) unhappy feature of this example is that we are not told enough about it. Does the husband know in each case that his wife is lunching with the man? Does he wish them to have lunch? Who is the man—her brother, her parish priest, her favourite film star? (Who could be Barry Fitzgerald.) If husbands and wives agree to this practice I find it hard to see how the so-called medievalist could hold his position. But I think we malign the medievalists. Suppose the issue is between A and B, and concerns whether wives should, *unknown* to their husbands, lunch with men whom they find sexually, or otherwise, attractive. A argues that they should not, unless they intend to tell him, and even then, they should not lunch with the man if they have reason to believe that they might become involved, even against their own wish not to. B argues that a woman has, like anyone else, the right to do what she has the desire to do, so long as she does not deliberately harm others; but that this involves, of course, risks of harm or complication, but she has, unless she intends simply to roll up in mothballs, to face these like anyone else. (A sort of secular version of: "He who would save his life shall lose it.") A replies: Suppose she knows that when she tells her husband he will be hurt? B replies: Then don't tell him. A: But then it is deceitful. B: It is deceitful only if he asks. A: Suppose he asks? B: Then tell him. A: But then he will be hurt, so she shouldn't go. B: Nuts. What is true is that he shouldn't *be* hurt.

The division between these two is, I think, clear. It is about what it is *reasonable* to do respecting others, and also about the weight to be assigned to certain *imponderables*. ("Will he make a pass at me?" "We haven't been getting on well lately, am I too vulnerable at the moment for this sort of meeting?") It is also a question of what one is oneself entitled to. This last is, of course, a moral question. For it involves consideration of the claims of one's self *against* the claims of others.

Briefly, I do not see how Nielsen is going to get these two (A and B) together, except he gets A to change his view about what is most important. But will that not be to get him to change his conception of what is part of 'human well-being' (this kind of 'existential' independence?)

This is connected to a slightly different aspect of the moral truth issue. It might be thought by someone (and certainly he would have good historical backing for this) that if there were such a thing as moral truth then a man could not escape recognizing its claims on him. It would stare him in the face, as the cat stares back from the mat, and how could he not admit that this or that was right or wrong to do? The idea is: If we can find out the truth in morals, we can then show *anyone* that there *is* a way he *ought* to live. ("There *is* such a thing as right and wrong!")

I do not wish to assert that Kai Nielsen has this idea. (Whether he has or not I don't know. The opening paragraph of the paper "Moral Truth" suggests it.) I want only to claim that it is not an idea which gets support from Nielsen's arguments. Ordinarily, if someone says "it's good to do that" he implies that, sometimes at least, he wants to do it. (You and I have just slammed into a bed of snow at the bottom of the ski run and as we lie back in the delightfully cool and sunlit powder you say, "Ah, it's good to do that! Skiing is heaven!" The priest replies to the boy who asks why he must always turn the other cheek, "It is good to do that, my son".) But it is Kai Nielsen's intention to overturn the idea that "in adopting the moral point of view, we [subjectively] attribute a certain content to 'good' ".[12] Nielsen wishes to show that there is, or could be found, a notion of 'good' or 'human well-being' which *every moral* agent must accept, such that all moral appraisals of what is good or right would, if carefully carried out, agree. Suppose Nielsen had accomplished this (which I have sought to give one reason for believing he could not), and had also got even amoral men to agree to a definition of what Baier calls in the third of his conditions "the good of everyone". What situation would obtain? Well, now everyone, moral and amoral alike, are agreed on what is for the good of everyone. What else has changed? I submit that so far nothing else has changed. If I may put it this way, it is not that in 'adopting' the moral point of view we attribute the same content to 'good (of everyone)'. It is that in 'adopting' the moral point of view *we want that good brought about. This* is 'the moral point of view'. This is what distinguishes the good from the bad man, or the good from the amoral man. The good man wants the good of others. The amoral, or evil, man wants only his own good. And he has reason to believe that what is for the good of everyone is not at all necessarily, or even probably, for his good. Even if it could be shown him that it was, *he* would only fall in because his good is served by doing so.

This is connected to the notions singled out above of 'endorsement' and 'warranted'. What is necessary for P's statement S to be capable of being true, according to Baier and Nielsen, is that S

be publicly warrantable, that is, that it admit of some publicly determinable procedure in virtue of which rational men could come to accept it.

We can properly call [S] . . . objectively true if it could be endorsed without doubt by informed, reasonable, reflective, and careful observers.

What do we have here? It seems that 'true' in morals is like 'true' in tennis. "It's forty-love, now love". "It can't be!" "T'is." "Harry, is that true?" "I'm afraid it's true my dear." Now talk of *endorsement* may obscure this. When I endorse a *cheque* I undertake to make good for the money. But when I endorse the statement "it's forty-love" I don't undertake anything in *that* sense. All I do, really, is say, "it's forty-love". Of course when I am challenged I can give reasons why I say it is, brandish a rule book, appeal to witnesses, and so on. But the bank wants more than reasons or witnesses. They want the money if the cheque is bad. They want a difference to be made here to which there is no parallel in the other case. (Unless I am the umpire, or paranoid, and *must* have others accept, or at least heed, my score etc.) That is, to endorse another's statement as true is no more than to acknowledge that it conforms to the principles of reasoning within which it is made, and is warranted by the facts. But I may care not a fig for that form of reasoning, or those facts, and still be *aware* that the statement is warranted. My endorsement amounts merely to a confirmation of the reasoning and the facts. It does not amount to an endorsement *of that form of reasoning*—it does not amount to undertaking to make those principles of reasoning my principles in the sense that I shall *live* by them. (And so one could imagine a gangster whose pastime was to keep track of the number of wrongs he committed a day, kept scores for each day, compared weeks, his record with other famous criminals, and so on.)

When Kai Nielsen writes: "[all that is necessary is] that it admit of some publicly determinable procedure in virtue of which rational men could come to *accept* it" (my emphasis) someone may think that this will give us a device for convincing any man that he ought to live a certain way, where this means, he will now *desire*, and conscientiously *seek*, to live this way. But nothing Kai Nielsen says warrants (if you will forgive me) an endorsement of that idea. Consider the following imaginary dialogue.

Tortoise: Put all the money in bags, Achilles.

Achilles: Tortoise, you know that Athene will punish you for this, and that my mother Thetis will intervene before Zeus, and you will be brought to justice.

Tortoise: I know all that, put the money in bags.

Achilles: But I shall suffer if you take it from me. How am I to live?

Tortoise: I know you'll suffer. Put the money in bags.

Achilles: You haven't a chance! You'll never get away!

Tortoise: We'll see. Put the money in bags.

Achilles: You are cruel Tortoise. You will be remembered forever as the most vicious and heartless of robbers.

Tortoise: Hmmm . . . I never thought of that. Put the money in bags. And the Jewels too.

Or (more subtly) these lines from Matthew, chapter 12:

At that time Jesus took a walk one sabbath day through the cornfields. His disciples were hungry and began to pick ears of corn and eat them. The Pharisees noticed it and said to him, 'Look, your disciples are doing something that is forbidden on the sabbath'. But he said to them, 'Have you not read what David did when he and his followers were hungry—how he went into the house of God and how they ate the loaves of offering which neither he nor his followers were allowed to eat, but which were for the priests alone? Or again, have you not read in the Law that on the sabbath day the Temple priests break the sabbath without being blamed for it? Now here, I tell you, is something greater than the Temple. And if you had understood the meaning of the words: *What I want is mercy, not sacrifice*, you would not have condemned the blameless. For the Son of Man is master of the sabbath.

I quoted above a remark by Kai Nielsen according to which the acceptability to the moral point of view of any statement must not depend "on some cultural or individual idiosyncrasy of the person(s) involved, [or] then the statement is subjective and cannot have the kind of truth required for an objective moral statement".[13] When we see the sort of thing 'objective moral truth' is it is clear that nothing in this statement contradicts anything I have said. The 'idiosyncrasy' I have isolated (caring, or not caring, about others) divides amoral (some of whom are also probably immoral) from moral persons. It does not divide moral reasoners *per se* one from another. The objectivity of moral judgments is itself a 'practice'-dependent or 'principle'-dependent objectivity, and to that extent is not subjective. But the 'practice' itself is subjective, in the sense that heeding moral considerations is a practice or principled activity—whose utterances possess this objectivity—*to which* not everyone is a 'committed participant'. So too, the calling of scores in tennis is objective, in the sense that you cannot call scores in tennis without calling them according to the facts and the rules. *Whether you play* tennis or not, is something which you, as a subject of desires and affections, must decide. The objective remarks of tennis may, with the game, leave you cold. (Still you understand and can assess them.)

Perhaps the most direct way to bring out the difference between truth ordinarily and truth in morals is that if everyone suddenly began to say that you, or I, do not exist, and we do, they would be saying what is false. Everyone else says what is false here, and only one's self says what is true. Now what one says here may be *shown to be* true because one can appeal to what is *there*. (In this case, to oneself.) One's statement is true in agreeing with what is there. True, it also agrees with what people used to say. But it is not true *in agreeing with that*. It is true in agreeing with what is there. Is the situation identical in morals? Suppose people suddenly began to claim that to kill you for no reason is not wrong to do. You insist that it is. And you are right in what you claim. It is true that it is wrong. But if they all *say* now that it is not wrong, but acceptable (or even right), to what can *you* appeal against them? To what is there? But what *is there* to appeal to? Well, one thing which is 'there' is: *what they used to say*:—how they used to regard the matter, and what they said to express that regard. But that is all one can appeal to here; to what they used to say, and so to the principles of reasoning according to which they used to decide what to say.

Perhaps one will be successful. Perhaps they will come to say "You're right and we're wrong". But one is not home free yet. For perhaps they will say: "So what? Don't let him get out that door, Harry."

IV

"But then morality on your account just is: blind reaction. You see something—and you respond. That's it. No rationality, no truth, no knowledge, no anything. Just reaction." This objection is misplaced, and could seriously be made only by someone who had both mistaken my argument and lost sight of human relationships and human understanding. One responds, but not blindly. One responds to human actions and human situations. I stressed this in chapters one to three. In caring about people, we understand and appreciate their needs, their ways of living, their hopes, aspirations, and pain, and we care that they not suffer. This is a response to people into which understanding and knowledge enter, and which makes possible moral argument, and moral wisdom.

Moral wisdom is a real fact. And it is not something intellectually empty. It is not mere reflex or a form of expertise. It is understanding suffused with love. It is not of the sort "shake before using", nor even "given every man thine ear, but few thy voice", but rather:

By and by came a decided external leading: a confidential subordinate partner died, and nobody seemed to the principal so well fitted to fill the severely felt vacancy as his young friend Bulstrode if he would become confidential accountant. The offer was accepted. The business was a pawn-broker's, of the most magnificent sort both in extent and profits; and on a short acquaintance with it Bulstrode became aware that one source of magnificent profit was the easy reception of any goods offered without strict inquiry as to where they came from. But there was a branch house at the west end, and no pettiness or dinginess to give suggestions of shame.

He remembered his first moments of shrinking. They were private, and

were filled with arguments; some of these taking the form of prayer. The
business was established and had old roots; is it not one thing to set up a new
gin-palace and another to accept an investment in an old one? The profits
made out of lost souls—where can the line be drawn at which they begin in
human transactions? Was it not even God's way of saving His chosen? 'Thou
knowest,'—the young Bulstrode had said then, as the older Bulstrode was
saying now—'Thou knowest how loose my soul sits from these
things—how I view them all as implements for tilling Thy garden rescued
here and there from the wilderness.'

Metaphors and precedents were not wanting; peculiar spiritual experiences
were not wanting which at last made the retention of his position seem a
service demanded of him: the vista of a fortune had already opened itself, and
Bulstrode's shrinking remained private. Mr. Dunkirk had never expected
that there would be any shrinking at all: he had never conceived that trade
had anything to do with the scheme of salvation. And it was true that
Bustrode found himself carrying on two distinct lives; his religious activity
could not be incompatible with his business as soon as he had argued himself
into not feeling it incompatible.

Mentally surrounded with that past again, Bulstrode had the same
pleas—indeed, the years had been perpetually spinning them into intricate
thickness, like masses of spider-web, padding the moral sensibility; nay, as
age made egoism more eager but less enjoying, his soul had become more
saturated with the belief that he did everything for God's sake, being
indifferent to it for his own. And yet—if he could be back in that far-off spot
with his youthful poverty—why, then he would choose to be a missionary.[14]

Or further:

Bulstrode gathered a sense of safety from these indications that Raffles had
really kept at a distance from Middlemarch since his memorable visit at
Christmas. At a distance and among people who were strangers to Bulstrode, what satisfaction could there be to Raffle's tormenting, self-
magnifying vein in telling old scandalous stories about a Middlemarch
banker? And what harm if he did talk? The chief point now was to keep
watch over him as long as there was any danger of that intelligible raving,
that unaccountable impulse to tell, which seemed to have acted towards
Caleb Garth; and Bulstrode felt much anxiety lest some such impulse should
come over him at the sight of [the doctor] Lydgate.

Bulstrode's native imperiousness and strength of determination served him
well. This delicate looking man, himself nervously perturbed, found the
needed stimulus in his strenuous circumstances, and through that difficult
night and morning, while he had the air of an animated corpse returned to

movement without warmth, holding the mastery by its chill impassibility, his mind was intensely at work thinking of what he had to guard against and what would win him security. Whatever prayers he might lift up, whatever statements he might inwardly make of this man's wretched spiritual condition, and the duty he himself was under to submit to the punishment divinely appointed for him rather than to wish for evil to another—through all this effort to condense words into a solid mental state, there pierced and spread with irresistible vividness the images of the events he desired. And in the train of those images came their apology. He could not but see the death of Raffles, and see in it his own deliverance.

Strange, piteous conflict in the soul of this unhappy man, who had longed for years to be better than he was—who had taken his selfish passions into discipline and clad them in severe robes, so that he had walked with them as a devout quire, till now that a terror had risen among them, and they could chant no longer, but threw out their common cries for safety.[15]

Earlier in this chapter I acknowledged that we often distinguish someone's thinking something to be right (or wrong) and its being right (or wrong). I wish now to take this issue up, since someone might still consider that this distinction presents difficulties for my account of moral statements. The discussion in chapter two of the children and Marie is relevant to this question, but I shall discuss it here in terms of the passages quoted immediately above.

The man Raffles has knowledge of Bulstrode's early life which he has used to extort money from Bulstrode. Raffles now lies in a state of acute alcoholic poisoning in Bulstrode's house. The doctor has told Bulstrode that Raffles is to be given food, but not alcohol, and made to rest. The following day the doctor returns and as the symptoms are worse he prescribes a change in the treatment:

The chief new instruction that Lydgate had to give was on the administration of extremely moderate doses of opium, in case of the sleeplessness continuing after several hours. He had taken the precaution of bringing opium in his pocket, and he gave minute directions to Bulstrode as to the doses, and the point at which they should cease. He insisted on the risk of not ceasing; and repeated his order that no alcohol should be given.[16]

Later events develop as follows.

At six o'clock, Raffles having had only fitful perturbed snatches of sleep, from which he waked with fresh restlessness and perpetual cries that he was sinking away, Bulstrode began to administer the opium according to Lydgate's directions. At the end of half an hour or more he called Mrs. Abel and told her that he found himself unfit for further watching. He must now consign the patient to her care; and he proceeded to repeat to her Lydgate's directions as to the quantity of each dose. Mrs. Abel had not before known anything of Lydgate's prescriptions; she had simply prepared and brought whatever Bulstrode ordered, and had done what he pointed out to her. She began now to ask what else she should do besides administering the opium.

'Nothing at present, except the offer of the soup or the sodawater: you can come to me for further directions. Unless there is any important change, I shall not come into the room again to-night. You will ask your husband for help, if necessary. I must go to bed early.'

'You've much need, sir, I'm sure,' said Mrs. Abel, 'and to take something more strengthening than what you've done.'

He had say an hour and a half . . . by the fire-light only, when a sudden thought made him rise and light the bed-candle, which he had brought down with him. The thought was, that he had not told Mrs. Abel when the doses of opium must cease.

He took hold of the candlestick, but stood motionless for a long while. She might already have given him more than Lydgate had prescribed. But it was excusable in him, that he should forget part of an order, in his present wearied condition. He walked up-stairs, candle in hand, not knowing whether he should straightway enter his own room and go to bed, or turn to the patient's room and rectify his omission. He paused in the passage, with his face turned towards Raffle's room, and he could hear him moaning and murmuring. He was not asleep, then. Who could know that Lydgate's prescription would not be better disobeyed than followed, since there was still no sleep?

He turned into his own room.[17]

Let us suppose that the next morning Raffles lies dead as a result of an overdose of opium. Is what Bulstrode did wrong to do? Is he responsible for Raffles' death? Of course he may tell himself that he is not, and strive to bend his thoughts to the shape of his desires. But I want to say that even Bulstrode knows that he has murdered Raffles.

Now this is not how events in the novel unfold. Moments after Bulstrode turned into his bedroom,

Before he had quite undressed, Mrs. Abel rapped at the door; he opened it an inch, so that he could hear her speak low.

'If you please, sire, should I have no brandy nor nothing to give the poor creetur? He feels sinking away, and nothing else will he swaller—and but little strength in it, if he did—only the opium. And he says more and more he's sinking down through the earth.'

To her surprise, Mr. Bulstrode did not answer. A struggle was going on within him.

'I think he must die for want o' support, if he goes on in that way. When I nursed my poor master, Mr. Robisson, I had to give him port-wine and brandy constant, and a big glass at a time,' added Mrs. Abel with a touch of remonstrance in her tone.[18]

In the novel Bulstrode thrusts through the two inches of doorway the key to the spirits cupboard. Here the murder is deliberately done. But I wish to introduce a change in the story as follows: Bulstrode tells the servant that the doctor does not wish liquor to be given the man. The servant snorts and scuttles away. Half an hour later Bulstrode hears her slippered feet on the floor outside his door, and after a short time he hears the hinge on the spirits' cupboard whine. Moments later, the slippered feet again pass his door and he hears the dulled clink of glass on glass hugged to a shawled breast. He sits a long time in the dark, in silence. In the morning Raffles is dead.

Suppose two men judge differently of what is done here. One says: "Bulstrode killed him, though he did not put the glass to Raffles' lips himself. But he knew what would be the result. He let him die." Another says: "He didn't kill him. The old servant did. He told her the doctor's orders. Bulstrode didn't *know* that she would give him liquor anyway." "But he heard her fetch it." "How did he know she meant to give it to Raffles? Perhaps she meant to take a little herself." "Get off it." "Well, all right. I'll give you that much. But still *she* did it. Bulstrode had *no duty* to go after her and return the brandy to the cupboard. He told her not to give the man any. She went against what he told her. Bulstrode is not responsible." "Bulstrode let her give it to him. He let Raffles die." "So he is guilty of a wrong then?" "Yes." "I disagree. I don't think he is guilty at all. I think he did what he had to do. He told her no. And that's enough."

I want to say that Bulstrode did wrong. I also wish to claim that in time the second man may come to see this. He may come to have the thought: "Perhaps you're right. Perhaps Bulstrode ought to have gone after her. Yes, I see now he should have. I thought he was not wrong to before. But now I see that he was in the wrong."

"*Perhaps you are right.*" "*I once thought it was not wrong to do that, but now I see that it is.*" These are thoughts (and so distinctions) which are possible on my account of morals. They are possible because they almost always involve changes (and disagreements) in judgment about the *contribution* persons make to human suffering, the responsibility they have for what takes place, and about the weight to be given *competing* moral considerations. The distinction between "think to be right" and "is right" is not a distinction which only the 'objectivist' can claim. A man who cares that others not be wronged has yet to discern what *is* a case of someone wronging them (and what, say, is a misfortune for which no one is responsible). Here he may sometimes make judgments from which he himself wishes later to retreat.

V

We have been urged to accept that P's moral statement S is true if it is required or acceptable from the moral point of view. Yet at the same time we are told that only if we can get beyond "thinking makes it so" can we be justified in claiming that there are objective moral truths. It should be clear by now that on an unexceptional construction of the word "thinking", the first of these claims defeats the second. For, *pace* Nielsen and Baier, the moral point of view *is itself a case of* "[human] thinking making something so". For it is a matter of our regarding an act as what ought not to be done because of what is wrought by the act in human (or, as I shall argue in chapter X, in animal) life.

Achilles: Ah, here we are, old and feeble and forgotten, Tortoise.—Do you yearn for youth as I do?

Tortoise: No, Achilles. My youth, as you know, was not a well-lived one. I have no desire to re-live it; except perhaps if I could do it the right way, as a good man would have lived it.

Achilles: Do you remember Tortoise that time you wronged me? It seems so long ago, now. You know, you were a very callous person then. Didn't you know that what you did—leaving me destitute in that foreign land where my enemies were everywhere—was a very great wrong?

Tortoise: I knew you would suffer. And I knew that what I did would be condemned by everyone as heartless and cruel. But somehow it didn't seem to matter. I wanted what you had. If you suffered or died, well, forgive me Achilles, but it seemed to me then of no very great importance.

Achilles: But now you regret it?

Tortoise: I deeply regret it, Achilles. I see now that what I did was deeply wrong, and something I ought never to have done.

Achilles: But you just said that you knew it was wrong even when you did it.

Tortoise: I knew that, Achilles, but only in the sense that I knew, from the point of view of morality, I ought not to do it. From the point of view I had then, callous libertine that I was, it seemed that I ought to do it. (Else why would I have done it?)

Achilles: Still you knew that it was morally wrong to do it?

Tortoise: Yes.

Achilles: But you didn't *appreciate* that you *ought not to do it*?

Tortoise: Sadly, I did not.

Achilles: So you knew what you were doing was wrong, but you didn't appreciate that you ought not to do it?

Tortoise: Yes.

Achilles: Why not?

Tortoise: As I said, it didn't seem to me to make much difference that it was wrong.

Achilles: But now it does?

Tortoise: Yes. Now it makes all the difference to me.

It is this *difference* that I am searching after in this essay.

Now it may be thought that a consequence of my view is that if there should come a time when no human being possesses what I have called moral sensibility or moral understanding, which involves caring about others, then nothing which human beings do is wrong. If no one cares there can be no appreciation that acts of brutality (for example) ought not to be done. Therefore these acts no longer are wrong.

This idea is a mistake. But it is prompted by something important here half caught sight of. Consider first works of art. Certain works of art, for example Rembrandt's *Stallmeesters*, or Monet's *Rouen Cathedral*, have inestimable value. Now compare the following positions.

(1) "A thing has value in being valued."

(2) "Wrong! The reason is that if (1) were true, then if at some future time T_F Monet's *Rouen Cathedral* is not valued by anyone, it is valueless. But suppose at some future time, when we are all dead, those living have no regard at all for art. They count it nothing. Are we to accept that Monet's painting is now—i.e. at this time T_F—without value? Surely, despite these people, it has exactly the value then as it is appreciated by us to have now?"

Suppose I try to hold (2). I hold that it does *not* follow that if a thing is not valued by anyone it is valueless.—If at some future time Monet's painting is not valued by anyone alive, still, *it has value*.

But look: my appreciation that it will still have value is itself *a valuation*. That is, if we ask 'Will it still have value?' *someone has to answer this question*. And my (or your) answer "It will still have value—despite them", *expresses* our valuation, our appreciation, of what Monet has achieved here in paint on canvas. *Someone has to have this thought*: 'It will yet have value." This is the sense in which value is a human creation.

It is also the sense in which morals are a human creation. For if we say that in the amoral future time spoken of a moment ago, the brutal and vicious acts of persons will still be wrong, these words express *our* moral appreciation of those acts. When I say that what the young people in Selby's story do to the soldier is wrong to do I do not mean it is wrong to do it now, for a time. I mean it will always be wrong to do it. In saying this I am expressing a judgment one implication of which is that nothing could justify a recall of that judgment. Something (application to the rack, or corruption) might provoke, or issue in, a different judgment. But nothing could *justify* that change of judgment. This is because that moral judgment upon the acts of the young people is an expression of values (or what I prefer to call, a certain regard) *in terms of which anything which might subsequently happen is itself judged*. The present judgment searches out, as it were, anything which might come, and judges it to be incapable of justifying a change of judgment.

It is this which gives a character of 'absoluteness' even to our own particular moral judgments of human acts. If its being wrong to treat persons in certain ways were dependent, say, on their being *for something*, it is conceivable that that something could be realized in some other way (for example by humanoids), and then it would not matter to us any longer that other persons *were*; and so it would no longer be wrong to let them die or even to kill or abuse them. But because the sense in which we should not kill or violate is tied to the absolute and unconditional significance to us of human life, and of persons not suffering, that cannot be so. For if in time what I have just described came about, and we ourselves were to act as indicated, this would be condemned (as I have argued earlier) by our own moral judgments. Even if we no longer cared about persons, being now less efficient means to our purposes, what we did would be wrong to do. True, no one would be there to appreciate that it was. Still, it would be wrong.

Thus the brutal and vicious acts of persons not yet born will be wrong—whatever these persons think. But their *being* wrong is a matter of the judgment upon those acts of what Baier and Nielsen speak of as the moral point of view. And this points up something related to what I said at the beginning of this section. We need to distinguish between

(i) A particular act (or type of act, or social institution) can be morally wrong, even if all the people who have ever lived (or ever will live) think that it is not.

(ii) A particular act (or type of act, or social institution) could be morally wrong, whatever all the people living, dead, or yet to be born, *think of human life or one another*.

The context in which (i) is true is our context: the human world in which there is, and has been, moral regard and understanding. The context in which (ii) is false is any context: i.e. there can be no context in which (ii) is true, for the reason that there is a *logical* dependence of moral wrong upon human 'thought'; upon human regard. An example of (i), so Proudhon and others have alleged, is private property. Another, less controversial, example is slavery. What (i) claims is that, properly understood, these things are morally indefensible—though people fail (or once failed) to realize this. And what one would seek to do to show this would be to trace the connections between *these* institutions or human relationships, and denials, sufferings, injustices, and deprivations which people already acknowledge to be wrong.

The impossibility of producing an example of (ii) this entire book seeks to establish.

NOTES

[1] Kai Nielsen, "On Moral Truth", in Nicholas Rescher (ed.), *Studies in Moral Philosophy* (Oxford: Blackwell, 1968) p. 25.

[2] Ibid., p. 9.

[3] Ibid., p. 10.

[4] Ibid., p. 14.

[5] Ibid., pp. 13–14.

[6] Ibid., p. 13.

[7] Kai Nielsen, "Problems of Ethics", in Paul Edwards (ed.) *The Encyclopedia of Philosophy* (New York: MacMillan and Free Press, 1967) Vol. 3, pp. 126–127.

[8] Ibid., p. 126.

[9] Ibid., p. 126.

[10] See note 5 above.

[11] "On Moral Truth", pp. 21–2, 24.

[12] Ibid., p. 22.

[13] See note 7 above.

[14] George Eliot, *Middlemarch* (Harmondsworth: Penguin Books, 1965) pp. 664–665.

[15] Ibid., pp. 756, 757, 758.

[16] Ibid., p. 759.

[17] Ibid., pp. 761–3.

[18] Ibid., p. 763.

V
Two Objections

If I resolve to take vengeance on someone, and when an opportunity offers, the better consciousness in the form of love and humanity speaks its word, and I am influenced by it rather than by my evil resolution, this is a virtuous act, for it is a manifestation of the better consciousness. It is possible to conceive of a very virtuous man in whom the better consciousness is so continuously active that it is never silent, and never allows his passions to get a complete hold of him. By such consciousness he is subject to a direct control, instead of being guided indirectly, through the medium of reason, by means of maxims and moral principles. That is why a man may have weak reasoning powers and a weak understanding, and yet have a high sense of morality and be eminently good; for the most important element in a man depends as little on intellectual as it does on physical strength.

SCHOPENHAUER

I shall seek in this chapter to meet two different objections which will be made against the argument, to this point, of my essay. I shall first consider the objection that morality does not in fact involve anything affective. I shall then confront the charge that my account of moral life is unacceptable because it is a form of ethical subjectivism.

I

The figure I must address in the first part is Kant. Consider these remarks from the *Groundwork of the Metaphysic of Morals*:

To help others where one can is a duty, and besides this there are many spirits of so sympathetic a temper that, without any further motive of vanity or self-interest, they find an inner pleasure in spreading happiness around them and can take delight in the contentment of others as their own work. Yet I maintain that in such a case an action of this kind, however right and however amiable it may be, has still no genuinely moral worth. It stands on the same footing as other inclinations—for example, the inclination for honour, which if fortunate enough to hit on something beneficial and right and consequently honourable, deserves praise and encouragement, but not esteem; for its maxim lacks moral content, namely, the performance of such actions, not from inclination, but *from duty*. Suppose then that the mind of this friend of man were overclouded by sorrows of his own which extinguished all sympathy with the fate of others, but that he still had power to help those in distress, though no longer stirred by the need of others because sufficiently occupied with his own; and suppose that, when no longer moved by any inclination, he tears himself out of this deadly insensibility and does the action without any inclination for the sake of duty alone; then for the first time his action has its genuine moral worth. Still further: if nature had implanted little sympathy in this or that man's heart; if (being in other respects an honest fellow) he were cold in temperament and indifferent to the sufferings of others—perhaps because, being endowed with the special gift of patience and robust endurance in his own sufferings, he assumed the like in others or even demanded it; if such a man (who would in truth not be the worst product of nature) were not exactly fashioned by her to be a philanthropist, would he not still find in himself a source from which he might draw a worth far higher than any that a good-natured temperament can have? Assuredly he would. It is precisely in this that the worth of character begins to show—a moral worth and beyond all comparison the highest—namely, that he does good, not from inclination, but from duty.

It is doubtless in this sense that we should understand too the passages from Scripture in which we are commanded to love our neighbour and even our enemy. For love out of inclination cannot be commanded; but kindness done from duty—although no inclination impels us, and even although natural and unconquerable disinclination stands in our way— is *practical*, and not *pathological*, love residing in the will and not in the propensions of feeling, in principles of action and not of melting compassion; and it is this practical love alone which can be an object of command.[1]

Kant appears flatly to exclude love from moral life as being an inclination, and so not generative of actions having moral worth. He distinguishes love of others from inclinations such as self-interest, and he accounts the second less valuable than the first, but he refuses the first moral worth. On Kant's account, those actions alone are moral actions which are done for the sake of duty. Actions which proceed from love, or what Kant calls compassion, or what St. Paul speaks of as charity, are not instances of morality. The important proposition is this one:

An action done from duty has its moral worth, *not in the purpose* to be attained by it, but in the maxim according with which it is decided upon; it depends therefore, not on the realisation of the object of the action, but solely on the *principle* of *volition* in accordance with which, irrespective of all objects of the faculty of desire, the action has been performed.[2]

The moral worth of what one does resides in the *formal* principle or maxim in following which one does what one does. This principle Kant considers to be: doing one's duty *because it is* one's duty. Kant does not want the results of human action, or any human desire, to constitute the moral worth of actions. He resists this because in the first place he thinks there will be a depreciation of the primacy of the human will in morals, since any effects which a human action could introduce into the world could conceivably be introduced by something which was not a human action, and secondly, because he considers human desires too mercurial and contingent to be the basis for the inescapable and eternal character of morality. Kant does speak of reverence for the law, but he does not locate moral worth in that reverence either. Rather he locates the moral worth of actions in the idea of the moral law so far as it is the ground determining the will. Reverence for the law is the 'subjective principle' which determines the will to obey; but that which is '*moral good*' is the person acting on the idea of the law out of reverence for it. It is Kant's notion of a good will (see page 66), or 'reverence', that I wish to examine. But before doing so I should like to make some preliminary remarks with the figure of Kant in the background.

Is there a necessary connection between *not doing wrong* and either (1) appreciating that one does not, or (2) consciously acting according to moral considerations? I believe it is obvious that there is no necessary connection in the first case. In the course of walking down a crowded street, or eating breakfast with his family, there are countless possibilities of wrong that a man might do. He might strike his child for no reason, insult passersby, push people into traffic. A man does not do these things. In order to keep from doing them does he have to appreciate that he does not do them? The answer is no. 'It never occurs to him', we say, to do them. And it never occurs to him therefore (except perhaps if he gets to doing philosophy) that he does not.

But then the answer in the second case is also no. In order not to do wrong a man does not have to keep from doing it because he appreciates that it is wrong to do it. A man may not do wrong because (as we have seen) it does not occur to him to do what it is wrong to do. And a man may not do what is wrong because he appreciates that it is wrong to do it. All I want to insist upon is that an enormous number of persons keep from wrong, throughout an enormous number of opportunities to do wrong (and in some of these cases they could do it without suffering any penalty for it), without even appreciating them *as* opportunities to do wrong, because without appreciating them as *opportunities* at all. These persons may of course be brought to realize that this situation obtains. All I am insisting upon is that this absence of wrongdoing does not depend on this realization (the realization that wrong is not done here). This of course still leaves all the cases of resistance to wrong: keeping from wrong because it is wrong.

Consider now a second question: whether there is a connection between a man's *doing what it is right to do* and either (1) appreciating that he does it, or (2) consciously acting from moral considerations. This question is connected to the one just discussed. That very many men do not *see* many possibilities of wrongdoing, and do not do wrong when they could, or even when it would be easy to—that a man worried about the rent does not even think to lie in wait in the dark for his more well-off neighbour; that a man who wishes he did not have to tell someone something does not think to lie—is enormously important in human life. Though a man who is, as we might say, naturally honest or generous, who has an honest or generous character, does not have to be at all innocent of the possibilities there are for meanness or dishonesty in human life. This man may even be especially wise concerning the ways in which people are liable to hurt or be careless of one another. It just never occurs *to him* to do these things in his relations with others and in his response to the flow of life. His question, if he does have a question he sometimes asks himself, is not "Should I not do this—it's dishonest?", but only, "What *is* the honest thing to do here?" This man is not drawn toward dishonesty. Still, the proof that he is morally aware of dishonesty is that one has only to suggest to him a dishonesty (which one may not present as such) to see him detect and repudiate it.

Now there is, I believe, an absurd moral prejudice which sees the excellent moral character in someone who is inclined toward the evil that one could do but who struggles to resist it in a zealous keeping to duty. This prejudice comes out, I think, in some remarks by Wittgenstein concerning Moore. Norman Malcolm had remarked to Moore that a well-known philosopher tended to react with hostility to criticisms of his published philosophical views. Moore seemed to be surprised at this information. Malcolm asked Moore whether Moore did not understand how professional vanity might make a man resent criticism of his writings. Moore replied that he did not. Malcolm related this story to Wittgenstein in a letter, and what follows is Wittgenstein's reply.[3]

Now as to Moore—I don't really understand Moore, and therefore, what I'll say may be quite wrong. But this is what I'm inclined to say:—That Moore is in some sense extraordinarily childlike is obvious, and the remark you quoted (about vanity) is certainly an example of that childlikeness. There is also a *certain* innocence about Moore; he is, e.g. completely unvain. As to it's being to his '*credit*' to be childlike,—I can't understand that; unless it's also to a *child's* credit. For you aren't talking of the innocence a man has fought for, but of an innocence which comes from a natural absence of a temptation. I believe that all you wanted to say was that you *liked*, or even *loved*, Moore's childlikeness. And that I can understand. I think that our discrepancy here is not so much one of thoughts as of feelings. I *like* and greatly respect Moore; but that's all. He doesn't warm my heart (or very little), because what warms my heart most is human kindness, and Moore—*just like a child*—is not kind. He is kindly and he can be charming and nice to those he likes and he has great *depth*.—That's how it seems to me. If I'm wrong, I'm wrong.

Now in the case of Moore it cannot have been that Moore was unaware of the difference literary or professional renown could make in a man's life. Nor could he have been unaware of vanity in human affairs. (Moore, remember, was a classicist.) What he was (apparently) without knowledge of was that some men can so prefer their own opinions as to resent criticisms of them, criticism which might of course get nearer the truth. What matters to them in the criticism is the attribution to their work of mistake. Moore was someone in whom this response would simply never arise. Moore's innocence in this matter was connected perhaps to the innocence of his desires, and to a love of truth, and also to humility. Now in some moral traditions the innocence of the child is not value-less at all. It is precisely to become as children that we are enjoined, for example, by Christ. Anyone who has ever responded to the transparent goodness of another person in whose company one's own self-centered concerns or preoccupations ran off one like water, and one's very conception of what was worthwhile was restored, will know something of what the sense of this injunction is. Of course all children are not what Christ hoped we would become. The point is that innocence of the kind that a child *may* possess is, many would wish to say, a blessing. That is a possible moral response. In Moore's case the innocence is almost certainly only in part like that of the child (the purity or undefiled nature of his sensibility, the unwordliness of his desires). For there is an innocence appropriate to a good man; a man who is not ignorant of the world, but who is not *drawn* toward evil; a man of whom we say, he is 'naturally good', he has a good nature. This is not, I want to insist, necessarily a man who never desires things he is without. But these are, ordinarily, desires for what are good or harmless things; and where on occasion they are not he repudiates them and condemns his desiring them. And he never *considers* getting any of these things by immoral means. (As for Wittgenstein's remark that Moore "*just like a child*, is not kind", I am inclined to confess I don't understand it—partly because it seems so obviously untrue both that a child cannot be kind or that Moore was not.)

Now Kant is one who wants to insist that those actions alone have *moral worth* which are done for the sake of duty, i.e. which are cases of consciously acting in accord with the moral law out of reverence for that law. This tenet of Kant's doctrine is very different from my own understanding of morals. Suppose a man walking through a wood comes upon another man in need of help. The second man has been pinned by a tree, which has fallen on him as he cut it down. The first man, immediately he hears the other's cries, hurries in the direction from which they come, and sees the man under the tree. Instantly he rushes forward and seeks to lift the tree off the man, all the while encouraging him to lie still, that he will be free in a moment and then they will together make their way to the village. He struggles with the tree for a few minutes and it does not come free. Instantly he sees he must go for help. He tears open his bag, gives water to the injured man, tells him to lie quietly while he goes for help. He turns and runs to the village, his breath tearing at his lungs by the time he reaches it. He summons help and they run back to the clearing and free the man. Now on Kant's account, except this man does these things *for the sake of duty*, his actions have no moral worth. And notice that on Kant's account, to act for the sake of duty one must be *inclined to do* otherwise than duty requires. But consider this man who helps the other pinned by the tree. What *accounts* for his actions? What brings him to do what he does? He hears what he takes to be cries of pain. He hurries toward the place from which they come. He comes upon the man caught under the tree. He goes forward to help. Suppose we ask him why he rushes forward to help. I expect he will give us a blank stare. "The man was caught under the tree", he will reply. "But is *that* why you hurried to help?", we ask again. "Is that not reason enough?" he might reply. "Then you went to help because the man was pinned under the tree, and that's *all* you considered?", we insist. We shall take his silence as assent. "Well, what you did was to be encouraged, but not esteemed. It had no moral worth." Are we honestly to say this?

What sort of consideration other than that a man is pinned under a tree is to be the *moral* consideration on which this man acts? Is he to have the thought "It is my duty to help"? Is he to do it because it is his *duty to*? That is Kant's answer. He is to do it for the sake of duty. He is to do it out of reverence for the moral law. I cannot accept this claim, since it seems to me that the most morally excellent man is the man who responds as this man does and who does not even 'present' the situation to himself in terms of what his duty is. He has no thought of duty. He has thoughts of the man and how he is to help him.

I have come upon a remark by Bernard Williams which confirms me in my judgment.

[I]s it certain that one who receives good treatment from another more appreciates it, thinks the better of the giver, if he knows it to be the result of the application of principle, rather than the product of an emotional response? He may have needed, not the benefits of universal law, but some human gesture. It may be said that this is obviously true enough in many cases, but it has nothing to do with morality; it just shows that people place other sorts of value on human conduct besides moral value. Well, this may be said, and Kant indeed said it, but it leads to an uncomfortable dilemma. Either the recipient *ought* to prefer the ministrations of the moral man to the human gesture, which seems a mildly insane requirement; or, alternatively, if it be admitted that it is perfectly proper and rational of the recipient to have the preference he has, the value of moral men becomes an open question, and we can reasonably entertain the proposal that we should not seek to produce moral men, or very many of them, but rather those, whatever their incon- sistencies, who make the human gesture. While there might be something in that conclusion, I feel fairly sure that this very restrictive, typological use of the word 'moral' is not the best use to make of it.[4]

My first objection to Kant then is that a man may do many morally excellent actions, may often do what he should do, though he does not decide to do them because they are right to do. Kant seems to identify acting from moral considerations with *having difficulty* acting from them. But many men respond spontaneously and deliberately to human situations as they should—generously, charitably, pitiably, honestly, loyally, mercifully, courageously, trustingly, forgivingly—because that is the way they are drawn to respond, the kind of person they are. If someone were to draw the attention of one of these men to what he does, and ask him if he acts on moral considerations, I do not know what he would say; *I* would say he does act on them. For he acts upon considerations of the situation or plight of these people, the trouble or need or anxiety or difficulty in which they are caught. These, I want to claim, are moral considerations. Is it necessary for this man to appreciate (at the moment he acts) that he should act as he does? Not if this is to mean that he is to *decide* to do it *because* he should. Perhaps he does not 'decide' to do it at all. He does it. If after, someone asks him if he should have done what he did he will answer yes. But *while* he responds in the way one should he does not do so *because he should* (because it is his duty) but because these are people in difficulty, with trouble, and so on.

In those cases where a person is drawn by some desire or emotion to ignore or neglect the difficulties others are in, we do get a situation where a man may decide to do what he should do because he appreciates that he should do it. This man does what he does *because he should*. Admittedly, to *appreciate that* he should, this man must see that these people are in difficulty, and care to help them for their sake. But there is still a difference between him and the first man, which is that the first man's acts toward these people are at no point something he must 'bring himself' to do. But why should that make a difference to the 'moral worth' of what he does? Is it not precisely because they are in difficulty that he should help them?

In the *Groundwork* the appreciation that one should do one's duty is explained in part as a subjective feeling, reverence for the law. But Kant hastily seeks to rid this notion of any sticky emotional content, as I shall show in a moment. This subjective feeling is said to be itself the result of recognizing the obligatory character of the moral law:

Duty is the necessity to act out of reverence for the law. For an object as the effect of my proposed action I can have an *inclination*, but *never reverence*, precisely because it is merely the effect, and not the activity, of a will. Similarly for inclination as such, whether my own or that of another, I cannot have reverence: I can at most in the first case approve, and in the second case sometimes even love—that is, regard it as favourable to my own advantage. Only something which is conjoined with my will solely as a ground and never as an effect—something which does not serve my inclination, but outweighs it or at least leaves it entirely out of account in my choice—and therefore only bare law for its own sake, can be an object of reverence and therewith a command. Now an action done from duty has to set aside altogether the influence of inclination, and along with inclination every object of the will; so there is nothing left able to determine the will except objectively the *law* and subjectively *pure reverence* for this practical law, and therefore the maxim of obeying this law even to the detriment of all my inclination.[5]

In a note at the bottom of the page Kant gives this account of reverence for the law.

It might be urged against me that I have merely tried, under cover of the word '*reverence*', to take refuge in an obscure feeling instead of giving a clearly articulated answer to the question by means of a concept of reason. Yet although reverence is a feeling, it is not a feeling *received* through outside influence, but one *self-produced* by a rational concept, and therefore specifically distinct from feelings of the first kind, all of which can be reduced to inclination or fear. What I recognise immediately as law for me, I recognise with reverence, which means merely consciousness of the *subordination* of my will to a law without the mediation of external influences on my senses. Immediate determination of the will by the law and consciousness of this determination is called '*reverence*', so that reverence is regarded as the *effect* of the law on the subject and not as the *cause* of the law.[6]

Reverence is the effect of the law; not the 'cause' of the law being appreciated *as a law*, as binding on one. The reverence we have for the law is not our appreciation that the law is valid. Our recognition of its validity is what awakens *in us* moral feeling or reverence. In the *Groundwork* Kant considers the appreciation of the moral law's validity as an assent which *reason* makes, or imposes on the will, and it is this which makes it look as though Kant completely repudiates any attempt to tie moral appreciation to "love"—to charity and caring about others.

But consider the following sentences:

There are certain moral dispositions such that anyone lacking them could have no duty to acquire them.—They are *moral feeling, conscience, love* of one's neighbour, and *reverence* for oneself (*self-esteem*). There is no obligation to have these because they lie at the basis of morality, as *subjective* conditions of our receptiveness to the concept of duty, not as objective conditions of morality. All of them are natural dispositions of the mind (*praedispositio*) to be affected by concepts of duty—antecedent dispositions on the side of *feeling*. To have them cannot be a duty: every man has them and it is by virtue of them that he can be obligated.[7]

These words are Kant's, taken from Part II of the *Metaphysic of Morals*. The love spoken of here cannot be the so-called practical love, since it is a love which makes possible the conception of duty. Practical love is action according to duty. The love spoken of in this passage is something which exists before the duty of practical love, and without which that duty would not be recognized. In case anyone should think this account of Kant eccentric I shall summon H. J. Paton in support of it.

Love, [Kant] tells us, is a matter of feeling, not of volition. I cannot love because I will to love, and still less because I ought to love. Hence a duty to love is an absurdity (*ein Unding*). But, unlike some of his critics, Kant does not suppose that this leaves no more to be said.

In the first place, love, even as a natural emotion, is—he tells us—one of the subjective conditions without which our minds would be incapable of receiving the concept of duty. It is indeed absurd to regard it as an emotion which we ought to feel, but it is, nevertheless, a natural predisposition which every man has and in virtue of which he can be subject to duty.[8]

Kant of course still holds a position importantly hostile to mine. He wishes to exclude actions done *from* love or caring from the realm of the moral.—Though he seems not to be always consistent about this, since he expressly (unless he is mistranslated here) calls these dispositions noted above *moral* dispositions. But the evidence that he wishes to exclude love from morals is greater than the reverse, as this passage which follows two pages after the one above shows.

Love is a matter of *feeling*, not of *will*, and I cannot love because I *will* to, still less because I *ought* to (i.e. I cannot be necessitated to love). So a *duty to love* is logically impossible. But *benevolence (amor benevolentiae)*, as conduct, can be brought under a law of duty. We often call unselfish benevolence to men *love* also (though this is most inappropriate); indeed we speak of love which is also our duty when it is not a question of another's happiness but of the complete and free surrender of all one's ends to the ends of another (even a supernatural) being. But every duty implies *necessitation* or constraint, even if the constraint is to be self-imposed according to a law. And what is done from constraint is not done from love.[9]

Still, Kant does admit that the *receptiveness to the notion of duty* depends upon certain 'empirical' states, and not upon formal principles. One of these states is love, that love which is sometimes spoken of as charity. This is near to my own claim that moral appreciation involves caring about persons; since in both cases the appreciation that something should or should not be done requires that one cares. I hope then to have shaken the confidence of those who consider that Kant rightly dispelled 'the affective' from morals a long time ago.

Let me try to shake it further by examining briefly the notion of action for the sake of duty (here I am arguing directly *against* Kant). To act for the sake of duty is to act for the sake of what? It seems it must be: to act for the sake of the moral law (because it is "the *moral* law" that one do it). So adamantly does Kant insist upon the claims of the *law*, while at the same time emptying duty of any material "inclination", that he ends up at this result:

Reverence is properly awareness of a value which demolishes my self-love. . . . All reverence for a person is properly only reverence for the law (of honesty and so on) of which that person gives us an example. Because we regard the developments of our talents as a duty, we see too in a man of talent a sort of *example of the law* (the law of becoming like him by practice), and this is what constitutes our reverence for him. All moral *interest*, so-called, consists solely in *reverence* for the law.[10]

I find this claim repugnant; but also confounding. I want to know why the law is *deserving* of reverence. Reverence, Kant tells us, "is properly awareness of a value which demolishes my self-love". But when I am aware of persons, or of any living thing, as having value, this value they have need not be a value for me—that they are useful for me. If my response to other living things is a caring about *them*, is this not awareness of a value other than myself, and into which my self does not enter? If a man tells me, then, that when he acts for the sake of duty he acts for the sake of these creatures, in whose lives his dutiful actions make a difference, I shall appreciate why it is that he does what he does, and why he considers what he does his duty. Kant himself sometimes speaks in ways which themselves support such an account. For we find him on page 9 of the *Groundwork* speaking of a grocer who acts honestly "from duty *or from principles of fair dealing*". Is anyone to trace our 'reverence' for fairness to some endpoint apart from the persons who are to be treated fairly?

II

But, it will be asked, is it *love* one has for others when one appreciates that one should not harm or injure them? Let me first remark that I am not seeking to *replace* the forms of virtue and moral response with which we are familiar with an injunction to love, or care. I am trying to show what it is that explains why these things—honesty, justice, mercy, loyalty, courage, charity, and so on—*are* the virtues, and how it is that we appreciate them as such. In the second place, I am not altogether alone (I have discovered since beginning this essay) in being prepared to speak of caring in connection with moral life. But those who are prepared to speak in this way conceive of this caring as limited only to some persons, and while they may admit that caring is the foothold for the beginning of moral appreciation, they do not see it as something which accompanies it afterwards (since caring is still considered to be restricted to a few persons among the many one encounters in life). I have claimed that this caring must extend to all cases where one appreciates that morally one ought not to do something, and I have shown a willingness to speak of this caring as 'love'. It is these things which will vex many persons.

Moral life involves concern with how human beings are, which springs from an appreciation of what they are and a certain response to them. This response I consider appropriately described as a form of love. But nothing important really turns on this. I for one am entirely content to keep to the expression 'caring about others'. What is important (and what I shall return to again in a later chapter) is to appreciate that if we seek to help persons, or prevent harm to them, and we do this from moral considerations, then we do it for their sake, not because of some personal or social purpose to which these actions contribute. If we ask, for example, of a man who comes upon the young people beating the soldier, and goes to the soldier's defense, "What does he do it for?", the answer is, he does it for him.

This man will not have seen the soldier before, as the man walking in the wood perhaps saw for the first time the woodcutter pinned under the tree. Why does each respond to the one in difficulty? I want to say that each cares about the plight of the one he comes upon in difficulty. And he cares about that plight because he cares about the one whose plight it is. Someone is sure to ask how this is possible, since each has only seen the other for the first time, and only for as long as took him to see that the other was in difficulty.

It seems to me that the only real answer to such a question is *to point to the reality*—as I have, in examples, done. And examples are legion. Here is one from fiction. A man is about to encounter a person he has seen before, but has never spoken to, and whom he has dread of, because he suspects the person means to betray him to the police. The man is the protagonist of Orwell's *Nineteen Eighty-Four*.

It was the middle of the morning, and Winston had left the cubicle to go to the lavatory.

A solitary figure was coming towards him from the other end of the long, brightly-lit corridor. It was the girl with dark hair. Four days had gone past since the evening when he had run into her outside the junkshop. As she came nearer he saw that her right arm was in a sling, not noticeable at a distance because it was of the same colour as her overalls. Probably she had crushed her hand while swinging round one of the big kaleidoscopes on which the plots of novels were 'roughed in'. It was a common accident in the Fiction Department.

They were perhaps four metres apart when the girl stumbled and fell almost flat on her face. A sharp cry of pain was wrung out of her. She must have fallen right on her injured arm. Winston stopped short. The girl had risen to her knees. Her face had turned a milky yellow colour against which her mouth stood out redder than ever. Her eyes were fixed on his, with an appealing expression that looked more like fear than pain.

A curious emotion stirred in Winston's heart. In front of him was an enemy who was trying to kill him: in front of him, also, was a human creature, in pain and perhaps with a broken bone. Already he had instinctively started forward to help her. In the moment when he had seen her fall on the bandaged arm it had been as though he felt the pain in his own body.

'You're hurt?' he said.[11]

Compassion claims this man even in the midst of dread and fear. That is how (some) human beings are. Many of us respond with compassion to people we have never seen before. Except this were so it is hard to see how there could be moral concern: concern that one does not harm, or concern to help, other human beings, because one cares that they should not suffer. Morality has to do with those who 'enter one's life', as well as those who are in it now. Caring about others, even as one comes upon them for the first time, is possible. But it cannot be 'explained'. This is one of those places where explanation comes to an end.

The foundation upon which all our knowledge and learning rests is the inexplicable. It is to this that every explanation, through few or many intermediate stages, leads; as the plummet touches the sea now at a greater depth, now at a less, but is bound to reach it somewhere sooner or later.[12]

III

Before turning to the objection concerning ethical subjectivism, there is something in the Orwell passage that I wish to comment on. I refer to the words: "it had been as though he felt the pain in his own body".

These words will almost certainly call up the claim (respecting Winston's emotion and his starting forward to help the girl): "He sees *himself* in the girl's predicament, and so responds to *his own* pain. He does it *for himself*." And indeed there is a perennial and astoundingly widespread view of human beings according to which—in the idiom of its most famous exponent—

> of the voluntary acts of every man, the object is some *Good to himselfe*.[13]

The arguments against such a view have been given so many times as to weary in repetition. They are expressed with perhaps the greatest economy and force by James Rachels in an essay entitled "Morality and Self Interest". Accordingly I shall quote directly from his essay here:

A. The first argument [in favour of this view] goes as follows. If we describe one person's action as selfish, and another person's action as unselfish, we are overlooking the crucial fact that in both cases, assuming that the action is done voluntarily, the agent is merely doing what he most wants to do. [For example, Smith gives up a trip to the country, which he would have enjoyed very much, in order to stay behind and help a friend with his studies . . .] If Smith stays behind to help his friend, that only shows that he wanted to help his friend more than he wanted to go to the country. And why should he be praised for his "unselfishness" when he is only doing what he most wants to do? So, since Smith is only doing what he wants to do, he cannot be said to be acting unselfishly.

. . .[S]uppose we were to concede, for the sake of the argument, that all voluntary action is motivated by the agent's wants, or at least that Smith is so motivated. Even if this were granted, it would not follow that Smith is acting selfishly or from self-interest. For if Smith wants to do something that will help his friend, even when it means forgoing his own enjoyments, that is precisely what makes him unselfish. What else could unselfishness be, if not wanting to help others? Another way to put the same point is to say that it is the object of a want that determines whether it is selfish or not. The mere fact that I am acting on my wants does not mean that I am acting selfishly; that depends on what it is that I want.

B. The second argument for psychological egoism is this. Since so-called unselfish actions always produce a sense of self-satisfaction in the agent, and since this sense of satisfaction is a pleasant state of consciousness, it follows that the point of the action is really to achieve a pleasant state of consciousness, rather than to bring about any good for others. Therefore, the action is "unselfish" only at a superficial level of analysis. Smith will feel much better with himself for having stayed to help his friend—if he had gone to the country, he would have felt terrible about it—and that is the real point of the action. According to a well-known story, this argument was once expressed by Abraham Lincoln:

Mr. Lincoln once remarked to a fellow-passenger on an old-time mud-coach that all men were prompted by selfishness in doing good. His fellow-passenger was antagonizing this position when they were passing over a corduroy bridge that spanned a slough. As they crossed this bridge they espied an old razor-backed sow on the bank making a terrible noise

because her pigs had got into the slough and were in danger of drowning.
As the old coach began to climb the hill, Mr. Lincoln called out, "Driver,
can't you stop just a moment?" Then Mr. Lincoln jumped out, ran back,
and lifted the little pigs out of the mud and water and placed them on the
bank. When he returned, his companion remarked: "Now, Abe, where
does selfishness come in on this little episode?" "Why, bless your soul, Ed,
that was the very essence of selfishness. I should have had no peace of
mind all day had I gone on and left that suffering old sow worrying over
those pigs. I did it to get peace of mind, don't you see?"

This argument suffers from defects similar to the previous one. Why should
we think that merely because someone derives satisfaction from helping
others this makes him selfish? Isn't the unselfish man precisely the one who
does derive satisfaction from helping others, while the selfish man does not?
If Lincoln "got peace of mind" from rescuing the piglets, does this show him
to be selfish, or, in the contrary, doesn't it show him to be compassionate and
good-hearted? (If a man were truly selfish, why should it bother his conscience that others suffer—much less pigs?) Similarly, it is nothing more
than shabby sophistry to say, because Smith takes satisfaction in helping his
friend, that he is behaving selfishly. If we say this rapidly, while thinking
about something else, perhaps it will sound all right; but if we speak slowly,
and pay attention to what we are saying, it sounds plain silly.

Moreover, suppose we ask why Smith derives satisfaction from helping his
friend. The answer will be, it is because Smith cares for him and wants him
to succeed. If Smith did not have these concerns, then he would take no
pleasure in assisting him; and these concerns, as we have already seen, are the
marks of unselfishness, not selfishness. To put the point more generally: if
we have a positive attitude toward the attainment of some goal, then we may
derive satisfaction from attaining that goal. But the object of our attitude is
the attainment of that goal; and we must want to attain the goal before we
can find any satisfaction in it.[14]

I would like to be able to stop right here; but Rousseau, who I have
invoked in support of my own understanding of morality, in at least
one place says something disturbingly evocative of the Hobbist
view, and I feel the need to remark upon this. Hobbes at one point in
Leviathan declares that

Griefe, for the calamity of another, is PITTY; and ariseth from the imagination that the like calamity may befall [one]selfe; and therefore is called
also COMPASSION, and in the phrase of this present time a FELLOW-
FEELING: And therefore for Calamity arriving from great wickedness [of

the one so afflicted], the best men have the least Pitty; and for the same calamity, those have least Pitty that think themselves least obnoxious to the same.[15]

Now in the remarks by Rousseau concerning pity which open my first chapter, "the most passionate detractor of human virtues" spoken of is, of course, Hobbes. It is therefore more than a little surprising to find Rousseau, on several key points Hobbes' most acute and effective critic, asserting (in *Emile*) that

The precept . . ., to act towards others as one wishes that others act towards oneself, has no true foundation other than in conscience and sentiment; for what precisely is the reason for acting, being oneself, as though I were another, especially when I am morally certain of never finding myself in the same situation? And who will reply that in following this maxim very faithfully, I will get others to follow it in the same way with me? The evil man gains his advantage from the honesty of the just and his own injustice; he is quite content that all the world should be just except himself. That arrangement, whatever one may say, is not very advantageous for good men. But when the force of an expansive soul identifies me with my fellow man, and when I feel myself so to speak in him; it is in order not to suffer myself, that I wish him not to suffer; I interest myself in him for the love of myself, and the reason of the precept lies in nature itself, which inspires in me the desire for my well-being wherever I may feel myself to exist. From which I conclude that it is not true that the precepts of natural law are founded on reason alone, they have a more solid and certain base. The love of men derived from the love of self [amour de soi] is the principle of human justice. The essence of all morality is given in the gospel by that of the law.[16]

I.e. the law: "Love thy neighbour as thyself". Now, as the remarks by Rachels quoted above will have made clear, there is something deeply troubling in this passage; I refer particularly to the expressions

(a) "when I feel myself so to speak in him"

(b) "it is in order not to suffer myself, that I wish him not to suffer".

To take (b) first, which is the least ambiguous of the two, it would take rather too much stretching to interpret this to mean: "if he suffers, *I* suffer *on his account*, and so seek to bring it about that neither he suffers nor I am distressed at his suffering." Rousseau himself goes on explicitly to declare that "I interest myself in him *for the love of myself*", and identifies this as a natural inclination to seek my own well-being "wherever I . . . feel myself to exist". This is precisely the position we began from. Winston sees himself in the girl, and responds to 'his own' pain 'in her'—i.e. we arrive at (a) above.

Consideration of why Rousseau falls into this analysis of pity, which is strikingly in conflict with a number of other things he says in his writings,* would take me too far from my own inquiry, and into the scholary excavation of eighteenth-century notions of the relation of reason to the passions. I shall confine myself to two remarks.

First, the injunction "Love thy neighbour as thyself" admits of two other interpretations which are at least as plausible as the one Rousseau fixes upon. The first involves simply reading it as: Love your neighbour as you love yourself—i.e. *as much as*. The second (which I believe I take from Simone Weil) is: Love your neighbour *in place of* yourself—i.e., love your *neighbour* as you now love yourself.

---

* "It is with pleasure we see the author of the Fable of the Bees, forced to acknowledge man a compassionate and sensitive being; and lay aside, in the example he offers to confirm it, his cold and subtle style, to place before us the pathetic picture of a man, who, with his hands tied up, is obliged to behold a beast of prey tear a child from the arms of his mother, and then with his teeth grind the tender limbs, and with his claws rend the throbbing entrails of the innocent victim. What horrible emotions must not such a spectator experience at the sight of an event *which does not personally concern him*? What anguish must he not suffer at his not being able to assist the fainting mother or the expiring infant?

Such is the pure impulse of nature, anterior to all manner of reflection; such is the force of natural pity, which the most dissolute manners have as yet found it so difficult to extinguish . . . Mandeville was aware that men, in spite of all their morality, would never have been better than monsters, if nature had not given them pity to assist reason: but he did not perceive that from this quality alone flow all the social virtues which he would dispute mankind the possession of. In fact, what is generosity, what clemency, what humanity, but pity applied to the weak, to the guilty, or to the human species in general? Even benevolence and friendship, if we judge right, will appear the effects of a constant pity, fixed upon a particular object: for to wish that a person may not suffer, what is it but to wish that he may be happy?" Rousseau, *Discourse on the Origin of Inequality* (my emphasis). Directly following these words Rousseau lapses into the position that "commisseration is no more than a sentiment, which puts us in place of him who suffers".

This second interpretation is the exact contrary of Rousseau's, being the injunction to 'die to the self'. The first is midway between, enjoining love of neighbour, but not calling for the cauterizing of love of self.

Secondly, Rousseau himself gives essentially an anthropological argument to the importance of self-love, finding "in nature itself" the explanation of "[this] principle of human justice". But if self-love is given in nature, why not love of others? Why is the one allowed as possible, unmysterious, "a solid and certain base", *but not the other*?

IV

Is my account a form of 'ethical subjectivism'? It is, but I shall argue that this does not tell against it.

The burden of the accusation against subjectivism is sometimes expressed: "It's only your feelings against theirs. There is nothing substantial or concrete or objective in morality as you draw it. You give examples of things which you say are wrong. But your saying they are wrong is simply a matter of your not wanting them done. This is simply a case of imposing upon phenomena a label expressive of *your reaction* to it. But if others do not react as you do, and go on to treat others brutally, in what sense is what they do *wrong* to do, since it's being wrong *in your mind* is just a matter of how you feel about it? It's just a matter of your feelings against theirs."

Now in a sense it is my feelings against theirs. But it is also the well-being of the persons threatened against their being harmed or injured. This last, the difference between their well-being and their suffering, is not something my feelings and my concern have created. It is something which is there in the facts, and which I call upon the other to admit to and appreciate. That some actions ought—morally—not to be done is not *just* a matter of caring that they are not done; it is a matter of what would be done *and* my concern, my caring, that it not be done. But my caring that it not be done is not something in which I figure as I often figure in my wants. Often what I want I want for myself. But I want these actions not done on account of those to whom they would be done. Moreover, a man may sometimes be mistaken in his moral judgment of a human situation. But if moral judgments are simply expressive of what a man feels about a situation, well, that is what he feels about it, and that is the end of the matter. But sometimes (as I have tried to show) we can get a man to see that his response to a situation is confused, or ignorant, or prejudiced. Sometimes we cannot. But if morality *were* *prejudice* there would be no sense in our moral condemnation of prejudices, such as people have against persons of another race, or concerning certain forms of sexual relation, and so on. Moreover, there have been in morals, perhaps as much as in any other realm of human life, profound moral *teachers*. But how in something which was mere 'feeling' could there arise the distinction between wisdom and ignorance, between integrity and corruption, between understanding and blind prejudice? (I shall return to this later.)

"But there is nothing *objective* in morality as you draw it." By this charge (that morality as I understand it is not objective) is meant: the claim which morality makes on human beings is not on my account accessible to any man solely by activity of his *reason*. (In this my objectors are Kantians, often despite themselves, for this too was an anxiety of Kant's.) The idea is that if morality is a rational phenomenon, then there must be *some reasons*—if not 'in' morals, then at least for acquiring morals—which are reasons for *any* man. Science, we are told, is objective, because in science the reason there is for accepting a claim or proceeding in a certain way does not depend upon, and is in no way affected by, what a man feels about the issue, or desires, or hopes. In science, a reason is a reason for any man, whether he cares to have a reason or not; and reasons are not generable by desires or cares. The same must be true in morals.

This view of the place of reason in morals is very different from mine. On my account there could not be morality except men cared for other persons. It is that caring which is generative of moral reasons. But I deny that this is in any way crippling or destructive of morals. It does make it possible that some men shall care nothing for moral considerations. But why does that in some way threaten our moral convictions? It is by an appeal to the facts, to what there is and to what would be done, that we justify our moral claims and judgments. Of course we cannot justify our *responding* to those facts as we do. We cannot justify our caring for persons. It is our caring which explains our keeping from or preventing harm, and our appealing to *others* not to harm; but how are we to justify *that* we care? It will not do to point to what we care about and say, "Well, because it is that—what it is." What will this achieve, except to make sense to another who also cares? But if someone does not care (and it is to him we are to give our justification), to ask him to consider what we care about will not justify to him our caring, unless he is able to appreciate (to perceive) that these creatures do matter—unless he comes to care about them too. We will never be able to convince someone who does not care about persons that some things should not, whatever he desires, be done. But why should we expect that we should be able to? The account I have given is of an agreement between many persons that some things should not be done which proceeds from their shared concern about the creatures whom these actions would touch and affect. What more is looked for by the objector?

Bernard Williams brings out something of what presses forward this objection in the following remarks.

[A] philosopher who had been arguing with the subjectivist all this time might at last turn around and say: of course the contrast exists; morality is not just like science or factual knowledge, and it is essential that it should not be. The point of morality is not to mirror the world, but to change it; it is concerned with such things as principles of action, choice, responsibility. The fact that men of equal intelligence, factual knowledge, and so forth, confronted with the same situation, may morally disagree shows something about morality—that (roughly) you cannot pass the moral buck on to how the world is. But that does not show (as subjectivism originally seemed to insinuate) that there is something *wrong* with it.

We observe that when men of equal scientific or historical competence, equal perceptual and intellectual abilities, etc., disagree strongly about some scientific or historical matter, there is good reason for them to stop dis-agreeing so strongly, and recognize something which their very dis-agreement, granted their knowledge and skills, reveals, namely that the matter is *uncertain*: it is rational for them, and third parties, to suspend judgment. One may be tempted to think that the same should obtain in cases of moral disagreement; but this will be a mistake. It depends on first contrasting morality and factual knowledge, and then assimilating them. For the vital difference is that the disagreement in morality involves what should be done, and involves, on each side, caring about what happens; and once you see this difference, you see equally that it could not possibly be a requirement of rationality that you should stop caring about these things because someone else disagrees with you.

But now we might reply: you said that it was not its business to mirror the world of empirical facts, and we agreed. But did we agree that it mirrored no facts at all? And here the focus of our dissatisfaction may become clearer in the thought that the reason why even defused subjectivism seems to have left something out is that moral thinking *feels* as though it mirrored something, as though it were constrained to follow, rather than be freely creative. When we see further that many defusing philosophers express the essential difference between the intellect and the *will*, and represent the responsibilities of morality in terms of our *deciding* on certain moral principles—then we have reason to be dissatisfied, either with them, or, if they are right, with moral thought. For certainly the consciousness of a principle of action as freely decided upon is very unlike the consciousness of a moral principle, which is rather of something that has to be *acknowledged*. If it is then said that there is just a psychological explanation of that—then moral thought seems a cheat, presenting itself to us as too like something which it is not.[17]

I am inclined to reply: it is not our moral thought which is a cheat, but rather our thought *about morality* is an attempt to cheat. We are disposed (partly by our religious traditions) to look for and expect something which cannot be delivered; and we are kept from seeing this because of an anxiety we have about the implication of detecting that impossibility. What we wish for and expect is some Archimedian point against which morality is to rest, and upon which we can base and justify our actions. It seems to us that this point cannot lie in human compassion and concern, since this looks just too much like some persons calling on others to do what they want them to do. And *why* should they, or we, do that? The short answer is, because of what will be done if we do not heed this calling.

"The consciousness of a moral principle is of something which has to be *acknowledged*". It needs first to be asked in *whom* these principles are experienced as something which has to be acknowledged. It is clear that the amoral man is not conscious of them in this way. It is the man who appreciates the claims of moral considerations who feels them confront him as things he has to heed. And the suggestion is that this is somehow very odd if there are no 'objective' grounds—grounds independent of human concern or caring —which claim the assent of his judgment. The idea is that what "has to be acknowledged" must have its basis in something outside of one, else how is it to demand acknowledgment? "Moral thinking *feels* as though it mirrored something, as though it were *constrained* to follow."

But moral considerations do have their basis outside us; they do *confront* us. And they *demand* acknowledgment because these considerations of suffering or harm to persons *claim* us if we care about persons. Often of course we are able to disregard them. We are able, for example, to keep ourselves from acknowledging the effects of our actions—to believe that what we do will have no real effect upon anyone; that others will get on despite what we do. This tendency to self-serving deception can sometimes make it hard to appreciate that (for example) a piece of dishonest selfishness is really wrong, since (we tell ourselves) it is not at all clear that anyone else will in fact be benefited by our giving up what we want, or that anyone will be harmed by our keeping it. A man who receives two different forms of support for his research keeps both, though he is not by the terms of each entitled to, because he persuades himself that those whom he knows are without any support at all will not necessarily be in a better position if he resigns one. They might still not be given support. Why then should he not keep both, since they will somehow or other get by anyway? (Of course he may perhaps care nothing for what happens to others, in which case no persuasion is required.) This tendency to self-serving 'blindness' is reinforced by the fact that in the ordinary relations of life we are often unable to *see* a direct connection between our actions and the well-being or suffering of other persons, so that while there may be a connection it is insulated and hidden from us by the nice complexity and comfortable anonymity of our community's relations and affairs. It is not for us as it would be, say, in a small village of a simple economy, where the momentum of action or inaction is more easily discerned. This creates for us a difficulty which selfishness thrives upon and in which compassion may sometimes expire for want of understanding or appreciation of what *is* done. But just as importantly, when we are aware of the very real difference which our actions will make, even to strangers, or when we are confronted by or caught up in a human difficulty, we are often not able to disregard it; for it is here before us, and if we do care, then, however much we might wish not to be claimed by the moral considerations that obtrude upon our consciousness, we are so claimed. We are claimed because we care. Even if we disregard them we shall perhaps be unable to escape appreciating that we have done the worse thing, not the better. A lover is *claimed* by his love. He has a concern which he cannot just put away, which pursues and binds him, and presses insistently upon him, even if he sometimes wishes he were rid of it. So too in morals we are claimed by that concern we call 'moral'; by our caring. In moral life we *are* 'constrained' to follow. We are constrained by our caring about persons—to whom these things must make a difference.*

But how do we know that we are not *cheated* in caring, someone might ask. How do we know that what we value indeed *has value*? Perhaps we should seek to care only for ourselves. For if a man cares for others this may often keep him from things he desires or would enjoy; indeed it may even destroy him, as many men have been destroyed who sought to help those who were wronged. Would these men not have been better to mind their own affairs? How do we *know* that they chose the better part?

Who asks this question? The man who does care for others? I do not deny that it is possible mistakenly to value what is valueless. But this is only possible where something is valued *for* some use which it has, or where the value it has is in terms of something which can be *got* for it (money, for example). But in morals, and also in art, we have something valued (by some persons) for itself. As John Anderson has remarked,

> What art . . . is most sharply contrasted with is utility. Utility insists on conditions and consequences, its sharp distinction of means and ends is bound up with hierarchy, with the master-servant relationship. But for art all things are on an equality; they are all alike aesthetic material; in any of them *character* can be discovered. Art, in other words, is concerned not with what things are "for" or what they are "by means of" but with what they are. And this is hard to find just because of utility, because in human life things become cluttered up with meanings and purposes. It is this which gives point to the description of the painter as restoring "the innocence of the eye", breaking up conventional associations; and in the same way the literary artist can be described as restoring the innocence of our sense of humanity, as against adventitious commendations and condemnations. On this basis, too, we can see that the artist is supremely productive or crea-tive—in fundamental opposition to the "consumer's view". That is to say, the good artist; for all arts can degenerate, and the bad artist is the supreme purveyor of consolation, the most efficient caterer to the consumptive or servile mentality.[18]

When a thing is valued for itself there is no *justifying* its value. It's having value is its being what is valued. Where we are able to justify a value put on a thing, this will always be a case of something being valued *for* something. So if we are not able to show that art is good

---

* See however pp. 195–198 below.

for something there will be those who can make no sense of art. These people cannot see in art what is there to be valued. They will want it shown to them. But to show a man that a thing has value you have in some way to connect it to what he does value. If what *has* value in art means nothing to him, then all you can do is show that something he does value is served by art, and that will be 'to show him that art is valuable' (for what it can contribute in the way of that service). This is the only way one is able to *show* that something is valuable; by connecting it to what someone wants. This fact takes the ground from under the one who sincerely asks if moral concern is a cheat or a fraud. For in the first place, even the things he now frankly admits to be valuable (because they visibly serve his purposes) are so because *he has* those purposes. Value is the shadow cast by human affection or desire. In the second place, where it is a case of persons being valued for what they are, no one can 'justify' their having that value. To justify here would be to *show to be* valuable (in that way). We are thus to bring a man who does not admit the value of persons, to value them, yet without making this value reduce to the relation these persons have to some desire or desires of the man, to the satisfaction of which these persons may instrumentally contribute. (I.e. without reducing the value he is to place on them to *extrinsic* value:—valuing persons only for what use they have to you.) But even if this could be done, which I believe it cannot, it would, if it were done, still not constitute justification. For *he* is the one who must make the change here. He must come *to value* them for what they are. That is not justification but conversion.

NOTES

[1] Immanuel Kant, *Groundwork of the Metaphysic of Morals* [*The Moral Law* (London: Hutchison, 1962) pp. 66–7. (Trans.: H. J. Paton.)]

[2] Ibid., pp. 68–9.

[3] Norman Malcolm, *Wittgenstein: A Memoir* (London: Oxford University Press, 1966) p. 80.

[4] Bernard Williams, "Morality and the Emotions", in John Casey (ed.), *Morality and Moral Reasoning* (London: Methuen, 1971) pp. 22–3.

[5] Op. cit., pp. 68–9.

[6] Ibid., p. 69.

[7] Immanuel Kant, *The Doctrine of Virtue* [Part II of *The Metaphysic of Morals*] (New York: Harper and Row, 1964) p. 59.

[8] H. J. Paton, 'Kant on Friendship', *Proceedings of the British Academy*, Volume XLII (London: Oxford University Press) 1956, p. 49.

[9] *Doctrine of Virtue*, p. 62.

[10] *Groundwork*, p. 69 Note.

[11] George Orwell, *Nineteen Eighty-Four* (Harmondsworth: Penguin Books, 1954) p. 87.

[12] Arthur Schopenhauer, *Essays* (London: George, Allen & Unwin, 1951).

[13] Thomas Hobbes, *Leviathan*, Part I, Chapter 14.

[14] James Rachels, "Morality and Self-Interest", in James Rachels and Frank Tillman (eds.), *Philosophical Issues* (New York: Harper and Row, 1972) pp. 118–20.

[15] Part I, Chapter 6.

[16] *Emile*, ed. Garnier (Paris: 1961) p. 278–9. (Transl.: J. Charvet).

[17] Bernard Williams, *Morality* (New York: Harper and Row, 1972) pp. 34–8.

[18] John Anderson, "Art and Morality", *Australasian Journal of Philosophy and Psychology*, Vol. XIX, 1941, p. 265.

VI

Rationality and Morals

The heart has its reasons which reason does not know.

PASCAL

You think that after all you must be weaving a piece of cloth: because you are sitting at a loom—even if it is empty—and going through the motions of weaving.

WITTGENSTEIN

In this chapter I wish to take up what is perhaps the oldest question in philosophy, whether a man can be given a reason to live rightly. Some philosophers have wished to insist that we must be able to give people a reason to live as morality requires, because unless we can do so morality must be adjudged something arbitrary and irrational. But while urging that it must be possible to give persons a reason to live rightly, these thinkers have divided over what that reason is; and some even allege that we have yet to uncover it. Most, however, do claim to be able at least to indicate the sort of reason it must be. This last group included at one time Phillipa Foot. In 1958, in her influential paper "Moral Beliefs", Foot argued that certain facts about human life, and the conditions in which that life is lived, both give rise to the goodness of morally good actions and enable us to give any man a reason to live rightly. Moreover, it then seemed to Foot, living rightly *had* to admit of such a justification, since if it did not, it must look as though we are at a loss in our dealings with unjust men. For if all we can do in appealing to men to be just is to appeal to their benevolence, or at least to their desire not to injure others,

many people certainly do not have any such desire. So that if justice is only to be recommended on these grounds a thousand tough characters will be able to say that they have been given no reason for practising justice, and many more would say the same if they were not too timid or too stupid to ask questions about the code of behaviour which they have been taught.[1]

It seemed in 1958 to Phillipa Foot that the way to proceed in justifying morality was to trace the very real and enduring connection of right living to a man's self-interest.

Those who think that [a man] can get on perfectly well without being just should be asked to say exactly how such a man is supposed to live. We know that he is to practise injustice whenever the unjust act would bring him advantage; but what is he to say? Does he admit that he does not recognise the rights of other people, or does he pretend? In the first case even those who combine with him will know that on a change of fortune, or a shift of affection, he may turn to plunder them, and he must be as wary of their treachery as they are of his. Presumably the happy unjust man is supposed, as in Book II of the *Republic*, to be a very cunning liar and actor, combining complete injustice with the appearance of justice: he is prepared to treat others ruthlessly, but pretends that nothing is further from his mind. Philosophers often speak as if a man could thus hide himself even from those around him, but the supposition is doubtful, and in any case the price in vigilance would be colossal. If he lets even a few people see his true attitude he must guard himself against them; if he lets no one into the secret he must always be careful in case the least spontaneity betray him. Such facts are important because the need a man has for justice in dealings with other men depends on the fact that they are men and not inanimate objects or animals. If a man only needed other men as he needs household objects, and if men could be manipulated like household objects, or beaten into a reliable submission like donkeys, the case would be different. As things are, the supposition that injustice is more profitable than justice is very dubious, although like cowardice and intemperance it might turn out incidentally to be profitable.[2]

Now the argument of these passages rests upon a mistake which Foot herself later acknowledged in this way.

. . . I had supposed—with my opponents—that the thought of a good action must be related to the choices of each individual in a very special way. It had not occurred to me to question the often repeated dictum that moral judgments give reasons for acting to each and every man. This now seems to me to be a mistake. Quite generally the reason why someone choosing an A may 'be expected' to choose good A's rather than bad A's is that our criteria of goodness for any class of things are related to certain interests that someone or other has in these things. When someone shares these interests he will have reason to choose the good A's: otherwise not. Since, in the case of actions, we distinguish good and bad on account of the interest we take in the common good, someone who does not care a damn what happens to anyone but himself may truly say that he has no reason to be just. The rest of us, so long as we continue as we are, will try to impose good conduct upon such a man, saying 'you ought to be just' . . .[3]

'He has no reason to be just.' Does this mean that he has no reason *sometimes* (or even often) *to act as though* he were just? I think it is clear that he may frequently have a reason to act as though he were just. He has such a reason whenever something he wants is to be gained, or something he fears is to be avoided, by the pretence of justice. The question at issue is not whether we can give a man a reason sometimes (or even always) to act *as though* he were a good man. The question is whether we can give a man a reason to *be* just, *to be a good man*. (The importance of being able to do this turns, briefly, on our wish to be able to *count* on a man not to do evil, even where his advantage or pleasure would be served by his doing it.)

It will perhaps be thought that there is no point in pursuing this question any farther, as Phillipa Foot, and those writers whose effect upon her own view she here acknowledges, have already settled the matter. As Foot states, in the remark just quoted, the possibility of giving a man a reason to be just is logically dependent upon his caring about what happens to other persons. He cannot be given a reason to be just *except* he cares what happens to others. For except he cares what happens to them, anything which does happen to them as a result of his injustice will be so much water under the bridge so far as he is concerned. To show him the effects of his injustice can only be to give him a reason to be just, *if he cares about those effects in a certain way*—if he gives a damn about what he inflicts on others. If he doesn't, you will never be able to give him a reason to be just.

Nevertheless there is, apparently, something incomplete in this answer by Foot to those who ask, can you give a man a reason to be just? For people continue to insist since the above argument was made that the question of giving men reasons to be moral is still an open one. (Indeed, exactly what Mrs. Foot's remarks amount to is itself, apparently, controversial.) For this reason alone I shall, I hope, be forgiven for enlisting one more discussion into the battle array of this ancient controversy.

I

Some sorting out needs to be done first. As already noted above, we can sometimes give a man a reason to do what it is right to do, without it being the case that we have given him a reason to act on moral considerations. The reason we give the man in the sort of case I have in mind is that it is in his interest to do what it is (in fact) right to do. But to comply with the requirements of morality is not *eo ipso* to act morally, since it depends on why you comply whether you act from moral considerations or not. Self-interestedly to do what in relation to others it is right to do is 'acting rightly', in the sense of 'acting as morality calls for', but it is not *acting morally*, since to do this one must act from moral considerations.

It is this dichotomy which gives rise to the question which is our subject. If having regard to one's self-interest is one thing, and having a regard for moral considerations is another, why should anyone leave off attention to their own interest to take up the 'moral point of view'? If moral action is not self-interested action, why should any person 'take up morality'? *Why should anyone be moral?* As one philosopher who has asked, in order to consider, this question, remarks:

It is a truism that, morally speaking, we should always do what is right, but it is also a truism that from a self-interested point of view an individual should always do what is in his self-interest.

Kai Nielsen, whose words these are, holds that:

Viewed purely in the abstract, there indeed is and can be no non-question-begging answer to the question "why should I be moral?" [That is, no answer which does not presuppose the very point of view which is supposed to be justified.] However, for human beings as we find them and as we are likely to find them in the future, with the needs, personalities, and wants that they have or even are likely to come to have, consistently failing to act in accordance with a moral point of view will lead to a miserable life for the person who so acts. In short, there are solid self-interested reasons for a man not to override moral considerations. Indeed, *only* to be a man of good morals is not, as Kant stressed, to be a morally good man. But there are generally good self-interested reasons for becoming genuinely unselfish and for becoming a moral agent.[4]

Professor Nielsen distinguishes in this passage between 'a man of good morals' and 'a morally good man'. This is, I take it, the distinction between a man whose actions are (or at least very often are) of a certain sort (they are of the sort a good man would perform), and a man who acts, or at least attempts with considerable success to act, from moral considerations. What we seek are reasons which are to convince a man to become the second sort of man: someone who is genuinely unselfish. He is not merely for self-interested reasons to keep from doing selfish acts. He is (for self-interested reasons) to become someone who is unselfish. (That is, someone who is at least not only self-interested.) Kai Nielsen also speaks in this passage of a 'moral agent'. I take it that he means by this description someone who appreciates and is claimed by moral considerations. 'To be moral' then is to be a morally good man, a moral agent, in these senses. And the question before us is, can we give a man a reason to be this sort of person?

We are to GIVE *him* a reason.—Is it that he does not yet have a reason, and we are to give him one? Or is it that he has one, but does not see that he has? In the passage Nielsen asserts that the reasons we are to give him are to be self-interested reasons. This suggests that Kai Nielsen has in mind the second situation. We are to give the man a reason by pointing out to him a reason which is there but which he does not perhaps appreciate. We are to point out to him self-interested reasons which he has for becoming someone who is not completely selfish.

Finally, the assumption throughout is that the man we are seeking to convince is a rational man.

I am talking of the man who is resolved to be guided by reason, who has what has been called a 'commitment to rationality'. Can we show this individual that simply considering his own point of view, if he is to act rationally, the best thing for him to do is to adopt that moral point of view[?][5]

II

There is an argument which one might make at this point which goes as follows. We are dealing throughout this discussion with a man who is not just, who is not moral, who does not take the moral point of view. We are to produce reasons for this man to become just. Nielsen (and other philosophers) attempt to do this by connecting living justly with a man's flourishing in terms of his self-interest. But these philosophers assume that once a man opts for justice as a way of living, as a way of conducting his life, he will henceforth be just no matter what. He will be prepared perhaps even to die, rather than to participate in or condone injustice. *But preparedness to do this* requires (unless it is the preparedness of an insane man) that the man at some point *give up his initial position of self-concern*. But at what point did he have a reason to do this? So long as he *is* self-concerned we cannot give him a reason to do what may cost him everything in self-satisfaction. If he does accept what we say, and follows our proposal, and goes to his death for justice, he acts (on his own terms—the terms from which he began) irrationally; for he does what, as a self-concerned man, he ought not to do. But to be guided by reason, to be rational, is what from the beginning he is supposed relentlessly to be committed to.

This arrow passes over Kai Nielsen and leaves him unconcerned. For Nielsen considers that his man does not stand at the crossroads between morality and self-interest, *self-interestedly* looking down each road for the best policy. He stands there possessed of the human condition and reason, and deliberates whether *to be* self-interested or moral. He is neither one or the other yet. Nielsen would in fact agree that if a man chooses justice he will (since he is just) be just, come hell or high water. The question is: Had he a reason to choose justice? Had he reason to adopt the moral point of view? Before going farther then I must spell out more clearly Kai Nielsen's position.

Nielsen is aware that the question 'Why should I be moral?' needs to be stated with care to avoid confusion. Nielsen makes clear in the following remarks what he is *not* asking by this question.

It is indeed true that *if we are reasoning from the moral point of view* and if an act is genuinely the right act to do in a given situation, then it is the act we should do. Once a moral agent knows that such and such an action is the right *one to do in* these circumstances he has *eo ipso* been supplied with the reason for doing it. But in asking 'Why should I be moral?' an individual is asking why *he* should (non-moral sense of 'should') reason as a moral agent. He is asking, and *not* as a moral agent, what reason there is for his doing what is right.

It will, [as the philosopher John Hospers has pointed out], be natural for an individual to ask this question only when "the performance of the act is *not* to his own interest". It is also true that *any* reason we give other than a reason which will show that what is right is in his rational self-interest will be rejected by him. Hosper remarks "What he wants, and he will accept no other answer, is a self-interested reason" for acting as a moral agent. But this is like asking for the taste of pink for "the situation is *ex hypothesi* one in which the act required of him is contrary to his interest. Of course it is impossible to give him a reason *in accordance with his interest for acting contrary to his interest*". 'I have a reason for acting in accordance with my interest which is contrary to my interests' is a contradiction. The man who requests an answer to 'Why should I do what is right when it is not in my interest?' is making a "self-contradictory request". We come back once more to Prichard and Bradley and see that after all our "question" is a logically absurd one—no real question at all. The person asking "the question" cannot "without self-contradition, accept a reason of self-interest for doing what is contrary to his interest and yet he will accept no reason except one of self-interest". [Emphasis in the original.][6]

Nielsen's own position respecting the question can now be stated. (The words are his own.)

The man asking 'Why should I do what is right when it is not in my self-interest?' has made a self-contradictory request *when he is asking this question as a self-interested question.* [i.e., when he is self-interested *already*.]

These two points must be accepted, but what if an individual says: As I see it, there are two alternatives: either I act from the moral point of view, where logically speaking I must try to do what is right, or I act from the point of view of rational self-interest, where again I must seek to act according to my rational self-interest. But is there any *reason* for me always to act from one point of view rather than another when I am a member in good standing in a moral community? True enough, Hospers has shown me that *from the moral point of view* I have no alternative but to try to do what is right and from a *self-interested point of view* I have no rational alternative but to act according to what I judge to be in my rational self-interest. But what I want to know is what I am to do: Why adopt one point of view rather than another? Is there a good reason *for me*, placed as I am, to adopt the moral point of view or do I just arbitrarily choose, as the subjectivist would argue?[7]

I shall put the remark about the subjectivist aside. What I want to point to here is the way the question about choosing morality or self-interest is put. It is in fact put in two ways.

A. Is there any reason for me always to act from one point of view rather than another?

B. Why adopt one point of view rather than another?

I think it is reasonable to claim that these two are not the same. Which does Nielsen mean to ask? If frequence of occurrence is a sound guide B is the question we are considering. But there is a better reason for taking B to be what Nielsen intends. If all the man wants is a reason always *to act* as morality requires, perhaps a plausible reason ("as a rule you'll get on better") is ready to hand. But if this reason appeals (as this one does) to the man's self-interest, why does he want a reason *always* to act as morality requires? Why not just sometimes (when it pays)? The answer is that the reason we are to provide is to be a reason *always* to act as morality requires, because A is in fact intended as a variant of B. What the man is to do is not merely to act 'according to', but *to adopt*, one or other of these points of view. But what will this consist in? It cannot simply be that he is to "reason from one point of view" or the other; for the good man might do this once in a while to avoid falling into the hands of villains, and the evil man might do it once in a while in order to pretend to be what he is not. "Reasoning from one point of view or the other" may mean only: seeing what each viewpoint calls for or allows. But this need not even yield *acting* as one or the other points of view requires. *Adopting* one or other point of view has got to be: having a certain sort of reason *for* acting as that point of view requires. In respect of say, the moral point of view, your reason has got to be the reason the "morally good man", the "genuinely unselfish" person, has.

We have, then, the picture of a rational man who is to choose between morals or self-interest. He is to choose for a reason. To repeat Kai Nielsen's remarks quoted above:

[W]hat I want to know is what I am to do: Why adopt one point of view rather than another? Is there a good reason *for me*, placed as I am, to adopt the moral point of view or do I just arbitrarily choose, as the subjectivist would argue?[8]

Nielsen's answer is that ordinarily (that is, in most human situations) a man has reason to choose the moral side. The reason he has to choose it is the one already cited at the beginning of this chapter.

[F]or human beings as we find them and as we are likely to find them in the future, with the needs, personalities, and wants that they have or even are likely to come to have, consistently failing to act in accordance with a moral point of view will lead to a miserable life for the person who so acts. In short, there are solid self-interested reasons for a man not to override moral considerations . . . [T]here are generally good self-interested reasons for becoming genuinely unselfish and for becoming a moral agent. We have good reasons, as individuals in a system of social control which is at least predominately moral or morally directed, not only to support that system of social control *or* some better moral system of social control, but also generally to act in accordance with a moral system of social control ourselves. And there are decisively good reasons, considering society at large, why moral systems of social control should prevail.[9]

III

Let us suppose that Nielsen's questioner *is* an ordinary man placed in ordinary circumstances. Let us suppose further that the man undertakes to adopt the moral point of view. Now there are difficulties with this notion of adopting morality which I wish for the moment to ignore. I shall assume that no difficulties attach to the notion of the man's adopting the moral point of view, and for the moment attend only to the question of the sort of thing he does *if he does adopt it*—how that adoption is to be characterized in terms of reasons and points of view.

Now if the man adopts the moral point of view because it is in his interest to, has he not already adopted the self-interested point of view? If he hasn't, how is the fact in question (that acting from the moral point of view will be in his interest) to be a reason for him to adopt that point of view? If a man undertakes to do something *because it is in his interest to*, that means that he is concerned to do or secure what is in his interest. But to be concerned to do or secure what is in your self-interest is to be self-interested. How then are you to *adopt* EITHER the moral view OR the self-interested view? You are already self-interested.

It may be objected that the man is not exclusively self-interested, and what he is to do is to adopt the moral point of view, *or*, the exclusively self-interested point of view.

But the man is to adopt one or other of these points of view as a way to act always. He is to choose henceforth always to act on moral grounds, or from self-interest. And the justification which is to incline him to adopt one or the other of them is the connection of the point of view adopted to his self-interest. He is now to choose, he is now to prefer, what will be in his interest. If he sees that the moral viewpoint is the one he is justified in adopting, what justifies to him his adopting it is the self-interest he has *in* that way of proceeding. But if this is what justifies to him adopting the moral point of view, is this not because to have his interest realized is what he prefers? But is this not the preference of a self-interested man?

It will not help to insist that it is not the preference of an exclusively self-interested man, and that this saves the question. For it is not, necessarily, the preference of a *not* exclusively self-interested man either. This is because as things stand the use of these expressions is effectively ruled out here. We are not placed to say of someone who chooses, on self-interested grounds, the *moral* way of life, whether or not, in so choosing, he is concerned exclusively with his self-interest. For he chooses here once and for all and after he may have to sacrifice his interest *for the sake of others*. (And presumably he knows that.) He *may* at the beginning be exclusively concerned with his self-interest. He may not be. But except we are told we shall never know here. For the only other way we can know that a man is exclusively self-interested is by how he acts. But this man chooses to live justly.

Where however a man opts self-interestedly to choose the self-interested point of view the same opacity does not hold. But there is a difficulty nevertheless. If a man chooses always to consider only his own self-interest, is he not exclusively self-interested? I think he clearly is; since if he was concerned about the interests of others he could (and would) surely act differently. He does not *need* to choose to consider *always* only his self-interest. He could elect sometimes to sacrifice his interest for others, if his own interest does not suffer greatly. If he does not so choose, but chooses the policy of exclusive self-interest, he does so because that is in fact what he is: exclusively self-interested.—But then the man who is to choose the exclusively self-interested point of view is in fact not able to *choose* at all. For he needs that point of view to choose it.

In the case of the adoption of the moral point of view this particular difficulty does not seem to obtain. True, there is to be no appeal to altruism to motivate the choice. The reasons which are alone to be admissible are self-interested reasons (this, that we might catch Everyman). If our man *does* have a concern for others it simply is not to be operative, for it is precisely *the rationale of heeding*, over time, that concern (i.e., acting morally) which is at issue. The reasons which are to move our chooser are to be self-interested reasons. It seems that there is possible a point of view, limited self-interest, from which morality—the moral point of view—could be chosen. The question, why should he, or we, adopt morals, appears on *this* score, and from this perspective, to be coherent.

But a different difficulty remains, which is whether anyone *can* *adopt* the moral point of view. My own answer to this question I have given elsewhere.[10] It is, briefly, that since caring about others is integral to 'the moral point of view', you cannot *adopt* morality; for adopting morality, adopting the 'moral point of view', would be deciding to be someone who cares about others. But you cannot *decide* to care about others. Therefore you cannot decide to be moral. At best, you can strive to care about others. And you may, or may not, succeed. Furthermore, you may (if you do not now care) see no sense in striving to care; and so no sense in morals. Whether someone could give you a reason to strive to care I shall consider later in this chapter.

IV

We have now to consider the possibility that Kai Nielsen's questioner is not an ordinary man, but different (more 'abstract'). The man I have in mind is neither self-interested, nor interested in the good of others; he is disinterested in everything. He has no point of view. He does not prefer any state of affairs over another. (For to prefer for some reason one state of affairs over others is to have a point of view from which it is seen as preferable. Unless the preference is an irrational one. But one of the conditions given is that the man is perfectly rational.)

The idea is that there is a reason which this man can be given to choose between exclusive self-interest or morals. (He does not just have to toss a coin, as it were.) And if there is a reason favouring one choice over the other, it has to be in the facts somewhere. My problem is not with this last part of the account. My problem is to see how anything could be a reason to this man.

In a note to a later work entitled *Reason and Practice*, Nielsen has this to say about rational action.

In speaking of a man behaving rationally, I need say no more for my purposes here than that a man behaves rationally when he is a man who has a sense of his own interests and has the ability to act in accordance with his interests and will act in accordance with his own interests where moral consideration, considerations of friendship and/or family do not intervene (what he will do when such considerations intervene I leave open), is willing to listen to evidence, and is willing to grant that if X is a good reason for B doing Y in Z, it is also a good reason for anyone else relevantly like B and similarily situated. That is not all that is meant by 'behaving rationally', but such a characterization is all that is intended by my use of 'behaving rationally' and my other references to 'rational'.[11]

The open question about moral considerations is of course meant to allow for precisely the issue of what a man is to do when he has to decide between self-interest and moral considerations. However the part of the passage which interests me are the words "has a sense of his own interests" and "will act in accordance with his own interests" (everything being equal—where no one else is involved, say). Now having interests and acting on one's interests are not the same. Any man has interests. Simply as an animal he has needs, for air, food, water, rest, and so on, and so it is in his interest to have or to be able to get these things. But a man is not rational simply in *having* interests. Nor is he rational simply in being aware of them. Of course, if he intends to act on his interests, he will be irrational not to seek to find them out. But the passage from *having* interests to *acting* on them is precisely what is at issue here. Why *will* the rational man *act* in accordance with his interests? The answer (or better, the assumption) is: because it is in his interest to; *and, he is interested in what is in his interest.* Being rational, he will therefore do what it is in his interest to do.

(If someone interjects that it is logical truth that "If P is rational, then, everything being equal, P will do what he sees to be in his own interest," I shall reply that this is false. To see that something is in your interest is not to desire it. Still less is it to do it. And if you desire nothing (except death, say) then you may quite rationally disdain what is in your interest. Moreover the objection depends on the phrase 'everything being equal' (i.e. no oddities obtain). In our case there is an 'inequality'. For the man we are discussing has no point of view, not even limited self-interest.)

If the man we are discussing is not concerned about himself (i.e. self-interested), and if he is not concerned about others (i.e. morally interested), what interest is he to have in either of these "points of view". What *reason* is he to have to adopt one or the other? It seems to me that nothing could be a reason for him. A fact is a reason for you to do something because of some interest you have in that fact. But this man has no interest in anything—except, of course, in being rational. Which in his case is an insane interest, since as he has no interest in himself or others what does it matter whether he is rational or not?

I hope it will not be objected that the man has reasons, even if he is not interested in acting on them. I granted this at the beginning. "He has a reason" is, as everyone knows, like 'The children want discipline'; an ambiguous remark. But it needs to be noticed that it is a remark; and someone therefore makes it. In the case of my remark above that this man has need of some things, whatever he wants or feels or knows, it is *I* who appreciate that he has these needs as a man; that is, as one who is alive and vulnerable. But if the man wishes to die has he need of them? Ordinarily we assume that a man does wish to live; and we say therefore that he has interests, to which he perhaps does not attend. He has reason to secure food, drink and shelter, even if he is not himself concerned to. I shall speak of this as 'has* a reason'.

If these are the sort of reasons the man has* for choosing one or other of the two points of view, it needs to be seen that they are self-interested reasons. *He could not*, then, for these reasons adopt one or other of the moral or self-interested points of view. If he did so, he would already be self-interested. To adopt for a reason is to have a reason, not in the sense of have* a reason but in the sense that you 'take in' the reason. It must be a reason for you in the sense that you feel the force of the reason. This difficulty will not be exorcised by invoking the distinction between justification and choice. This man is to have a reason to adopt one or other of these points of view. Now at the moment when admission that one choice is justified passes into adoption of that choice, then, if this adoption is not still to be an arbitrary, 'reasonless' choice, but a rational act, the reasons there are for this choice have got to engage this man. They have to be, not just reasons*, but *his reasons* for choosing. It is this that I cannot see to be possible.

If this man cannot, then, self-interestedly, or morally interestedly, choose one or other of these views, how then is he to choose (except wilfully, arbitrarily)? For nothing can be a reason for him. Therefore to choose rationally he has at some point to acquire a concern of one sort or the other. He has, for example, to become at least limitedly self-interested. (If he does not, perhaps some people will even say he is not a rational man at all. For he does not even prefer living to, say, dying (even in ordinary circumstances).) Until he does so, he just chooses, and while perhaps he has* reason to do what he does, these reasons are not reasons for him. This unfortunate man cannot feel the force of—because he cannot take any interest in—reasons, because he has no interest in anything.

It seems, from this discussion, that some of the assumptions at back of Kai Nielsen's position need to be modified. The man who is to 'choose' the moral point of view need not be completely self-interested, as may on first reading seem to be so. He need only be 'completely' self-interested in the sense that the reasons on which he is to base his decision are to be completely self-interested reasons. He is (so far as we *know*) perhaps only limitedly self-interested. Still he is self-interested, and this leaves intact the question at what point he has reason *to give up* his self-concern (limited though it may be) for a just life which might even require his death. I do not see how he is ever, rationally, to choose the just life, *so long as the reasons which are to move him* are self-concerned reasons. For it seems that if he opts for justice knowing that it may cost him dearly to live this way then he does what it is least rational for someone prompted by self-concern to do. Surely a self-concerned man ought to adopt the pretence of justice, or, if you prefer, a moderate sort of commitment to justice—leaving the option open for withdrawal if his 'justice' proves too dear. For remember, the good he is to see in justice is to be his own good. If he goes for justice because of what that way of life will mean for others with whom he has relations, he acts for disinterested reasons. And that, *ex hypothesi*, is what he cannot do.

Of course if he can only choose: genuinely just *or* exclusively self-interested, he is caught. And if self-interest is all that is to engage him, then whether it is more rational for him to choose justice or not will depend enormously on where and at what time he lives. Harlem? Vietnam? Revolutionary Paris? Post-war Berlin? The White House?

V

I should like now to return briefly to the 'adoption' side of this question. Kai Nielsen has suggested to me that perhaps the most objection-free way to put the matter is this:

We all desire our own happiness. This is something that we seek, or at least hope or wish for. Now consider this: what *reason* can be given to us to put the interests of others on a par with our own interests? To be fair, to be moral, is to do so, but why be moral or fair? Granted that if I am to be a man of principle—to be a morally good man—I must be fair and that to be fair I must be prepared to put the interests of others on a par with my own interests. And further grant that Thrasymachus [in Plato's *Republic*] is mistaken and morality is not just what is in the interests of the stronger. But even after we have granted all these things, might we still not individually ask the question: why *do* what I recognize (acknowledge) to be right and indeed through and through morally mandatory, when it is not in my self-interest to do so? This is a question a non-evasive man will put to himself. And while this is not a moral question, all the same it appears at least to be a perfectly intelligible question about human conduct.[12]

We are first asked what reason can be given us to attach to others' interests the importance we attach to our own. We are then told that to be moral is to attach this importance to others' interests. We are also told that to be fair is to do so. I would have thought that to be fair was to act in a certain way, and to attach importance to others' interests was to attach importance to being fair. In any case, to be moral, remember, is to be someone who appreciates moral considerations and heeds them in one's relations with others because of the claim they make on one. The question Nielsen proposes is, what reason can be given us to attach to the interests of others the importance we attach to our own? The answer is, no reason can be given. This, if it could be done, would be to give a man a reason to care about others. But in the first place no reason to *care* (which involves more than simply a preparedness sometimes to sacrifice) could be a reason for someone who does not care in the first place. And secondly, the person could not do what was needed if a reason *could* be given him, since he cannot just decide to care. He cannot choose to attach that importance to others' interests. (If I try to admire someone because I think it important to admire him I have of course attached an importance to him. But that importance is not admiration. *That* is what I am trying for.) A man may try to attach importance to others' interests. In time, if he is able to care about others, he may succeed. Their interests may come to be as important to him as his own. But he cannot decide that they will. What proves this is that one can set about considering the interests of others, confining and adjusting one's own projects and demands so as to

accommodate the interests of others, but all along resent that confinement and adjustment, and covet what it costs. What this resentment and covetousness show is that *so far* the interests of others are
not sufficiently important to one after all. (So obviously I cannot just
decide that they will be.)

The second question put by Kai Nielsen is, why *should* I do what I
acknowledge it is right to do, if (and when) it is not in my *interest* to
do it? We have here two questions, though one of them is uppermost
as it were. If you acknowledge that it is right that you should do a
certain thing, you cannot then go on to ask from 'within morals' *why*
you should do it. You have already acknowledged why: it is right to
do it. This much Kai Nielsen agrees to. If, at the same time, it will
cost you something you want if you are to do the right thing, and it is
this that moves you to ask why you should then do it, you can only
receive one reply: make up your mind. Do you want most to do
what it is right to do (that is, heed the good of others), or do you want
most what you stand to lose if you do the right thing? If the last is
what you truly want, then the answer is simple. Since you have in
mind the attainment of that, and its desirability, the answer is: you
should not do the right thing—since that other is what you want. No
one can give you a reason to give up what you indeed want most,
unless it can *be* a reason to you to give it up. *But then it would be that*
(what the reason points to) *that you wanted most.* If, as is the case here,
you do not want it most, it can never be a reason to give up what you
do want most. (Notice, I do not say here 'make up your mind what
you want most' in the sense (if it ever has this sense) of 'decide that
you will want such-and-such most'. I say, make up your mind what
you do want most, i.e. find out, discover, get clear about, what your
wants are.)

It has been objected to me that reasons can be given for caring
about others. One of them is that in a world in which men do not care
about each other much unnecessary suffering will occur. And if a
man asks why he should care about that, the answer is that suffering
can be seen to be intrinsically evil. Even an exclusively self-interested
man sees its badness. But since he can see that it is bad for him he can
see that it is bad for others; for he can see that these others are in no
relevant respects different from him. But if suffering is bad for him,
and for everyone else, then being bad it should be avoided, and so he
should favour its being avoided for everyone.

This argument seems to me a case of *petitio principii*. In the first place the appeal to *unnecessary* suffering is a moral appeal—an appeal which springs from human concern. (Do we have a conception of unnecessary suffering touching the relations between antelope and lions?) Unnecessary suffering is, well, it is *unnecessary*, and something we want not to obtain. If we do not care whether it does obtain, to whom, or to what, is it unnecessary? In the case of the claim about there being no relevant difference between the completely self-interested man and others, surely a most relevant difference, for his purposes, obviously does obtain. He is 'me' and they are 'them'. When pain is concerned that *is* a relevant difference. In the third place, concerning the claim that everything is equal, the fact is that everything may not be equal. It may be in his interest to act in ways such that others suffer. If it is in his interest, then this is an inequality between him and them, and one which forestalls any appeal to him to favour their not suffering.

A second argument has been made to me.

[A]s far as caring for others is concerned, even the hard bitten utterly ego-centred man, if he is also tough-minded, can see that his own happiness and well-being is not independent of caring for others. Kierkegaard would surely say, and rightly, that that is a paradigm of doublemindedness. But while it is not on my view of the matter an ethically appropriate justification for caring for others, it is a prudential justification, clearly showing that *reasons* can be given for others. Moreover, we need not even stop there with plainly prudential reasons; we can also appeal to the fact that there could hardly be the sense of community and the human flourishing and the happiness that goes with it if people did not care for others.[13]

This can be taken to show that there are good results of caring. But are these good results reasons to care? (Can you even appreciate these results *as* good *except* you care?) Certainly they are not reasons which those who do care have *for caring*. They could not be; for caring is not something you can, for a reason, do. These results may at best be reasons those who do not care have to try to care. "But surely that is enough. If there are good results of caring there are good reasons to care." Good self-interested, or good disinterested, reasons to care? Of course if the reasons are disinterested this is to say: one cares already. If they are self-interested, why are they reasons *to care*? If a man *seeks* 'to care' how does he know what he seeks to do, if he does not already care about some persons? Perhaps he senses there is something missing in his life, and people tell him "you should care about someone other than yourself''. They tell him the good results of persons' caring. But if these are results in others' lives, why will they touch him? If they are results affecting *him* does he need to care in order for them to continue? Suppose he does; and now 'he tries to care'. But first, at what point does he have a reason, not to continue *trying*, but *to care* (and continue caring)? And secondly, it seems that what this man has therefore to do when he starts out is to chance his arm at something he knows not what. When the time comes when he can truly be described as striving after what he *understands,* he will be one to whom these words by Pascal will apply: "comfort yourself, you would not seek me if you had not found me."[14]

VI

No one, it seems to me, *can give* a man a reason to care. If I am right, we cannot then give a man a reason to live a good life. At best we can give the man who does not care reasons which *may* move him to *try* to care, and so to come to be capable of living that way. But when (if he does) this man comes to live that way, his reason for doing so will not be any reason we were able to give him for trying to.—"But then the man who does live rightly *has* a reason to do so?" I think the answer is, he has a reason. But it is not a reason anyone gave him, or that he decided to have. His reason is that, living as he does, he harms no one and helps some. That is, for him, reason to live that way, because he cares about others.

"But if you are right, then the immoral man has just as much reason *not* to live rightly. The immoral man is (or can be) every bit as rational as the moral man. To do evil may for him be just as sensible as for the good man to do good. Each has as much—*or as little*—justification for what he does as the other.—I say 'as little', because on your view there is no way of showing that the view of one or the other of them is correct. But then isn't it quite *arbitrary* which of these views, or points of view, one adopts or lives in accordance with?"

If the question is, do immoral men have reason to choose to do the acts that constitute their immorality, I do not see how this conclusion is to be avoided. Immoral men are not paradigms of rationality, any more than good men are. Some (like some basically good men) are a sort of flotsam in the current of their desires. But this is not necessarily, or perhaps even ordinarily, the case. An immoral man may be quite firmly in control of his life, so far as is humanly possible. And as for having reasons for what he does, he will, ordinarily, have reasons, some of them very good reasons, for all that he does. But they will be reasons, and projects, which the good man will condemn and resist. Why is this supposed to be surprising? If men *could have no reason* to act wickedly, why should we strive morally to educate our children in the hope of *keeping* them from wickedness?

As for the questions about the correctness of each 'point of view', and the alleged arbitrariness of choosing to go one way rather than the other, these proceed from an unwillingness to accept the argument presented in this chapter. The first claim is that in my view the immoral, or the amoral, man (it does not matter which) is as much justified in what he does as the morally good man. Each has as much, *or as little*, reason for living as he does as the other. Each is as correct in his view of, and relation to, the world as the other. The appeal to correctness expresses the desire for some foothold against which moral life can be appreciated as a 'best policy'. If there were some properties of the world which were its moral properties then the man whose conception of the world admitted them would indeed be more correct in his view of the world than another man who did not. But if the moral 'flows onto' the world from 'within the human breast', the amoral man is different from the morally good man, but it makes no sense to speak of him as less correct in what he does. *Unless of course one wants to say as a moral judgment*: "he chooses the lesser good and passes over the better". All justification is justification from a point of view. If a man desires a pipe of opium, though he knows that in his present condition one more pipe may well kill him, is he justified if he takes it? If he wants to live more than to die, he is not (from his own viewpoint) justified. Though notice that the pipe of opium is what he desires, and taken by itself his desire surely justifies his reaching for it. From the point of view of someone desiring the pipe of opium more than to live, the man is justified in taking and smoking it. Smoking it gets him what he most desires. (From the point of view of someone who values human life over any satisfaction he is again not justified.) It is the same way in the case of a man who is trying to decide whether deceitfully to take money from old people or not. The use he has for the money justifies his doing so. The hurt he will give does not. But of course when I say (and write) this *I am judging morally*. I am appealing to considerations which matter to me. Still, if they don't matter to him, and he goes ahead—*on his own terms*, is he not justified?

It does not follow, however, that it is an arbitrary choice whether one chooses to heed moral considerations or self-interest in living day to day. It can only be an *arbitrary* choice if one has no point of view. Then it has to be arbitrary, since one can have no reason to do anything. (And notice that I put it in terms of choosing to *heed*, not choosing to *be someone who is claimed by*, moral considerations or self-interest. The first—'choosing' to heed—but without any point of view, would indeed be a choice which was arbitrary. But the second would be choosing to *have* a particular point of view, a choice not arbitrary, but impossible.)

NOTES

[1] Philippa Foot, 'Moral Beliefs', *Proceedings of the Aristotelian Society*, New States, Volume LIX, 1958–9, p. 102.

[2] Ibid., pp. 102–3.

[3] Philippa Foot (ed.), *Theories of Ethics* (London: Oxford University Press, 1967) pp. 8–9. From the introduction.

[4] *Reason and Practice* (New York, Harper & Row, 1971) pp. 317–18.

[5] Ibid., p. 314.

[6] Kai Nielsen, 'Why should I be moral', Methodos, Volume XV, Number 59–60, 1963, pp. 290–1. See also John Hospers, *Human Conduct* (New York: Harcourt, Brace and World, 1961).

[7] Ibid., pp. 291–2.

[8] See note 7.

[9] See note 4.

[10] R. Beehler, "Reasons for being moral"; Kai Nielsen, "On giving reasons for being moral"; and R. Beehler, "Morals and Reasons", *Analysis*, Vol. 33, No. 1, 1972, pp. 12–21, 1972. See also R. Beehler, *Moral Life*. Ph.D. Dissertation, 1972. National Library, Ottawa, Chapter 5.

[11] Op. cit., p. 319.

[12] Kai Nielsen, unpublished MS[1972].

[13] Kai Nielsen, unpublished MS[1972].

[14] Blaise Pascal, *Pensées*, 553. (Brunschveig edition.)

VII
Moral Education and Moral Understanding

1st Gent: Our deeds are fetters that we forge ourselves.
2nd Gent: Ay truly: but I think it is the world that brings the iron.

GEORGE ELIOT

What we are supplying are really remarks on the natural history of human beings . . .

WITTGENSTEIN

I shall seek in this chapter to give an account of how persons come to be capable of appreciating that certain ways of treating other persons are wrong. To put it differently, I shall try to show how the claim moral considerations make upon a person comes to be understood and admitted.

I

I shall begin by calling attention to an account of what might be called the moral character of a person, which might be thought virtually to do away with moral education as traditionally understood. On this view, since every action which a person performs is deliberately performed, from a motive which either is consciously appreciated or could be consciously appreciated, it follows that a person *chooses* his character. He does so, since he deliberately chooses to act, and so chooses whatever the action may bring about, even if this is a change in (or a contribution to the formation of) his character. Hence it follows that a person is not helpfully said to be morally educated; since if he has or comes to have any morals these are or will be the result of deliberate *choices* he has made, and the most he could have learned from others is a range of possible choices, and the reasons favouring each, from among which he chose.

This view can, I think, be seen obviously to rest upon a mistake. It does not follow from the fact that an action is deliberately performed that a character is deliberately chosen. This would only be true if (1) persons recognized (and sought) the consequences of their acts *for* their characters, which I do not believe they ordinarily do; or if (2) a person's acquiring a character were a matter solely of his performing certain actions. It is true that the possession by someone of a character is something which is ordinarily detected from his actions. Appreciation of a person's character involves an appreciation of his actions. But his actions, notice, are not his 'outwardly observed' performances, but *what he does*. These last are what they are depending upon the motives, intentions and background of the public performance. The apparently traitorous acts of a man may be the dangerous and unselfish acts of an espionage agent. The seemingly stupid questions of a teacher may be his attempt to encourage discussion. The fulsome attentions of a person may be his dishonest pretence at affection. It follows that the acquiring by a person of a *character* cannot be simply a matter of the performance of certain *actions*, even where the actions are repeated over time. This cannot be so, just because the relation of a man's actions to his character *is* the relation of his actions to his desires, emotions and affections, his humours, and so on. He cannot by deciding to act decide to change his desires, his affections, his interests. He can at best, by acting, so alter the world as *perhaps* to change the objects of his desire. No matter how often a man performs certain actions, the questions remain (1) whether acting that way is a revealing expression of this person's character, and (2) whether the performance of these actions has in fact an effect upon the man so as to bring about in time a change in his character. There is no one action which issues in a particular character, and no series of deliberately chosen actions gives a sufficient condition for redescribing a man as having a character different from what he had before. For it is always possible that though a man (even repeatedly) acts a certain way, and does so deliberately, yet he is not the sort of person his actions suggest—or that he aspires to become. He is not as he appears, or as he wants, to be. Accordingly, then, if someone were to claim "We choose our characters *and therefore* cannot be *taught* to be a good man or woman, but only that this is a possible choice each can make", he would be mistaken. But the important mistake is not the suggestion that we cannot be taught to choose one thing rather than another (for we can); the important mistake is in the idea that our character is one of those things which we choose.

The view concerning human character just sketched is close to, though not identical with, that held by Jean Paul Sartre. Sartre is aware of the complicated links that lie between the performance of actions and the development of character. Nevertheless he does want to insist that a character is chosen, though he accepts that the choice may be unknowingly made, because, say, the result of an action is not foreseen (or, at least, not consciously foreseen), or could not be foreseen. I see no reason to accept the claim that we choose our characters; but this leaves untouched Sartre's appreciation that there is a connection between the actions we choose to perform and what we are or become, and that a man may be at least partly *responsible* for his being, or becoming, a person of a certain sort. And it is, I believe, clear that there is nothing in this recognition by Sartre that rules out 'moral education'. For if to 'teach to be moral' is to bring someone to appreciate the claim that moral considerations make on one, then this indeed is something which persons can do, and have done; though at the same time one wants to say that, here, one can be 'taught' only up to a point—the point at which one is or is not claimed in the appropriate way. However if one thinks of moral education as getting persons to do (for whatever reason, or even unquestionably) what it is right to do, then teaching to be moral is teaching persons to act, or forbear to act, in certain ways. This notion of moral education is, I think, something to be jettisoned. For if it is the reasons why one acts or forbears to act which decide whether one acts or forbears from *moral* concern, and if what *can be* a reason for one depends upon one's desires and affections and attitudes, then in so far as these last are not simply given over to one by others one's moral education cannot be a process of being instructed or 'conditioned', but must take the form of being turned toward certain possibilities, and *appealed to* to recognize certain differences and to place certain values on things.

I think it will be obvious from what has gone before in this essay that my own account of moral education will essentially involve teaching persons to love others. If we cannot bring children to care about others, to be persons to whom the good of others unselfishly matters, they will never appreciate the claims of morality.

In a passage by Schopenauer quoted earlier there is expressed a contrast between a direct control of conduct by a "better consciousness, in the form of love and humanity" and an indirect control "through the medium of reason, by means of maxims and moral principles". If reason enters into moral understanding, as it does, then this antithèsis is obviously too crude. Nevertheless, it does call attention to the place of moral 'rules' or 'maxims' in moral education, and in the moral conduct of life which follows after. These rules must, if they are to inform as moral principles the life of the child and the adult, be seen by him as rules which he ought to follow. Now as this 'ought' cannot be located in the rules themselves it must lie in the human reality which these rules are to govern—that is, *in the child's relationship to others*. If the child's relationship to others is that he cares about others then he will be claimed by this caring, and the moral teaching he receives in the form of instruction and admonition will be an ordering and deepening through understanding of that 'inner principle' or 'better consciousness', and the creation of a capacity for self-discipline and resolve in its service.

The obvious question to ask now is how it is possible for a child to be brought by someone else to care about others. It will perhaps be enough for my purposes to sketch here briefly my own understanding of the development of 'moral concern'. If this seems a departure from philosophy into psychology it is hard to see how this can be avoided, since the question is whether, or in what sense exactly, a child can be *brought* to care about others. How is this question to be dealt with except by an appeal to the facts?

Whether the capacity to care about other persons is innate or acquired is a question I do not wish to consider. It is enough for my purposes that in certain circumstances a child does come to love some persons and (at least) to care about what happens to others. Some children, and adults, seem to be without love or care respecting others. The evidence of psychologists and other observers of human nature suggests that the capacity to love is developed, or arrested, according to how the child is raised, that is, according to the nature of his relationships to, and treatment at the hands of, other persons, especially in the first decade of his life. Human infants respond to affection and attention in ways which obviously show pleasure; and an infant who has over a period of months been attended to, held, caressed, and played with, exhibits if these things are withdrawn obvious signs of disturbance. Attention, once enjoyed, becomes something a child *needs*, something he suffers from the loss of. As the child grows older he continues to desire the attention and treatment which pleases and comforts him. He will also be affected by certain states of other persons, especially those with whom he is most familiar. He will be frightened and unhappy if they weep or show signs of distress or suffering. As he comes to understand more about persons and his environment, his fear and anxiety in response to their distress will be more and more accompanied by concern and unhappiness on their account—by sympathy. The child, as he grows, comes to know in his own case what it is to be in pain, to be afraid, to feel rejected or pilloried, to be alone or frustrated, and he learns to recognize these states in others. Because he cares, it touches him when these others are hurt or distressed. He comes to know what hurt is, and his caring for these others who look after him and love him makes him concerned about and affected by what happens to them, so far as he understands their situation.

How far the capacity to love can only arise within a situation where there is restraint upon a child and a need for him to recognize the claims of others is an important question, and one difficult to answer. It would seem, from what evidence there is, that there is a connection between acquiring discipline on the part of the child and the development in him of an affectionate nature. There is a connection, because self-discipline enters into the exercise of concern for others, and perhaps more importantly, because the greater the play given the self-centered desires of the child the greater is the possibility that the outcome will be selfishness. Once accustomed to getting what he wants, and coming to expect this command of his environment, the child may be disinclined to sacrifice the objects of his desires on account of others. He may even come so to enjoy his unfettered situation, and to resent constraint, as sometimes, when opposed, to want what he wants simply because he wants it. Allowed always to do what he desires to do, there is a risk that the child will never even be confronted with the claims or demands of others in such a way as to enable these to make any impression upon him. He is never made to take the claims of others into account, to amend or sacrifice his own projects for the sake of others. Because his attention and activity are always centered upon himself, he may literally remain ignorant of the desires, sentiments, attachments of these other persons. He may therefore never become interested in what others feel, or suffer, or do, or become so only for so long as these persons' states affect his own designs or pleasures, or engage him but are not troublesome. If he has never needed or been involved with persons in such a way that their good could ever become dear to him, how is he to be affected by what happens to others? He cannot care what happens to them if he has not come to care about them. And he may be kept from caring, or caring at all deeply, by his insulation from other's lives. This possibility is brought out vividly in the stories by F. Scott Fitzgerald about the rich. At the end of *The Great Gatsby*, the narrator takes leave of Tom Buchanan, and as he does he observes:

I couldn't forgive him or like him, but I saw that what he had done was, to him, entirely justified. It was all very careless and confused. They were careless people, Tom and Daisy—they smashed up things and creatures and then retreated back into their money or their vast carelessness, or whatever it was that kept them together, and let other people clean up the mess they had made. . . .

I shook hands with him; it seemed silly not to, for I felt suddenly as though I were talking to a child.[1]

The child, as he comes to care for those close to him, or for others in whom he discovers characteristics which he finds attractive, or loves already in those he knows, appreciates that his caring must make a difference to what he does. More accurately, he appreciates that *these persons* must make a difference to what he does. At the same time his understanding of persons and human relationships and activities continually grows. He comes to see what certain actions are, what they do to others, how they affect them. Coming to see what these actions are, and caring for others, he comes to see that some actions are actions he cares not to do. The more selfish, or the more immature, he is, the less concerned he will be to keep from these actions.

I have yet to say anything about persons teaching the child to care. Those who tend and love the child, who receive him into their lives as one who belongs and is cherished, make possible his caring for them and for others outside the family. But do they "teach him to love"? I think they can be said to do so, in so far as they acquaint the child with features of his environment and the people in it which are deserving of love, draw connections for him between things he does care about and things which he ought to care about, and love these things and these persons themselves. To teach a child to love the beauty of the world, for example, is not to *decide* that the child shall love it, but to strive to present to the child the world in such a way as to awaken that love. It is the same way with persons; though here the reality which is to be loved can itself strive to awaken love in the child by loving the child first, by receiving him with love. This is an important difference, perhaps the most important difference if love *is* only first called forth by love. The contrast between the relation of a person to natural beauty and his relation to persons is brought out in these lines by Housman.

> On russet floors, by waters idle,
> The pine lets fall its cone;
> The cuckoo shouts all day at nothing
> In leafy dells alone;
> And traveller's joy beguiles in autumn
> Hearts that have lost their own.
>
> On acres of the seeded grasses
> The changing burnish heaves;
> Or marshalled under moons of harvest
> Stand still all night the sheaves;
> Or beeches strip in storms for winter
> And stain the wind with leaves.
>
> Possess, as I possessed a season,
> The countries I resign,
> Where over elmy plains the highway
> Would mount the hills and shine,
> And full of shade the pillared forest
> Would murmur and be mine.
>
> For nature, heartless, witless nature,
> Will neither care nor know
> What stranger's feet may find the meadow
> And trespass there and go,
> Nor ask amid the dews of morning
> If they are mine or no.[2]

Mill was especially aware of the importance of other *persons* for the development of moral sensitivity, and in an early essay on marriage he stressed the unique and virtually irreplacable significance of those who nurture and are constantly in the company of the child:

The education which it does belong to mothers to give, and which if not inbibed from them is seldom obtained in any perfection at all, is the training of the affections: *and through the affections, of the conscience, and the whole moral being*. [My emphasis.] But this most precious, and most indispensable part of education . . . a mother does not accomplish . . . by sitting down with her children for one or two or three hours to a task. She effects it by being with the child; by making it happy, and therefore at peace with all things; by checking bad habits in the commencement and by loving the child and by making the child love her. It is not by particular effects, but imperceptibly and unconsciously that she makes her own character pass into the child; that she makes the child love what she loves, venerate what she venerates and imitate as far as a child can her example. These things cannot be done by a hired teacher; and they are better and greater than all [that can be].[3]

At the same time there is, in these remarks, the suggestion that Mill too would want to acknowledge the importance of a love of beauty, non-human as well as human, for the development of moral sensibility.* The connection of a love *of* nature, animate, and inanimate, to a loving human nature, and to a just treatment of persons, is shown in this remark by Iris Murdoch.

Beauty is the convenient and traditional name of something which art and nature share, and which gives a fairly clear sense to the idea of quality of experience and change of consciousness. I am looking out of my window in an anxious and resentful state of mind, oblivious of my surroundings, brooding perhaps on some damage done to my prestige. Then suddenly I observe a hovering kestrel. In a moment everything is altered. The brooding self with its hurt vanity has disappeared. There is nothing now but kestrel. And when I return to thinking of the other matter it seems less important.

* This son of James Mill wrote to his wife from Italy: "Nothing can be more beautiful than this place . . . now in this bedroom by candle-light I am in a complete nervous state from the sensation of the beauty I am living among—while I look at it I seem to be gathering honey which I savour the whole time afterwards."[4] (In the early essay on marriage from which the passage on maternal education is taken, Mill opens the next paragraph with the declaration that "The great occupation of women should be to *beautify* life" (sic); a view the limitations of which he himself later contributed more than any male, living or dead, to exposing and repudiating. This is perhaps the clearest piece of evidence that Mill, as he so often claimed, learned much from Harriet Taylor.)

And of course this is something which we may also do deliberately: give attention to nature in order to clear our minds of selfish care.[5]

Murdoch later connects this truth to art.

[A] good man may be infinitely eccentric, but he must know certain things about his surroundings, most obviously the existence of other people and their claims. The chief enemy of excellence in morality (and also in art) is personal fantasy: the tissue of self-aggrandizing and consoling wishes and dreams which prevents one from seeing what is there outside one. Rilke said of Cezanne that he did not paint 'I like it', he painted 'There it is'. This is not easy, and requires, in art or morals, a discipline.[6]

The importance to one's moral education, and to one's education generally, of the persons who raise one, who take, or fail to take, an interest in one's beliefs, one's awareness of the world, one's sensitivity to what there is and to the possibilities in life, who enrich one's experience and give a certain direction to one's thoughts and feelings, has been pointed out by many people, among them Rush Rhees:

[A] rat does not have to learn what it wants. But learning what one wants is a major part of the growth of understanding in human beings. Coming to understand better what one wants. Or perhaps more commonly, recognizing that this and that are not what one wants, although one thought they were. Socrates used to emphasize this.

[He wished also to insist] that the development of love comes about not from the success of the lover in finding his objective, but from the beauty under which his search is carried on and grows. . . .

I am trying to emphasize that in all this we have not to do with discovering more complex and more all-inclusive ways of satisfying one's responses: of achieving a better economy in one's responses, so that one may avoid frustration, and so on. It is not that one has found a better method of getting what one wants. It is that one's eyes have been opened. And this has been through what has *come* to one, not in the form either of reward or of punishment, but from people and from culture and from teachers. It is because one has *learned from* something, and one would never have grown otherwise.[7]

One can, then, come to care about people, and not just to appreciate with increasing understanding the ways in which they are hurt and made glad, the features of their lives on which their happiness and their dignity depend. Any person contributes to the moral awakening of the child who does all he can to create a loving human environment for the child, and to call the child 'out of himself' to become involved with and to hold precious persons, feelings, ways of living, achievements, relationships, natural phenomena, so as in time to create *claims* upon the child which spring from the child's *caring about* these persons, creatures, states of life, and natural objects.

Absence of such a loving human environment is the most certain contributor to the failure to develop what in the eighteenth century was spoken of as "the moral sense":

Tralala was 15 the first time she was laid. There was no real passion. Just diversion. She hungout in the Greeks with the other neighbourhood kids. Nothin to do. Sit and talk. Listen to the jukebox. Drink coffee. Bum cigarettes. Everything a drag. She said yes. In the park. 3 or 4 couples finding their own tree and grass. Actually she didn't say yes. She said nothing. Tony or Vinnie or whoever it was just continued. They all met later at the exit. They grinned at each other. The guys felt real sharp. The girls walked in front and talked about it. They giggled and alluded. Tralala shrugged her shoulders. Getting laid was getting laid. Why all the bullshit?[8]

I cite this, not as an example of sexual wrong, but as an example of an impoverished emotional life and the absence of certain realms of significance out of which affection and attachment might grow. So far as claims of friendship or compassion are concerned:

If a girl liked one of the guys or tried to get him for any reason Tralala cut in. For kicks. The girls hated her. So what. Who needs them. The guys had what she wanted. Especially when they lushed a drunk. Or pulled a job. She always got something out of it.[9]

This indifference to the feelings or attachments of others, or to others' suffering or loss, is manifest throughout Tralala's life.

As they grow older (and bolder) the boys Tralala is acquainted with

Werent satisfied with the few bucks they got from drunks. Why wait for a drunk to passout. After theyve spent most of their loot. Drop them on their way back to the Army-base. Every night dozens left Willies, a bar across the street from the Greeks. Theyd get them on their way back to the base or the docks. They usually let the doggies go. They didnt have too much. But the seamen were usually loaded. If they were too big or too sober theyd hit them over the head with a brick. If they looked easy one would hold him and the other(s) would lump him. A few times they got one in the lot on 57th street. That was a ball. It was real dark back by the fence. Theyd hit him until their arms were tired. Good kicks. Then a pie and beer. And Tralala. She was always there.[10]

Soon Tralala wants more than a share of what the others collect. She wants to get something on her own which she will not have to divide with the others. There then follows the episode discussed in chapter one above. After this episode things go from the terrible to the more terrible (as I shall later show).

Tralala is not simply indifferent to the people she wrongs. She is not only without compassion, affection or remorse. Tralala is constantly consumed with rage and hatred and resentment. Piteously wretched, she is without pity herself, without sorrow even. (One evening in a bar to which she has gone to pick up someone for his money she is ignored by all the men there, who have come with women in couples. "She didnt touch her third drink, but sat looking around, cursing every sonofabitch in the joint and growing more defiant and desperate. Soon she was screaming in her mind and wishing takrist she had a blade".) Her consciousness is a flickering play of appetite, boredom and hate. How is she to appreciate the wrong even in one action, let alone what the *corruption* of a person would be? She, and the two boys, are capable of appreciating the physical suffering they inflict upon the soldier their attack on whom was described earlier. It is because they see and sense their victim's physical torment that they beat him even more brutally until they tire. But do they comprehend the terror and anguish they raise in him? His fear and desperation are not only those of someone threatened with and now subjected to a violent beating, but also of someone who has expectations of comfort and love in the company of those he cares about and to whom he is going after a long absence, and who is threatened with the loss of these things. His pleas have no effect upon his hearers. How could they? They do not *know*, perhaps, *what* they threaten him *with*; of what he will be deprived. They themselves appear to be completely without affection.

The absence of caring (or trust) in the relationship of Tralala to the boys she spends almost all her time with is brought out when the boys rob a bar while Tralala watches on the street to make sure they are not discovered. The boys open the money box in the alley-way before going to Tralala. Finding two thousand dollars there, they distribute the money throughout their pockets and keep from Tralala the knowledge of how much they actually got. They tell her there was two hundred and fifty dollars in the box and give her fifty as her share. Events then develop as follows.

The next afternoon they went to the Greeks for coffee and two detectives came in and told them to come outside. They searched them, took the money from their pockets and pushed them into their car. The detectives waved the money in front of their faces and shook their heads. Dont you know better than to knock over a bookie drop? Huh? Huh, huh! Real clever arent you. The detectives laughed and actually felt a professional amazement as they looked at their dumb expressions and realized that they really didnt know who they had robbed. Tony slowly started to come out of the coma and started to protest that they didnt do nothin. One of the detectives slapped his face and told him to shutup. For Christs sake dont give us any of that horseshit. I suppose you just found a couple of grand lying in an empty lot? Tralala screeched, a couple of what? The detectives looked at her briefly then turned back to Tony and Al. You can lush a few drunken seamen now and then and get away with it, but when you start taking money from my pocket youre going too far sonny. What a pair of stupid punks . . . OK sister, beat it. Unless you want to come along for the ride? She automatically backed away from the car, still staring at Tony and Al. The doors slammed shut and they drove away. Tralala went back to the Greeks and sat at the counter cursing Tony and Al and then the bulls for pickinem up before she could get hers. Didn't even spend a penny of it. The goddamn bastards. The rotten stinkin sonsofobitches.[11]

Yet earlier in the story, when she steals the wallet from the soldier, Tralala herself hides most of the money and keeps from the boys how much the wallet contained. When they insistently press her to tell them, she lies. It is fear that the soldier will say something to indicate how much she actually got from the wallet that at first provokes her to scream and kick at him. She wants to get them to beat him so he cannot say anything.

This episode with the soldier is connected to a question I wish directly to confront—whether Tralala has a conception of justice. When the soldier confronts Tralala at the Greeks,

Tralala screamed in his face that he was a no good mothafuckin sonofabitch and then started kicking him . . . She spit in his face again, no longer afraid he might say something, but mad. Goddamn mad. A lousy fifty bucks and he was crying. And anyway, he shouldve had more.[12]

After the beating

they left and walked slowly to 4th avenue and took a subway to Manhattan. Just in case somebody might put up a stink. In a day or two he/ll be shipped out and nobodyll know the difference. Just another doggie. Anyway he deserved it.[13]

'He should've had more.' 'He deserved it.' Do these remarks issue from a conception of justice held by these persons? I do not *know* what to say here. If I am pressed to answer I should say that the remarks spring only from selfishness and frustration. They are the projection upon the order of things of the claims of self. Because Tralala wanted more he should have had more. Still, it might be thought that Tralala's sense of not getting what she should have got involves a sense of what she is entitled to. But the important question is, entitled to on what grounds? Has Tralala a sense that her chances in life are not what a person's chances in life ought to be? Does she see the taking of what she is without as a redress of some injustice in which she is caught? We are not told enough to settle the matter conclusively. What we are told suggests that Tralala's own desires and expectations are the only ground on which she decides whether a particular winnings are enough or not. That is to say, she has a primitive notion of what *she is entitled to*. But it is cauterized, as it were. She is unable to look upon others except as competitors (and so threats) or as accomplices—or as 'marks': someone to be preyed upon. These last she looks upon with a mixture of envy, hatred, contempt, and suppressed rage. She considers they get no better than they deserve. Her attitude toward her accomplices is not much better, except that she only directs her hate toward them when they threaten her own designs, or make demands on her which she wishes to escape.

The question has now to be answered, what effect is the morality of other persons to have on Tralala? It seems to me that the answer is, none. If Tralala was to encounter goodness in a person, one would expect her to respond to it either with contempt, or with cunning, depending on how she figured in their actions. A good treatment of *others* she would regard with resentment or contempt. A good treatment of herself would be accepted at first with satisfaction, but after there would almost certainly follow a calculation of how someone so dumb could be parted from what else he or she had. Her response to affection and generosity in the story bear this out. She meets a man in uniform at a bar. The next morning:

When they had finished eating he lit her cigarette, smiled, and asked her if he could buy her something. A dress or something like that. I mean, well you know . . . Id like to buy you a little present. He tried not to sound maudlin or look sheepish, but he found it hard to say what he felt, now, in the morning, with a slight hangover, and she looked to him pretty and even a little innocent. Primarily he didnt want her to think he was offering to pay her or think he was insulting her by insinuating that she was just another prostitute; but much of his loneliness was gone and he wanted to thank her. You see, I only have a few days leave left before I go back and I thought perhaps we could—that is I thought we could spend some more time together . . . he stammered on apologetically hoping she understood what he was trying to say but the words bounced off her and when she noticed that he had finished talking she said sure. What thefuck. This is much better than wresslin with a drunk and she felt good this morning, much better than yesterday (briefly remembering the bulls and the money they took from her) and he might even give her his money before he went back overseas (what could he do with it) and with her tits she could always make out and whatthehell, it was the best screwin she ever had. . . They went shopping and she bought a dress, a couple of sweaters (2 sizes too small), shoes, stockings, a pocketbook and an overnight bag to put her clothes in. She protested slightly when he told her to buy a cosmetic case (not knowing what it was when he handed it to her and she saw no sense in spending money on that when he could as well give her cash), and he enjoyed her modesty in not wanting to spend too much of his money; and he chuckled at her childlike excitement at being in the stores, looking and buying. They took all the packages back to the hotel and Tralala put on her new dress and shoes and they went out to eat and then to a movie. For the next few days they went to movies, restaurants (Tralala trying to make a mental note of the ones where the Officers hung out), a few more stores and back to the hotel. When they woke on the 4th day he told her he had to leave and asked her if she would come with him to the station. She went thinking he might give her his money and she stood awkwardly on the station with him, their bags around them waiting for him to go on the train and leave. Finally the time came for him to leave and he handed her an envelope as she lifted her face slightly so he could kiss her. It was thin and she figured it might be a check. She put it in her pocketbook, picked up her bag and went to the waiting room and sat on a bench and opened the envelope. She opened the paper and started reading: Dear Tral: There are many things I would like to say and should have said, but—A letter. A goddamn LETTER. She ripped the envelope apart and turned the letter over a few times. Not a cent. I hope you understand what I mean and am unable to say—she looked at the words—if you do feel as I hope you do Im writing my address at the bottom. I dont know if I/ll live through this war, but—Shit. Not veh-emently but factually. She dropped the letter and rode the subway to Brooklyn. She went to Willies to display her finery.[14]

So far as the moral *judgment* by others of her actions is concerned, it is hard to see how this is to have any effect upon Tralala's sympathies. Its likely effect (if expressed to her) would be to add to the objects of her hate.

How did Tralala come to be as she is? From the story we get a picture of the society in which Tralala was raised and now lives. It is of a kind which has been described by social psychologists in what must now be hundreds of books. A sample description from this literature is the following.

The district has . . . the highest incidence of the poverty diseases: tuber-culosis, venereal diseases, bronchial infections, skin infections, bad teeth.

The men are in unskilled, ill-paid, casual employment. They are often out of work: they obtain little satisfaction from their work; they express no interest in it.

The home is usually hopelessly overcrowded. Seldom, if ever, is a house occupied by one family only. Families have either two rooms or only one; occasionally a family will have two rooms and a kitchen, but this is rare. The rooms are poorly furnished, with probably two beds, one for the parents and youngest child, the other for the older children; if the family can afford another bed the children will be segregated by sex, but this does not always happen.

The average first child will have been born when both father and mother are round about twenty. The child is not likely to have been planned.

At first, the child sleeps with his mother, so that for much of the time the mother is readily available to give the warmth and contact he needs. At first, too, the child is breast-fed, and fed almost whenever he cries, so that in these very early days there is little frustration of his needs. Because he tends to be fed whether he cries from hunger or for other reasons, food comes to have attached to it a general feeling of comfort and consolation which it retains in later life. But since the mother does not always feel like feeding him when he cries, satisfaction does not come to the child at regular intervals or on predictable occasions. Thus there is some restriction on the infant's satisfactions, but it is not a systematic restriction.

Weaning involves the breaking or weakening of one of the ties which keep the child dependent on the mother. Though little is known for certain about this aspect of child-care, the psychological significance of such breaks seems to depend as much on the way they are brought about as on the age at which they are experienced. One such break occurs when the child is put on the bottle. This is not as sharp a break [here] as it is in some environments, for breast-feeding is not normally considered an opportunity for the expression of tenderness in Branch Street. Nevertheless, it does provide some occasion for contact between mother and child, and this ceases when bottle-feeding starts.

He is still apt to be fed whenever he cries. Food thus retains its consoling significance, but contact with the mother is removed from the general context of this gratifying experience.

Infancy comes to an end when the Branch Street baby leaves his mother's bed and goes to share the bed of his brothers and sisters. The parents now want him out of the way. He is sent out to play in the street, and at the earliest opportunity, to school.

. . . it is possible to identify among the adolescents and adults at least three well-established types of behaviour pattern: those normally attributed to an affectionless early childhood, and those attributed to a childhood in which affection was rather suddenly and permanently withheld. There is also a third variant in which affection is given, but not in a sustained way, being given unexpectedly or when not especially wanted, and withheld at times when the need for affection is strongly felt.

Many [parents] do not hesitate to lie to their children and to mislead them. At the children's hospital it is not uncommon for a child to be greatly shocked because his mother has said he is being taken to the seaside for an outing, when in reality he is put in the children's ward to have his tonsils removed. Children are promised treats to keep them quiet and the treats do not materialize. If their position in the family is irregular they are not told the truth about their parentage. They are lied to in countless little ways.

[The child] does not grow in a soil which allows to take root such ideas as that there is a time and place for everything, that good things arrive regularly though one may have to wait or even cry for them, that foresight and effort will please the parent and be rewarded by them. The absence of this kind of learning is to be connected with the absence of striving, the intolerance of frustration, the inability to wait for a gratification, which marks the adult personality.

As he grows older, he will join successive playgroups, composed of the children in his street, the boys in his neighbourhood, a gang.

In the street play-group the child learns that life is now catch-as-catch-can, look after number one for if you don't no one will, any good thing may be taken away by others, you had best enjoy it while you can. In this way the street confirms, and gives detail and substance to, such earlier pre-dispositions as greediness for food and other enjoyments, unwillingness to defer a present gratification, pessimism of the outcome of concentrated effort.

Having been accustomed to sleep in the same bed as their brothers and sisters, and parental control in general being minimal, the children tend to have engaged in sexual play with one another. All their information on sex will have come from other children. These are children who . . . ask a pretty new [social] worker whom they see for the first time, 'Are you Peter's tart?'; who in the painting sessions draw pictures usually to be found as an-onymous scribbles on the walls of lavatories; who incessantly accuse every grown-up person of promiscuity; who sleep three or four together in the same bed; who may sleep under their parents' bed on the nights father comes home drunk; who may return from school to find that a baby has been born in the bed which they have to share the same night with the young mother—an older and unmarried sister.

It is therefore not surprising that these children do not develop much of a conscience. They feel unloved or betrayed; the adults in their world define no behaviour as right or wrong on general grounds; rather, the rightness and wrongness of behaviour is dependent on its coincidence with a good or a bad temper in the adults. There is little opportunity to idealize any known person, because, with living conditions as they are, they see people in their real form, which may be very sordid.[15]

But the human reality which is this environment is here softened by the academic prose. A less deliberately heuristic, but compellingly more powerful description of this reality is given by Selby in the last pages of the story of Tralala. In time Tralala becomes a drunkard and an inhabitant of skid row. One afternoon she is thrown out of a bar, and in a rage she returns to the old neighbourhood. Here she

becomes drunk with some people she has met there, two of whom
are girls she knew before. Eventually with her own encouragement
and challenge she is dragged out to an old car in a vacant lot by some
of the men in the bar.

[A] sort of line was formed by everyone yelling and laughing and someone
yelled to the guys on the end to go get some beer and they left and came back
with cans of beer which were passed around the daisychain and the guys
from the Greeks came over and some of the other kids from the neighbor-
hood stood around watching and waiting and Tralala yelled and shoved her
tits into the faces as they occurred before her and beers were passed around
and the empties dropped or thrown and guys left the car and went back on
line and had a few beers and waited their turn again and more guys came
from Willies and a phone call to the Armybase brought more seamen and
doggies and more beer was brought from Willies and Tralala drank beer
while being laid and someone asked if anyone was keeping score and
someone yelled who can count that far.[16]

We have seen that some of the neighbourhood children are present.

[In time Tralala] lay unconscious on the seat in the lot and soon they tired of
the dead piece and the daisychain brokeup and they went back to Willies the
Greeks and the base and the kids who were watching and waiting to take a
turn took out their disappointment on Tralala and tore her clothes to small
scraps put out a few cigarettes on her nipples pissed on her jerkedoff on her
jammed a broomstick up her snatch then bored they left her lying amongst
the broken bottles rusty cans and rubble of the lot and Jack and Fred and
Ruthy and Annie stumbled into a cab still laughing and they leaned toward
the window as they passed the lot and got a good look at Tralala lying naked
covered with blood urine and semen and a small blot forming on the seat
between her legs as blood seeped from her crotch and Ruthy and Annie
happy and completely relaxed now that they were on their way downtown
and their deal wasnt lousedup and they would have plenty of money and
Fred looking through the rear window and Jack pounding his leg and roar-
ing with laughter. . . .[17]

It is not for nothing that Selby prefaced his story with these lines
from the song of Solomon.

I will rise now, and go about the city in the streets, and in the broad ways I
will seek him whom my soul loveth: I sought him, but I found him not.

The watchmen that go about the city found me: to whom I said, Saw ye him whom my soul loveth?

II

In conclusion, I want to consider briefly, for its relation to moral life, a feature of human awareness and sensibility which is identified by John Plamenatz in these remarks from an essay addressed against the utilitarians:

> [Man] is a self-conscious, self-communing, animal who sees life in the round, who knows that he must die, who is his own most constant companion, whose desires are often fantasies, who wants to be one kind of person rather than another and to live one kind of life rather than another. He is, as Hegel might put it, 'his own object'; he has some image of himself, more or less variable, more or less obscure, which it matters to him enormously should be true; some idea of what is proper to him or worthy of him. He is the happier and the more secure and easy in his mind, the more confident he is that the image is true and the better or the more impressive it appears to other people. Just as we are interested in ourselves as persons rather than as subjects of desire pursuing satisfactions, so too are we interested in others. It is as persons, much more than as competitors and collaborators for the satisfaction of wants, that we hate and love one another; that we feel pride, envy, and gratitude. Our wants flow largely from the ideas we have of ourselves and our neighbours, and of the kind of life we want to live. But the utilitarians, except for John Stuart Mill, speak as if the great object of our lives were to cater as best we know how for a multitude of desires; as if man were a collection or sequence of appetites, each to be fed in turn or to be sacrificed only to make the food go further.

> We are moral persons, not primarily because we follow rules which prevent our getting too much in each other's way as we strive to satisfy one desire after another, but much more because we try to see ourselves and our neighbours as whole persons leading whole lives. True, we do not see either ourselves or them as we and they really are; we are not in full possession of ourselves, or anywhere near it; we live fitfully and uncertainly and in a half-light. We do not exactly know what we want to be or how we want to live; our ideas are half-formed and change continually. Our heads float while our feet walk and we are often closer to the real world in our habits than our thoughts. We are often vague and restless; but we are so precisely because we need much more to make us happy than to see our way to satisfying as many of our desires as possible.[18]

When Plamenatz speaks of 'moral persons' he speaks within a tradition of inquiry which stems especially from Hegel, in which the 'moral' aspect of men's lives is its self-conscious, self-communing, *social* and *'picture-making'* aspect. The 'moral being' is the creature who has a conception of a social world, with parts for himself and others to play in it.[19] Now the idea I want to consider here is the idea: a man may keep from wrong because he wishes to be a certain sort of person. But before doing that I should like to make one remark about the features of our inner life which Plamenatz's remarks depict. It will be recognized by anyone who has any knowledge of criminality and criminals that many thoroughly immoral and callous men have a conception of themselves which figures importantly in their lives, and informs in many ways their actions. The professional criminal is perhaps possessed of some inhibitions, and may have loyalties. But he may be quite ruthlessly immoral to the point of being amoral. Still, he will have standards of conduct, and (this connects up with what was said above) rationality, which he will sneer at the neglect of by others. An example of this is the following comment by a professional workman on his tools.

The only pistol you can count on is a revolver. Every real character [criminal] knows that. So do the cops. Did you ever see a cop with an automatic? When you read about a job where an automatic was involved, you know the guy was an amateur. Sometimes an automatic won't go off. Yeah, not very often, but it happens. Once is all you need. When you pull that trigger your life depends on it. You can't take that chance. You don't have that worry with a revolver. And a revolver is balanced better. You can be more accurate with it.

Another thing, when you read about guys using .45's and such. That's just amateur stuff. You're giving up accuracy for a lot of power you don't need. Sure, maybe it makes sense for an FBI man to use a .357 Magnum sometimes, 'cause sometimes he has to knock down a door and things like that. For me a .38 is plenty. But you can't go much lower. A .32 is the bottom. You want a gun that if you have to shoot somebody, he goes down. Take a .25; that's a gun that's fit for nothing but a lady's purse.

Most times what you're supposed to do is just throw down on somebody [point the gun at him]. You don't really use that pistol if you don't have to. That's show-off stuff too. And when you use it you don't shoot if you don't have to. You have to fade enough heat without maybe killing somebody, so what you do is you try to slap somebody 'cross the head with it. That's another reason for a revolver. You slap somebody 'cross the head with an automatic, that mechanism gets loose and starts rattling, and maybe it jams next time.[20]

I do not deny therefore that we often act or keep from acting in order to make true some insistent picture of ourselves which it is important to us we maintain. And of course this can be a happy, or a crippling, thing, as the case may be. But in so far as morals go, if one keeps from wrong because one wants to be a good person the question arises why one wants to be this kind of person. If the answer is, in respect of someone, simply that he just likes this picture of himself, or that he wants to be this way because the persons he likes or depends on will show him favour if he does, or because the persons whom he dislikes are not upright or right-living, and he wants to be different from them, if the preference remains always at this level, we shall, I think, consider this man (*at best*) morally immature. For he fails to appreciate the moral claims of his practice on him. Where however there was once genuine moral appreciation but now there is also this type of 'picture-preference' we shall have (ordinarily) what Kierkegaard called the 'double-minded' man:

The Good is one thing; the reward is another that may be present and may be absent for the time being, or until the very last. When [a man], then, wills the Good for the sake of the reward, he does not will one thing but two. In ancient times this problem was also frequently an object of consideration. There were shameless teachers of impudence who thought it right to do wrong on a large scale and then to make it appear as if one willed the Good. In this way they thought one had a double advantage: the pitiful advantage of being able to do wrong, to be able to get one's own way, to let one's passions rage, and the hypocritical advantage of seeming to be good. But in ancient times there was also a simple sage, whose simplicity became a snare for the impudent ones' sophistry. He taught that in order really to be certain that it was the Good that man willed, one ought even to shun seeming good, presumably in order that the reward should not become tempting. For so different is the Good and the reward, when the reward is separately striven after, that the Good is the ennobling and the sanctifying; the reward is the tempting. But the tempting is never the Good.

The other aspect of the reward–centered man is willing the good only out of fear of punishment. For in essence, this is the same as to will the Good for the sake of the reward, to the extent that avoiding an evil is an advantage of the same sort as that of attaining a benefit. The Good is one thing. Punishment is something else. Therefore the double-minded person does not desire one thing when he desires the Good under the condition that he shall avoid punishment. The condition lays its finger upon just the double-mindedness. If that condition were not there, he would not fear the punishment, for punishment is indeed not what a man should fear. He should fear to do wrong.

[Furthermore] suppose a man wills the Good simply in order that he may score the victory, then he wills the Good for the sake of the reward, and his double-mindedness is obvious, as the previous section of the talk has sought to point out. Actually he does not care to serve the Good, but to have the advantage of regarding it as a fruit of conquest. When, on the contrary, a man desires that the Good shall be victorious, when he will not call the outcome of the battle "victory", if he wins, but only when the Good is victorious; can he then, in any sense, be called and be double-minded? Yes, and yet if he be double-minded (for the decision as to the boundary line between the pure and the double-minded is here of a singular complexity), then his double-mindedness is more subtle and concealed, more presumptuous than that obvious and out-and-out worldly sort. It is a powerful deception that seems nearest of all to approach the purity of heart that wills the Good in truth, even though it is at the other pole from it, just as the high place is from the deep chasm, just as heaven-storming pride is from humility's dwelling in the low places, just as if a pretentiously plausible approximation had been won by falsifying a line of separation that was eternally real. He does not will the Good for the sake of the reward. He wills that the Good shall triumph through him, that he shall be the instrument, he the chosen one. He does not desire to be rewarded by the world—that he despises; nor by men—that he looks down upon. And yet he does not wish to be an unprofitable servant. The reward which he insists upon is a sense of pride and in that very demand is his violent double-mindedness.[21]

What Kierkegaard means by calling these forms of 'moral' engagement double-minded is that if the true object of your desire (your reward, your escaping punishment, your self-admiration) were suddenly to be got in a different way, or threatened by the very thing you would claim to be pursuing—the Good—then you would forsake that which you now most emphatically claim (and even perhaps believe) to be the object of your desire: the Good. It will be revealed that you did not will only to live rightly all along. You willed that *and* something else. *And this last is what really mattered to you*. Kierkegaard wants to say that the Good is what must matter if you are truly to be moral. It will by now be clear that I wish to say that it is the good of persons, or as I prefer most of all to say, it is persons, who must matter to you.

The form of double-mindedness that I wish especially to point to here is the last; what Kierkegaard calls the 'egocentric service of the good'. I wish to emphasize the distance which this form of engagement with life throws up between the one who lives this way and the persons whom his actions touch or who figure in his deliberations. The one who lives this way (as opposed to the man who wants simply to be at the top) had once to appreciate the true importance of living rightly; it is precisely because he once had this appreciation, which involved a response to persons which was not wholly self-concerned, that he is now able to attach importance to his activities and to celebrate himself under this aspect, under the aspect of being someone who is a good man. But selfishness has so got a grip on his affections that in a very real way he is engaged, in his 'moral' life, not with the persons among whom he lives and follows out his activities, but with a 'form' of reality—in which *he* figures as a significant and central object, admirable, admired, and admiring. Peter Winch has remarked:

It may be asked . . . what is so attractive about being an object of admiration; and this is a pertinent question. Of course, if one is an object of admiration this may as a matter of fact be of assistance to one's further designs by, for example, bringing with it power or money. But it is not just that that one values in admiration. . . . [T]o understand people's behaviour as constituting admiration is to understand it as directed towards something good, something worthy of admiration. So the thought of something as really worthy of admiration is indeed involved when anyone takes pleasure in being admired. Only this thought is corrupted.[22]

I should like to introduce the words 'conceived as', 'accounted as' here; the behaviour may be directed toward something conceived as good, something accounted worthy of admiration. For of course the aspiring villain may admire the greater villainy of his idol. There can be admiration of corrupt things, as well as a corruption of one's relation to good things under the spell of others' (and one's self-) admiration. Furthermore Winch himself wishes now to acknowledge that the thought of something as worthy of admiration is not *necessarily* involved in taking pleasure in being admired. (One may just take pleasure in being admired—for whatever reason.) Still Winch's remark reveals the form corrupted appreciation of something once genuinely regarded takes, and its connection to true appreciation. What Kierkegaard called an egocentric engagement in moral life is a corruption of this kind. The center of this engagement is not others but a mode of self-existence. It is this mode of self-existence, conceived of as something worthy and beautiful and touching, even heroic, which is the object of contemplation and the focus of one's energy. This 'living rightly' is done, not for the sake of, for love of, those with whom one's life is involved. It is done for the sake of their—and one's own—*esteem* and *appreciation*; or (worse) for the sake of delighting in a comparison with others. This is not moral life, but style.

NOTES

[1] F. Scott Fitzgerald, *The Great Gatsby* (New York: Charles Scribner's Sons, 1953) pp. 180–1.

[2] A. E. Housman, *Collected Poems* (Harmondsworth: Penguin Books, 1961) p. 159.

[3] J. S. Mill and Harriet Taylor, *Essays on Sex Equality*, A. Rossi (ed.), (Chicago: The University of Chicago Press, 1970) p. 76.

[4] Ibid., p. 48.

[5] Iris Murdoch, *The Sovereignty of Good* (London: Routledge and Kegan Paul, 1970) p. 84.

[6] Ibid., p. 59.

[7] Rush Rhees, *Without Answers* (London: Routledge and Kegan Paul, 1969) pp. 156, 157, 158.

[8] *Last Exit to Brooklyn,* p. 93.

[9] Ibid.

[10] Ibid., p. 94.

[11] Ibid., p. 99.

[12] Ibid., p. 96.

[13] Ibid., p. 97.   [14] Ibid., pp. 103–4.

[15] Josephine Klein, *Samples of English Culture* (London: Routledge & Kegan Paul, 1965). Vol. I, pp. 4, 7, 9, 11, 13, 16, 18, 19, 38.

[16] Op. cit., pp. 112–13.

[17] Ibid., pp. 113–14.

[18] John Plamenatz, *The English Utilitarians* (Oxford: Blackwell, 1958) pp. 173–4.

[19] Ibid., p. 175.

[20] Quoted in Ned Polsky, *Hustlers, Beats and Others* (New York: Doubleday, 1969) pp. 130–1.

[21] Soren Kierkegaard, *Purity of Heart* (New York: Harper and Row, 1956) pp. 69, 70, 79, 99–100. (Trans.: D. V. Steele.)

[22] Peter Winch, *Moral Integrity* (Oxford: Blackwell, 1968) pp. 24–5.

VIII
Society and Morals

1st Gent: An ancient land in ancient oracles
         Is called 'law-thirsty': all the struggle there
         Was after order and a perfect rule.
         Pray, where lie such lands now? . . .
2nd Gent: Why, where they lay of old—in human souls.

GEORGE ELIOT

Say what you choose, so long as it does not prevent you from seeing the facts. (And when you see them there is a good deal you will not say.)

WITTGENSTEIN

Plato taught that morals have to do with harmony of the soul. In our own century the idea of harmony has again been introduced into moral philosophy, with the difference that the harmony now spoken of is a harmony, not of the soul, but of society. Representative of those who argue in this way is Ralph Barton Perry. A generation ago Perry declared that

Morality is man's endeavour to harmonize conflicting interests: to prevent conflict when it threatens, to remove conflict when it occurs, and to advance from the negative harmony of non-conflict to the positive harmony of cooperation. Morality is the solution of the problem created by conflict—conflict among the interests of the same, or of different persons.[1]

This conception of morality is held today by, among others, Kurt Baier and Kai Nielsen. In Nielsen's book *Reason and Practice* we are told that

Usually, typically, and understandably there has been concern, when morality has been at issue, to adjudicate and in some way harmonize conflicts of interest and divergent needs in such a way that life together remains or becomes humanly tolerable. Morality is—or so I would maintain—a system of social control that functions primarily equitably to adjudicate conflicting wants, needs, and human aims in such a way so as not only to make societal life possible and tolerable but also to diminish as much as possible human harm and suffering.[2]

I wish to show that the picture of morality cast by these remarks, a picture frequently encountered not only in philosophy but in political, sociological, and legal writings, obscures and distorts more than it reveals.

I

Perry speaks of a *solution* to the problem of conflict, and Nielsen of a *concern* to harmonize conflicting interests. Nielsen's emphasis upon making social life tolerable and Perry's upon the achievement of cooperation and non-conflict may seem to suggest that the *aim* of moral reasoning and action is social harmony. Persons, when they act from moral considerations, aim at harmony. Placing this construction upon Perry's and Nielsen's words leads immediately to obvious difficulties.

For the fact is that harmony can sometimes only be got by repudiating or ignoring the claims of morality. A woman who wishes to avoid conflict with her husband, who is determinedly involved in some cruelty or injustice, can only achieve the desired accord if she is herself willing to be an accomplice to wrongdoing. Disagreement and conflict frequently arise precisely because one or more parties to a matter insist upon doing what it is right to do. This fact shows that there is something radically mistaken about any view that what we seek in acting morally is to put harmony in the place of conflict. That people live in harmony does not of itself show that the relations between them—or between them and their neighbours—are just or humane. The absence of conflict and the presence of co-operation are never proof of moral ship-shapedness. Therefore they cannot be that in the achievement of which morality is realized.

Nielsen throughout (and Perry at least once) asserts that the harmony moral agents are bent on realizing is not mere agreement or cooperation but a harmony *of needs and interests*. The emphasis is upon the adjudication and *equitable treatment* of claims. This allows for the possibility of conflict provoked by morality, which may arise if such equitable adjudication is not achieved, or is refused to be acted on. The expectation however is that if this moral adjudication is ongoing, and if everyone does act as morality requires, then everyone's interests and needs will be equitably met; and the result will be social harmony (provided only that individuals are rational—on this more below). This moral adjudication contributes then to social harmony. But it does so by identifying as warranted, or unwarranted, the divergent claims and interests of persons according to some set of standards. These standards are 'the rules, or principles' of morality. Moral action consists in seeking to put the satisfaction of persons' needs and interests into harmony with the requirements of these principles. (Not, as the first interpretation suggests, simply to get harmony, whatever the level of persons' satisfaction). We are still, on this second picture, to speak of morality as "the solution to the problem created by conflict". But the solution consists *in trying to achieve equity* (where the efficacy of so doing is something still to be explained). Our aim in moral reasoning and action becomes, on this picture, not harmony between persons, but harmony between the satisfaction of persons' needs and interests *and* these standards of morality. It is this reasoning and action which comprises "a system of social control".

II

A morality which did not make a difference to what individuals should or should not do is an absurdity. Morality then 'controls action' in the straightforward sense that the consideration for others which morality involves marks out some actions as acceptable and others not. This however is not what those who describe morality as a system of social control mean to say. The key to their meaning is to ask *why* the equitable adjudication and settlement of conflicting needs and interests is supposed to make any difference to how individuals behave toward one another. The answer comes back:

To a very considerable degree the very *raison d'être* of morality is to adjudicate between the frequently conflicting and divergent desires and interests of people, in order to give everyone as much as possible of whatever it is that each will want when he is being rational, when he would still want what he wants were he to reflect carefully, and when his efforts to satisfy his own wants are constrained by a willingness to treat the rational wants of other human beings in the same way.[3] [See also page 153 above.]

In speaking of the *raison d'être* of morality Nielsen directly implies that morality is a *product* of *rational deliberation*. It is something men have made to achieve a quite specific purpose. Because the wants of all cannot simultaneously be satisfied, some sort of mutual accommodation is necessary. Since each wants as much as he possibly can get, rules or principles must be identified which spell out that accommodation between the competing interests and needs of each which will be optimally satisfactory for all—taking into account the desire each has for the others to show toward him tolerable behaviour, which tolerableness must depend on the others getting as much as possible of what they want (taking into account *their* interest in being tolerably behaved toward, etc.). These rules or principles (and their observance?—Nielsen does not say) men call 'morality'. They are a *system* of *social* control, which functions by identifying those claims and interests on which each is entitled to act, and whose rationale is the achieving of a social order in which each is best able to realize the optimum satisfaction of his or her wants consistent with the comparable satisfaction of the wants of all the others.

The Hobbesean ancestry of this picture (and its contemporary debt to John Rawls) is transparent. Morality is subsumed under politics. The political problems of scarcity and conflict are "solved" by devising rules of interaction which spell out the entitlements of each *vis-a-vis* the rest. Observance of these rules by all confers on each the most advantageous situation with respect to the satisfaction of his or her needs, compatible with the society of the others. Observance, then, is the most rational course for each individual to follow, since refusal to observe the rules puts in jeopardy the social order that most consistently favours one's realizing one's interests (where these include one's desire for life and the security of one's property). It is this compelling *rationality* of observance that is to explain why the equitable settlement of claims and needs is supposed to achieve social harmony. To be treated equitably by the rest is the most favoured situation one can hope for, all things taken into account. Therefore it is the most rationally attractive situation to contribute to. Moral rectitude is really the pursuit of happiness.

III

I shall raise four objections to this picture of morality. The first concerns the reduction of moral action in this account to *extrinsically valued, instrumental* activity. Observance of moral rules is made a rational policy whose object is to foster conditions under which one can best hope to get what one wants and needs.

A man stops on a highway to help a person who has fallen from drunkenness and lies ill and covered with vomit. He does this because the person is ill, and possibly in pain, and liable to suffer from exposure. He does it because the man needs care.

On the model under discussion the point of so acting, *qua* moral conduct, is to contribute to a structure of social interaction which enhances one's own interest. The rationale of moral action is that which makes it possible for the person whose action it is sensibly to do it. Suppose then that as our Samaritan bends over the drunken man, and tries to help him to his feet, it becomes apparent to him (how does not matter) that the man will die within the hour. Is this to make a difference in what he has reason to do? Is our Samaritan to cease to tend the man and tend only to his removal, as one whom the rational policy of acting morally does not now encompass, since the man will soon no longer be in society, and there is no question of reciprocity or of his affecting in any way the conditions of social life? Or is the first man to continue to tend the man, because of the beneficial example this gives others, or because it is a useful rein- forcement of his own disposition to perform in the prescribed fashion even where it is not strictly speaking productive?

Even in the approach of death we tend, and seek to comfort, the one who is dying. I do not see how this is to be explained as action to realize a social order in which the one who acts, and the one acted upon, will mutually flourish. What these actions aim at is: this tending, this comforting, this helping, nothing more. They matter, where they matter, for what they are; not for anything they make possible.

It is true (and this is my second point) that in a passage already quoted Kai Nielsen declares that it is the function of morality "not only to make societal life possible and tolerable *but also to diminish as much as possible human harm and suffering*" (my emphasis). These words suggest a rationale for moral action different from that ident- ified up to this point in Nielsen's and Perry's remarks. But one wants some explanation *why* the diminishing of human harm and suffering *tout court* should be an object of the system of social control we call morality. Nielsen in fact never gives an explanation why this should be so. The reasons he identifies never get beyond the interest each individual obviously has in a social order which accomplishes this object. Nielsen does at one place speak of "the value of life in society" but he means by this the value of 'social membership'—the advantage to each individual of being *in* society (as opposed to trying to subsist in isolation). The seeking to diminish human harm and suffering is something which a rational man can, Nielsen insists, be brought to cooperate in. But as I have tried to show in this essay, everything will turn on *why* this man cooperates whether his 'participation' will instantiate *morality* or not. On Nielsen's account, the motive throughout remains the fostering of the man's own concerns, which is perfectly compatible with caring nothing for people, but using and cooperating with them within the parameters set by 'the institution of morality'.

IV

My third objection to the picture of morality under consideration can be brought out by calling attention to an ambiguity in the expression "a system of social control". This ambiguity comes out in some words of Kai Nielsen's quoted above, where he speaks of the *raison d'être* of morality being

... to give everyone as much as possible of whatever it is that each will want when he is being rational ... *and when his efforts to satisfy his own wants are constrained by a willingness to treat the rational wants of other human beings in the same way.*[4] [my emphasis]

Strictly speaking, what we have here is a contradiction not an ambiguity. Being constrained and being willing are virtual opposites. To be constrained by a *willingness* to treat the rational wants of others as of equal importance with one's own is literally non-sense. What Nielsen is trying to express here is the necessity for individuals actually to refrain from any behaviour which would effectively deny others the satisfaction of their rational wants; otherwise the system of mutual accommodation will not work. But of course such restraint may be accomplished either because the individual wants so to refrain—i.e. willingly refrains—from denying others their reasonable entitlement; or because the individual is *constrained* to refrain by his wish to avoid some unpleasant consequence, such as the collapse of the system, or by something *more immediate*, such as ostracism, physical punishment, or some other form of socially-administered sanction. Nielsen's words seek to walk a line between *both* of these possibilities; "constrained" pulling one way, "willingness" the other. But the same ambivalence attaches to the notion of "social control". Is it that the individual controls his behaviour (i.e. heeds the rules), and his controlling his behaviour in this way is an instance of 'morality'? Or is that *morality* controls (or seeks to control) his behaviour, so that morality (this *system of social control*) constrains the individual to observe these ordinances? Nielsen wants it to be the first way: the system of social control which is 'morality' consists in individuals rationally controlling their conduct, so as to respect the systematically-related 'moral rules' of interaction, thereby creating the social order—the relationships, practices, mutual behaviour patterns—that favour the realization of each's interests. But it is at least as common to find the second story and surely more in keeping with the description "a system of social control". Thus we find it declared in H. L. A. Hart's justly celebrated *The Concept of Law* that

Rules are conceived and spoken of as imposing obligations when *the general demand for conformity* is insistent and *the social pressure brought to bear upon those who deviate* or threaten to deviate is great. Such rules may be wholly customary in origin: there may be no centrally organized system of punishments for breach of the rules; the social pressure may take only the form of a general diffused hostile or critical reaction which may stop short of physical sanctions. It may be limited to verbal manifestations of disapproval or of appeals to the individuals' respect for the rule violated; it may depend heavily on the operations of feelings of shame, remorse, and guilt. When the pressure is of this last-mentioned kind we may be inclined to classify the rules as part of the morality of the social group and the obligation under the rules as moral obligation. Conversely, when physical sanctions are prominent or usual among the forms of pressure, even though these are neither closely defined nor administered by officials but are left to the community at large, we shall be inclined to classify the rules as a primitive or rudimentary form of law. We may, of course, find both these types of serious social pressure behind what is, in an obvious sense, the same rule of conduct;

sometimes this may occur with no indication that one of them is peculiarly appropriate as primary and the other secondary, and then the question whether we are confronted with a rule of morality or rudimentary law may not be susceptible of an answer. But for the moment the possibility of drawing the line between law and morals need not detain us. What is important is that the insistence on importance or seriousness of social pressure behind the rules is the primary factor determining whether they are thought of as giving rise to obligations.[5]

According to Hart, rules imposing obligations—rules which it is obligatory that we obey—are of two kinds; moral rules, and legal rules. It is the form the social pressure behind a rule takes which determines whether a rule gives rise to legal, or moral, obligation. Ignoring the whole question of legal obligation (which I have examined in another place[6]), I wish to call attention to Hart's identification of *social pressure* as that which gives rise to the moral 'ought'. Now it is true that Hart speaks here of this social pressure perhaps "depend[ing] heavily on the operation of feelings of shame, remorse, and guilt". But it is also a tenet of Hart's legal and moral philosophy that "such feelings are neither necessary nor sufficient for the existence of 'binding' [i.e. obligatory] rules".[7] This suggests (what many writers explicitly avow) that these feelings are to be understood as 'internalizations' of the 'social norms' in question. They are 'internal' manifestations of society's pressure-for-conformity upon the individual. Indeed societies strive (so the story goes) to inculcate these psychological feelings (especially during childhood, when the human being is especially susceptible to suggestion and influence), precisely in order to assure the maximum constraint possible operating upon individuals to secure their observance of society's rules. These feelings, together with other forms of social pressure— "hostile or critical reaction", "verbal manifestations of disapproval"* —comprise, with the rules themselves, a system of *social control*. I.e., a system for controlling the behaviour of individuals so as to realize social peace, etc.

* Hart includes with these two: "appeals to the individuals' respect for the rule violated". But I do not see why this should be admitted as "social pressure" at all. Appeals to the individual's *respect for* the rule are surely appeals to his judgment as to the merits of the rule; and such appeals get what force they have from the individual's relation to that rule, and what it achieves in human life, not from society's "pressure" on him. (Unless of course Hart means by "respect" some sort of non-rational, socially inculcated "feeling".)

In other words, morality is a social device for the regulation and constraint of individuals in the interests of all. (Hobbes' *Leviathan* minus the sword.) One difficulty with this picture is that while the morality *of others* may constrain you (their decency making imprudent or inopportune some project you would otherwise initiate) *your morality* cannot. Your morality—your being claimed by moral considerations in the way we describe as moral concern—at best *restrains* you; where this means, your concern for, and sensitivity to, others' hurt triumphs over your desire for what would give harm. But even here what restrains you is not *society*. It is—your "better nature".

A second difficulty is that, on this picture of morality, an act's being morally obligatory does not depend upon the content of the act: it depends upon whether there is an insistent general demand for conformity backed by social pressure. If one is confronted by such a demand, and pressured to comply, one is *eo ipso* morally obligated to comply. There is no appealing to considerations *other* than the fact of social pressure, considerations such as what the specific act involves, what it works upon others, what it means for one's own life, for on this account morality is not conceived in terms of *considerations* at all. It is conceived in terms of social pressure and the demand that one comply.

V

My fourth comment concerns the attribution to morality of the description "a system". I take it that part of what forms the alleged system here is the body of moral 'rules' or 'principles' whose observance is to achieve the rationally optimal accommodation outlined in Nielsen's remarks. I have nowhere seen it made out that those principles, or, as I should prefer to say, considerations, which we acknowledge as *moral* in fact form such a system. I do not think it could be made out. Certainly there would seem to be considerable difficulties to overcome. Our regard for justice, mercy, and generosity is presumably to be captured by these principles or rules of action, and while these three are not necessarily incompatible (one can, in insisting upon the restoration of justice yet seek to be merciful to those who were unjust) still, justice, in so far as it calls for the equal treatment of cases, does tend to work against the exercise of mercy or generosity. Is there a covering rule which tells us when to be strictly just, and when to be merciful or generous, so as to make of our practice *a system* of actions? The provision of a rule of this kind, and of a rule which tells us in what cases to be honest and when to hide the truth, or when to be loyal and when, rightly, to repudiate (etc.), would seem to be one of the things which may reasonably be required of anything deserving of that description.

Lastly, the picture of morality as social control obviously puts a premium upon the achievement of cooperation and agreement. But when we are claimed by moral considerations, just as we are not seeking our 'rational self-interest', nor conforming under the weight of social pressure, neither are we aiming at agreement. Rather, what agreement we shall be able to reach will be limited by the preparedness of each of us to heed the moral considerations that bear on what we are considering. Agreement, accord, *is* important in social life. But more important is *what* we agree upon. Where moral considerations matter to the individuals involved in an issue, then sometimes, perhaps often, agreement may be reached. But even here, desire for agreement cannot determine what each should agree to. We think, perhaps, that if only moral considerations did matter to every member of our society we should then be able to live in peaceful agreement. But supposing (what is improbable) that this were true, we should not in each successive case agree *in order that* we should be in agreement. The hypothesis is that each of us will be truthful, just, and so on; and *as a result* we shall be able to reach, and live in, agreement with the rest. But we should, then, as now, *be* truthful, honest, and so on, *because of the importance of being so*; not because of the importance of achieving agreement.

VI

I wish in this concluding section to take up briefly the question of justice, and the difficulty it might be thought to make for my account. I shall seek to show that there is no difficulty. One consideration that may be urged is that while men who care for others will often be just to others, sometimes justice calls on one to act in a way which will favour someone for whom one cares little and injure someone for whom one cares a lot. What is to happen here, it may be asked. My answer is: If you care that justice obtains between persons you will act justly even at cost to the one you especially care about;

for if you *are* a lover of justice this will be because you care about persons, and about their situation and what happens to them, and not just about certain favoured ones. If, on the other hand, you care most for these special ones, and cannot bring yourself to do what it is just to do, well, then you are not a lover of justice, and what was one to expect?

Let us suppose that a man has for several months been obtaining money from people under false pretenses, all of it from elderly persons. It does not matter how he does it. (We shall suppose he gets knowledge of elderly persons who are retired, and he misrepresents himself to them as an agent of the assurance company which administers their pension. He tells them of an updating of the company retirement scheme which they are to be allowed to benefit from if they make a certain cash payment in contributions to the scheme. He gets money from a good many old people, most of whom are only able to raise the money at great hardship, but who do it on the assured greater security it will bring. He in fact shies away from those who do not depend only on their pension, as their relative independence bespeaks a likely sophistication about financial matters which would perhaps issue in suspicion.) This man, whom I shall call N, has a friend of whom he is very fond, and to whom he has often been generous. The friend is grateful for these things, and has himself an affection for the other. Eventually N is caught and the friend learns about what he has been doing. What is to be the problem here (as the situation is drawn so far)? Because the friend cares for N, is he supposed to be unable to appreciate that what N has done it is wrong to do? I do not see why this should be so. The friend loves and cares about N. But I am supposing that he also cares about what has been done to these people. He cares that they have been wronged and will suffer. Why is love of someone supposed to prevent an appreciation that something he or she has done is wrong to do? Perhaps what in fact will happen is that the friend will no longer love N as before. Perhaps he cannot love him that way now. Even deep personal love is not, or not necessarily, corrosive of moral understanding and concern. It is often sensitive to it.

The question of justice will perhaps be thought to arise only when the story goes this way. The friend (whom I shall call J) not only learns what N has done but is placed to do something about it. (N has not yet been caught on this account.) And J is drawn perhaps by his affection for N to do nothing, though he knows that if it were not his friend involved he would immediately act to stop and redress the wrong. He confronts N, and N begs him not to do anything that would take the money from him, now that he has enough once and for all to get on his feet and live securely. He promises not to do it again, but pleads to be let to keep the money. He cannot give it back, he says. It can make too great a difference for him. He is young. They are old. He deserves a chance. Now I have already argued that there is no reason why J cannot appreciate what justice requires. It is precisely because he is able to appreciate it that he is caught this way (and the supposed difficulty for my account is able even to be conceived of). The question here is: how is J to *do* what justice requires? If he does nothing these people have been callously wronged. Justice requires that he restore to them what his friend has taken, even if his friend suffers as a result. Now whether J acts to restore the money to these people or not is not a philosophical issue.

He either does or he doesn't. What is relevant for my inquiry is to see that considerations of justice can bring a man to act to protect those he does not know even against someone he loves. If justice matters to J it must matter to him because of what a just treatment of persons means in people's lives. These people have had taken from them what was theirs and what they have need of. Justice requires restoration. There is no counter appeal to mercy here, for mercy is here on the side of justice. Mercy too calls for restoration. If J acts as justice requires this will be an acting from concern for these people, out of a caring about what becomes of and is done to them—or it must seem an insane act that he does, to repudiate the one he loves for those he does not.

Once more, I do not seek to *oppose* love of persons *to* justice. I seek to explain our commitment to justice in terms of our caring about persons. If deep personal love were destructive of morality we could never explain how it is that our moral concern extends to those who even momentarily enter our life, not just those who are in it now, or how it is that we may condemn those close to us for their treatment of others whom we do not even know. We respond to the stranger as to one who matters. How is my *questioner* to explain this?

NOTES

[1] R. B. Perry, *Realms of Value* (Cambridge, Mass: Harvard University Press, 1954) Chapter 6.

[2] Op. cit., p. 308.

[3] Ibid., p. 308.

[4] Ibid., p. 308.

[5] H. L. A. Hart, *The Concept of Law* (Oxford University Press, 1961) p. 84.

[6] R. Beehler, "*The Concept of Law* and The Obligation to Obey", *American Journal of Jurisprudence,* Vol. 23, 1978.

[7] Op. cit., p. 56.

IX
God and Morals

Jesus Christ, without riches, and without any outward show of knowledge, is in His own order of holiness. He made no discoveries; He did not reign. But He was humble; patient; thrice holy to God; terrible to devils; without any sin. Oh, in what majesty, and with what wonderful splendour, He is come to the eyes of the heart, which perceive wisdom.

PASCAL

If my first and chief reason for worshipping God had to be a belief that a super-Frankenstein would blast me to hell if I did not, then I hope I should have the decency to tell this being, who is named Almighty God, to go ahead and blast.

RUSH RHEES

I

A tradition exists among more than one people which identifies morality with the commands of God. According to this tradition, if some acts are good and others evil, this is because God has commanded the first and forbidden the second. Thus if a man in choking life from his neighbour does what is wrong, this is because he does what God has forbidden. The force of this tradition is manifested in the widespread belief (and fear) that if there is no God, there is neither good nor evil. Anything goes.

A second tradition common to many nations tells not of God fashioning good and evil, but of His teaching men of their existence, and His commanding them to keep from evil and do only good.

Where God teaches men concerning good and evil it does not follow that morality originates in His will. God may reveal that some acts are to be done, because good, and others are to be avoided, because evil, and He may even require men, by threats, to avoid the one kind and to do the other, without good and evil being His creation. If God brings it about that there is in the world the possibility of virtue, of righteousness, He need do so on this second account only in the sense that He brings it about that mankind have knowledge of good and evil. It need not (on this view) be God who makes some actions virtuous and others evil. To this second view, therefore, an unbeliever may feel no need to object.

But where good and evil are thought to originate in the commands of God, difficulties arise. In the first place, acquaintance with the commands of God will be necessary for a moral appreciation of one's acts. Thus even if a people in fact deliberately keep from doing what (unknown to them) God has forbade, their keeping from these acts—whatever their reason for doing so—cannot be a case of virtuous behaviour. For they can have no moral understanding of the evil of these acts. Such a moral understanding can only be conferred by knowledge that these things are forbidden by God; since on this view their being evil consists in their being so forbade. Hence only a people to whom such a revelation has been made can be described as living a moral life.

Secondly, if choking life from one's neighbour is wrong *because forbidden by God*, the wrong lies not in what the victim suffers but in one's disobedience. One's wrongdoing consists not in what one does to this man but in what one does to God. One disobeys.

Thirdly, in respect of anything which God (to take one of the three possibilities) forbids, it is conceivable—i.e. logically possible—that He should have allowed, or even commanded it. What any man forbids he could conceivably not have forbidden. So too, whatever God forbids He conceivably could not have forbidden. This is a logical truth attaching to proscription. If then the wrong in choking life from one's neighbour proceeds from God's will toward this act, it is *logically* possible that the act should not in fact be morally wrong, but morally permitted—even morally commendatory. All that must change for this to be so is God's proscribing the act. If God were to cease to forbid it, then, though nothing else has changed—neither the humanity, innocence, or vulnerability of this man—the act is no longer evil. But are we able to accept that any act can become morally permissible simply by ceasing to be (or never being) forbidden by God? Can we accept, in other words, that whether an act is good or evil is a purely arbitrary matter, according to what God decides?

It may be replied that it is not conceivable that God should allow, or command, what He has in fact forbidden. The reason believers will give in explanation of this alleged inconceivability of God's allowing or commanding what He has proscribed is that God is good. Being good, He cannot sanction evil. It is *because* He is good that He has (for example) forbidden men to kill. And it is inconceivable that He should have allowed or commanded it.

It does not matter, for the purposes of this discussion, whether believers allege that God is necessarily good, or only as a matter of fact good. What is important is that on either view the reason why it is allegedly inconceivable that God should command what is evil, or forbid what is good, is not that good is whatever God commands. The reason is that good is what God is. But the incompatibility of this view with an account of good and evil as introduced by God's fiat is obvious. The goodness attributed by believers to God is a *moral* goodness. But on the view under discussion moral goodness consists simply in conformity to God's will. On this view then, God's moral goodness can consist only in observance of His own commandments—*whatever these are*. But the whole point of insisting upon God's goodness is to defend against the conceivability of God commanding what is evil. However where 'evil' just means 'in violation of God's commands' such a defense is both chimerical and quixotic. It is quixotic because there could never be the sort of possibility which is being envisaged. No act which God commands could on this view ever be evil because by definition whatever is commanded by God is good. (There is nothing to defend against.) It is chimerical because it first presupposes that good and evil are independent of what God commands—hence the insistence that, being good, God will never command what is evil—yet at the same time good and evil are identified with obedience or disobedience to God's commands; on which view the goodness of God, as the defense conceives of it, evaporates. (There is nothing to defend with.)

II

Anyone who has an informed acquaintance with Christian theology will know that this traditional belief about morality which I have been discussing, and which still exists among many communities today, is not straightforwardly identifiable with the Christian account of good and evil. The Christian moralists (or at least a significant proportion of them) have been concerned to resist any hint that God arbitrarily introduces the measure of good and evil. They have sought to represent 'the moral law' as rationally defensible. And some have even taught that it is discernible without revelation. Moreover all are committed to the view that the appreciation of God as good is a moral appreciation. Indeed it is the appreciation that God is good that is expected to claim the believer in the first place, and elicit from him a preparedness to submit his will to God's. This means that at least *God's* goodness (and mankind's recognition of His goodness) is inexplicable in terms of commands or obedience. True, this appreciation that God is good is expected to go along with a recognition that God is the Creator and Father, deserving of obedience from those who have received from Him life and grace. But these facts too are apprehended as moral considerations, giving rise to an obligation which is again inexplicable in terms of God's commands.

On the other hand, morality is repeatedly represented by Christian teaching as 'law'. And the requirement which this law makes—its being obligatory to obey it—is often represented as a matter of being obliged by a threat of hell. Throughout there is a tendency to represent sin as disobedience to God or to the moral law; and each of these is dangerously like an equation of wrong with disobedience *per se*. Moreover there often lurks in Christian apologetics a suggestion that the moral law is dependent in some way upon God's existence. Hence the doubt which may arise, for those who no longer believe, as to whether, if God does not exist, there is any longer good and evil. The vulgar moral theology which the Christian ministry can be found often to preach is the seed in our community of this popular anxiety to which I drew attention at the beginning. But it is a logical consequence of any doctrine which represents that wrong is non-observance of a law God has made for men.

This perennial belief, I have tried to suggest, has fatal difficulties. Yet at least one philosopher of the first order appears at one time to have favoured this view. Waismann tells us that Wittgenstein once remarked:

Schlick says [in *The Problems of Ethics*] that theological ethics contains two conceptions of the essence of the Good. According to the more superficial interpretation, the Good is good because God wills it; according to the deeper interpretation, God wills the Good because it is good.

I think that the first conception is the deeper one: Good is what God orders. For this cuts off the path to any and every explanation 'why' it is good, while the second conception is precisely the superficial, the rationalistic one, which proceeds as if what is good could still be given some foundation.

The first conception says clearly that the essence of the Good has nothing to do with the facts, and therefore cannot be explained by any proposition. If any proposition expresses just what I mean, it is: Good is what God Orders.[1]

"Good is what God orders" is the view just discussed. "God wills the good because it is good" implies that good and evil are independent of God's will. Wittgenstein says of this last view that it is superficial. The key to understanding this charge is his remark "The first conception says clearly that the essence of the Good has nothing to do with the facts, and therefore cannot be explained by any proposition."

At the time he made these comments Wittgenstein was still operating with the philosophical psychology of the *Tractatus Logico-Philosophicus* and the *Notebooks*. In these works Wittgenstein distinguishes between the human will as a 'phenomenon' in the world giving rise to action, and the human will as the subject of ethical attributes—as either good or evil.[2] He held that the first of these, the will as ordinarily conceived, is in actuality as much dependent for its 'movement' upon conditions outside the willing subject as is any other happening in the world. Wittgenstein at this time construed willing as a form of wanting, and held that just as my wants are not realized simply by dint of my wanting them, so my acts do not proceed from my will just by dint of my deliberately undertaking them. They happen, or not, *like other happenings in the world*, according to conditions outside the control of the 'agent' of these phenomenal changes: I do not stand in any special relation to those events which are said to proceed from my will. To find out what act I shall perform in the future, I must wait and see—as with any other event.

This conception by Wittgenstein of the will is expressed in a way particularly relevant to our inquiry in two remarks to which Peter Winch has drawn attention.

Even if all we wish for were to happen, still this would only be a favour granted by fate, so to speak: for there is no logical connection between the will and the world, which would guarantee it, and the supposed physical connection itself is not something that we could will.

"Willing too is merely an experience', one would like to say (the will too only 'idea'). It comes when it comes, and I cannot bring it about.[3]

The human will, which we all think of as the originator of actions, turns out to be an illusion. Wittgenstein is therefore forced by his conception of the will to conceive of the ethical as 'transcendental'. The human subject which is good or evil is not the will that acts or reacts in the world of flesh and bone but the will as the bearer of a certain *attitude* toward 'the world as a whole'. This transcendental will does not act in, or upon, the world.

I cannot bend the happenings of the world to my will:
I am completely powerless.
If the good or bad exercise of the will does alter the world, it can alter only the limits of the world, not the facts—not what can be expressed by means of language.[4]

It is this which explains why there can be no *explanation* why the Good is good. For such an explanation would of course have to be stated in language. But language, Wittgenstein then held, can state only facts, which it does by 'picturing' them. Ethical value, however, does not consist in any fact, or collection of facts. Consequently, to search through the world for some property or state of affairs which is to be identified (and asserted) as the basis of ethical judgments is doubly misguided. For the Good does not lie *in* the world; and about what does not lie in the world—what is not composed of facts—nothing can be said. Hence

If any proposition expresses just what I mean it is:
Good is what God orders.[5]

The difficulties which attach to this conception of ethics and the human will have been traced out with great patience and clarity by Peter Winch.[6] It will be sufficient for my purposes to remark that the central difficulty is the one which has already been seen to attach to any identification of good and evil with obedience or disobedience to

God's will. One might express this difficulty by saying that, on Wittgenstein's account, the goodness of an action has indeed nothing to do with the facts. Wittgenstein, by separating the ethical from the phenomenal will, separates ethics from human actions and their effects. Good and evil now literally transcend the sensual facts of the world, and attach to the world as 'a whole'. The moral quality of a life is not logically connected to its phenomenal manifestation in action and relationship, but is a function of a 'super'-phenomenal relation of the subject to something not *in* the world. This, I have argued, is just the difficulty which inheres in identifying (as Wittgenstein does) good with conformity to God's will.

III

I am tempted to leave the matter here. But there is, I believe, a further explanation of Wittgenstein's remarks concerning God and ethics which is worth examining. What suggests this explanation is the date of Wittgenstein's conversations with Schlick and Waismann (1929–1930), and his description of the conception "God wills the Good because it is good" as *rationalistic*. Wittgenstein explicitly remarks that he favours the conception "Good is what God orders" because it

cuts off the path to any and every explanation 'why' [the Good] is good, while the [first] conception proceeds as if what is good could still be given some foundation.[6]

Now the notion of 'giving the good some foundation' is in part the notion of finding what it is that the goodness of ethically good acts or states consists in. It is the notion of *explaining* their goodness; establishing *why* they are good. The implication, therefore, is that their goodness is something discernible, and so amenable to investigation (and articulation). It is some feature or property of good acts or states that is good. This can be discovered and stated. Against this suggestion Wittgenstein insists, as we have seen, that goodness is *not* some factual feature or property which these phenomena possess; and because it is not, it *cannot be said* in what ethical goodness consists.

There is however a further aspect to the notion of "giving the explanation why it is good", and it is this that I wish to suggest partly explains Wittgenstein's remarks against Schlick. At the time of these remarks it was still a doctrine of Wittgenstein's that whatever can be said is either true or false. Every proposition has a truth table. An important implication behind this doctrine is that every proposition which is syntactically well-formed (i.e. grammatically in order) can be understood by any speaker of the language. The whole notion of the truth table is of what is objectively—i.e. *inter-subjectively*—demonstrable. Propositions *convey* meaning from one speaker of the language to another; and what the proposition 'pictures', or 'expresses', can be publicly evaluated for its truth or falsehood. The paradigm of a proposition is the statement of fact, which empirical investigation—'science'—prove or disproves. Now in the lecture on ethics which I have already discussed briefly in Chapter three, and which Wittgenstein gave about the time of the conversations with Schlick and Waismann, he alludes to a conception of *ethics* as a science.* He declares:

. . . if I contemplate what Ethics really would have to be if there were such a science, this result seems to me quite obvious. It seems to me obvious that nothing we could ever think or say should be *the* thing. That we cannot write a scientific book, the subject matter of which could be intrinsically sublime and above all other subject matters. I can only describe my feeling by the metaphor, that, if a man could write a book on Ethics which really was a book on Ethics, this book would, with an explosion, destroy all the other books in the world. Our words used as we use them in science, are vessels capable only of containing and conveying meaning and sense, *natural* meaning and sense. Ethics, if it is anything, is supernatural and our words will only express facts; as a teacup will only hold a teacup full of water and if I were to pour out a gallon over it. I said that so far as facts and propositions are concerned there is only relative value and relative good, right, etc. And let me, before I go on, illustrate this by a rather obvious example. The right road is the road which leads to an arbitrarily predetermined end and it is quite clear to us all that there is no sense in talking about the right road apart from such a predetermined goal. Now let us see what we could possibly mean by the expression, "*the* absolutely right road." I think it would be the road which *everybody* on seeing it would, *with logical necessity*, have to go, or be ashamed for not going. And similarly the *absolute good*, if it is a describable state of affairs, would be one which everybody, independent of his tastes and inclinations, would *necessarily* bring about or feel guilty for not bringing

* At Cambridge, where Wittgenstein read the lecture, ethical studies were in fact then prosecuted under the title, the 'Moral Sciences'.

about. And I want to say that such a state of affairs is a chimera. No state of affairs has, in itself, what I would like to call the coercive power of an absolute judge.

I do not claim to understand all that Wittgenstein is seeking to express in this passage. I shall confine my attention to the idea of "*the* absolutely right road". Wittgenstein says that this is "the road which *everybody* on seeing it would, *with logical necessity*, have to go". All ordinary roads are right to go along, or not, according to the destination of the traveller. Whether a road is 'the right road' for you is a contingent matter. It depends on where you are headed, and it depends on where the road in fact goes (or whether it goes anywhere; whether it continues beyond that hill, in the same direction, or veers back sharply upon itself, or peters out into mud and stones, and so on). The 'absolutely right road', on the other hand, differs from ordinary roads in being the road which everybody, on seeing it, would *with logical necessity* have to go along. (It also differs from other roads in being the *ethically right* road—the road everybody would be *ashamed* for not going along. But this aspect I wish for the moment to ignore).

I think it is clear that Wittgenstein is trying to get his listeners to think of the drawing of a conclusion from premises. In reasoning, the right conclusion to draw—the conclusion you must, with logical necessity, accept—is the conclusion which *follows* from the premises according to the rules of semantic construction, syntactic formation, and logical connection. All that is required for the conclusion is there 'in the language'. And everybody must acknowledge the conclusion as that which the premises warrant, or be 'logically shamed' for not doing so. The conclusion *requires acknowledgement*, being the conclusion warranted by the premises. As Achilles declared to the Tortoise: ". . . Logic . . . take[s] you by the throat and force[s] you to [acknowledge] it!"[6] But the notion of a *road* which everybody must, on seeing it, acknowledge is the right road for them is a chimera.

No state of affairs has in itself . . . the coercive power of an absolute judge.

That is, no road, of itself, can require its acknowledgement as the right road for you, or for me. This is because the logic of taking roads is not the logic of drawing a conclusion. Whatever you wish for, or need, or dread in respect of a conclusion, if it is the logically warranted conclusion it will be the right conclusion—for you, and for everybody. But until you desire, or need, to get somewhere, no road can be the right road for you.

In the same way with the notion of "the absolute good": this is a chimera because the ethical too involves an attitude toward things. It has to do with "tastes and inclinations". Before a state of affairs can command my attention, before it can claim me as what I *have* to strive to realize, or *must* not bring about, I must be related to that state of affairs in a certain way. No state of affairs IN ITSELF—i.e. apart from my relation to it—can have the coercive power of an absolute judge: can confront me as what I *inescapably* must keep from, or do.

Thus the idea of a book containing 'the science' of ethics is confused. It involves a picture of ethical good as a state of affairs which the book will describe. Everyone who reads the book will be forced to admit to the absolute goodness of the ethically best state of affairs. They will be forced *by what is in the book* to acknowledge this, and by that only. Independently of their tastes and inclinations, simply by dint of the (inescapable) logical force of the argument, they will feel guilt at not striving to bring that state of affairs about. *They will be convinced by the book that this is how they ought to live.* (It is in this sense that this ethical book will destroy, as with an explosion, all other books. It will do so by destroying all corrupt and wayward tastes, inclinations, purposes, and goals. It will destroy them by replacing them with: being claimed by good.)

Wittgenstein's reply to this picture is that even if there were one absolute good, and it were possible to describe it (both of which ideas are mistaken), no series of remarks could have the power to bring it about, of itself, that you appreciate that absolute value. This is because the appreciation is not reducible to intellectual comprehension. To appreciate that it has that absolute value just is: to value that which is being represented to you. But this valuation is not something the utterance or representation can 'logically coerce' you to make. Whether you make that valuation or not, whether you can receive what is represented or uttered in the appropriate way, depends on what matters, and can matter, to you. It depends on your "tastes and inclinations". Hence those who ask for an explanation why the good is good either ask for what they do not need, or for what cannot be given them. If they already see that it is good, they do not need convincing; if they do not see it, they cannot be convinced.

If I need [only] a theory in order to explain to another the essence of the ethical, the ethical would have no value at all.

A theory gives me nothing.[6]

This is why the conception "Good is what God orders" is preferable to the conception "God wills the good because it is good". It is preferable (Wittgenstein feels) because it comes nearer to capturing not only the inexpressibility, but—if one may so express it—the *affectivity*, of the ethical.

But it is, I believe, clear that this second reason which inclines Wittgenstein to the formula "Good is what God orders" does not upset any I have given for opposing the view that there is a necessary dependence of morality upon God. It does not, because Wittgenstein's reason has no necessary connection to God at all. The argument he gives provides just as effective reason for preferring, say, the formula "Evil is: what men condemn", to the formula "Men condemn evil because it is evil".

IV

There is one last subject touching the relation of religion to morality on which I should like to comment. This concerns a seeming confirmation of the religious picture of good and evil which many may think is provided by our very language.

When people who are religious believers say that some act is wrong many of them do mean that it is forbidden by God. This alleged fact, that it is forbidden, is independent of what any human being thinks or cares concerning the act or its effects. Whatever any man or woman thinks or feels about the act, it is wrong, because forbidden by God. (If God himself were not actually to care whether such acts are done, it would still be wrong to act this way, provided only that He has in fact—senselessly—forbidden mankind to act in this way.) Now it may be thought that our ways of speaking confirm this non-human dependence of morality upon God. For expressions such as "the wrong he committed", "the person wronged", "the evil in her heart", may seem to imply an objective quality in the act or attitude which transcends any particular person's viewpoint. In fact, however, the explanation of this idiom does not require any implicit appeal to God. Part of the explanation obviously has to do with the objective features of the acts or attitudes themselves: what is, or was, done; what desires, or intentions, are harboured. The rest has to do with the origin of those utterances. We do, as I have said, frequently speak of 'the wrong' someone has done, or intends to do, as though the wrong were independent of our or anyone's appreciation of it as wrong. We do this naturally, *because on these occasions our attention to what is or would be done goes on within a moral examination of the matter.* We are agreed that what was done, or would be done, is wrong, and we are discussing (say) what to do as a result of it. And so we speak of 'the wrong done'—and try perhaps to show the person in question where the wrong lay in what he did. But (to take just this last case) what we are doing here is trying to get the person to *appreciate* what he did in a certain way. We are trying to get him to appreciate his act *as* something he ought not to do. But this, I have argued, must always involve some affective response on his part to what he has brought about. If such a response is at no point forthcoming the person will at best come to appreciate that others think it important, for some reason, not to do what he has done. (Included among these others, he may learn, is He who is called "Almighty God".)

NOTES

[1] "Notes on Talks with Wittgenstein", *Philosophical Review*, Vol. LXXIV, 1965, p. 15.

[2] See Peter Winch, "Wittgenstein's Treatment of the Will", *Ratio*, Vol. X, 1968. Reprinted in Peter Winch, *Ethics and Action* (London: Routledge & Kegan Paul, 1972) Chapter 6.

[3] *Tractatus*, 6.374. *Investigations*, I, s. 611.

[4] *Notebooks*, pp. 73, 74.

[5] Op. cit.

[6] "Notes on Talks with Wittgenstein", p. 15.

[7] "A Lecture on Ethics", p. 7.

[8] Lewis Carroll, "What the Tortoise said to Achilles", *Mind*, 1885.

[9] "Notes on Talks with Wittgenstein", p. 16.

X

Other than Humankind

[C]onfining myself to the first and most simple operations of the
human soul, I think I can distinguish in it two principles prior to
reason; one of them interests us deeply in our own preservation and
welfare, the other inspires us with a natural aversion to seeing any
other being, but especially any being like ourselves, suffer or perish. It
is from the concurrence and the combination our mind is capable of
forming between these two principles, without there being the least
necessity for adding to them that of sociability, that, in my opinion,
flow all the rules of natural right; rules, which reason is afterwards
obliged to reestablish upon other foundations, when by its successive
developments, it has at last stifled nature itself.

By proceeding in this manner, we shall not be obliged to make a man
a philosopher before he is a man. . . . By this means too we may put
an end to the ancient disputes concerning the participation of other
animals in the law of nature; for it is plain that, as they want both
reason and free will, they cannot be acquainted with that law; however, as they partake in some measure of our nature in virtue of that
sensibility with which they are endowed, we may well imagine they
ought likewise to partake of the benefit of the natural law, and that
man owes them a certain kind of duty. In fact, it seems that, if I am
obliged not to injure any being like myself, it is not so much because he is a reasonable being, as because he is a sensible being; and
this quality, by being common to men and beasts, ought to exempt
the latter from any unnecessary injuries the former might be able
to do them.

ROUSSEAU

There are two issues touched upon by Rousseau in these remarks. I
wish, in this final chapter, briefly to consider both of them. I shall
take up the second of the two first.

I

Throughout this essay I have represented morality as connected to what is wrought in *human* life by certain ways of acting, and to our caring about other *persons*. This has been deliberate. One cannot say everything at once, and it seemed necessary first to give an account of what every reader would unequivocally consider the domain of morals—the relations of human beings one to another. But I must now confront the question whether morality extends to living things other than the human.

The issue was in fact raised in the second chapter, in a long passage quoted from Warnock:

... Moral *agents*, we have said, are rational beings; if we now say that the beneficiaries, so to speak, of moral principles are, unrestrictedly, persons, should we take 'person' here to mean 'rational being'? There is plain reason, I believe, to hold that we should not so take it—to hold, indeed, that 'person' is itself too restrictive a term here. Notice, first, that we do not in fact place this limitation upon the class of beneficiaries of moral principle. We do not regard infants and imbeciles as moral agents, as liable to judgement for their conduct on moral principles, since we take them not to possess those rational capacities which are a condition of being capable of moral thought and decision; but we do not for that reason regard them as morally insignificant, as having, that is, no moral claims upon rational beings. Why is this? Is it that they are in some sense, though not actual, yet potential rational beings, members, so to speak of a potentially rational species? I do not think so. Infants no doubt could be said to be potentially rational; but is it for that reason that they are not to be, say, physically maltreated? Not all imbeciles, I dare say, *are* potentially rational; but does it follow that, if they are reasonably judged to be incurable, they are then reasonably to be taken to have no moral claims? No: the basis of moral claims seems to me to be quite different. We may put it thus: just as liability to be judged as a moral agent follows from one's general capability of alleviating, by moral action, the ills of the predicament, and is for that reason confined to rational beings, so the condition of being a proper 'beneficiary' of moral action is the capability of *suffering* the ills of the predicament—and for that reason is *not* confined to rational beings, nor even to potential members of that class.[1]

Warnock reproduces here the position taken by Rousseau (and by others), but which is most widely identified with Bentham, who in *The Principles of Morals and Legislation* declared:

The day may come when the rest of the animal creation may acquire those rights which never could have been withholden from them but by the hand of tyranny. The French have already discovered that the blackness of the skin is no reason why a human being should be abandoned without redress to the caprice of a tormentor. It may one day come to be recognized that the number of the legs, the villosity of the skin, or the termination of the *os sacrum*, are reasons equally insufficient for abandoning a sensitive being to the same fate. What else is it that should trace the insuperable line? Is it the faculty of reason, or perhaps the faculty of discourse? But a full-grown horse or dog is beyond comparison a more rational, as well as a more conversable animal, than an infant of a day, or a week, or even a month, old. But suppose they were otherwise, what would it avail? The question is not, Can they *reason*? nor Can they *talk*? but, Can they *suffer*?[2]

There are two questions at issue here. The first is whether animals are entitled to moral consideration; or as I should prefer to put it, can one do wrong by acting in certain ways toward creatures who are not human beings? The second question is whether animals are entitled to the same—i.e. to *equal*—consideration with human beings; or (again) as I should prefer to put it, is it morally permissible to do things to other animals which it would not be morally permissible to do to human animals? Only the first of these two questions properly falls within the province of my inquiry, but I shall exceed my brief far enough to say something (though not very much) about the other. That the second is a question that requires to be considered is not difficult to show. Many—perhaps most—human beings do account it morally wrong to treat animals viciously or to kill them with unnecessary cruelty. Yet equally as many—perhaps most of them *the same* people—do not consider it morally wrong to kill animals for food; though they would condemn the gratuitous infliction of suffering in the course of killing them. Still, the man who kills *even cruelly* in the slaughterhouse is regarded differently from the mercenary who kills, though with more dispatch, in the villages or cities. Is this a failure of imagination on our part? Or *is* wanton cruelty to other animals less condemnable than even the painless homicide of human beings? (The same question arises in a slightly different way in Rachels' question, in the passage quoted in chapter five: "If a man were truly selfish, why should it bother his conscience that others [i.e. other persons] suffer—*much less pigs*?" (My emphasis.))

II

To give my remarks a focus, and to overcome the most insistently present obstacle in our culture to any progress in this matter—ignorance of animal life—I shall begin by reporting at length an encounter between three animals, one of them a human being.

The word had come through to get them alive—birds, reptiles, anything. A zoo somewhere abroad needed restocking. It was one of those reciprocal matters in which science involves itself. Maybe our museum needed a stray ostrich egg and this was the payoff. Anyhow, my job was to help capture some birds and that was why I was there before the trucks.

. . .

I pushed the door open, the hinges squeaking only a little. A bird or two stirred—I could hear them—but nothing flew and there was a faint starlight through the holes in the roof. I padded across the floor, got the ladder up and the light ready, and slithered up the ladder till my head and arms were over the shelf. Everything was dark as pitch except for the starlight at the little place back of the shelf near the eaves. With the light to blind them, they'd never make it. I had them. I reached my arm carefully over in order to be ready to seize whatever was there and I put the flash on the edge of the shelf where it would stand by itself when I turned it on. That way I'd be able to use both hands.

. . .

I snapped on the flash and sure enough there was a great beating and feathers flying, but instead of my having them, they, or rather he, had me. He had my hand, that is, and for a small hawk not much bigger than my fist he was doing all right. I heard him give one short metallic cry when the light went on and my hand descended on the bird beside him; after that he was busy with his claws and his beak was sunk in my thumb. In the struggle I knocked the lamp over on the shelf, and his mate got her sight back and whisked neatly through the hole in the roof and off among the stars outside. It all happened in fifteen seconds and you might think I would have fallen down the ladder, but no, I had a professional assassin's reputation to keep up, and the bird, of course, made the mistake of thinking the hand was the enemy and not the eyes behind it. He chewed my thumb up pretty effectively and lacerated my hand with his claws, but in the end I got him, having two hands to work with. He was a sparrow hawk and a fine young male in the prime of life. I was sorry not to catch the pair of them, but as I dripped blood and folded his wings carefully, holding him by the back so that he couldn't strike again, I had to admit the two of them might have been more than I could have handled under the circumstances. The little fellow had saved his mate by diverting me, and that was that. He was born to it, and made no outcry now, resting in my hand hopelessly, but peering toward me in the shadows behind the lamp with a fierce, almost indifferent glance. He neither gave nor expected mercy and something out of the high air passed from him to me, stirring a faint embarrassment.

. . .

In the morning, with the change that comes on suddenly in that high country, the mist that had hovered below us in the valley was gone. The sky was a deep blue, and one could see for miles over the high outcroppings of stone. I was up early and brought the box in which the little hawk was imprisoned out onto the grass where I was building a cage. A wind as cool as a mountain spring ran over the grass and stirred my hair. It was a fine day to be alive. I looked up and all around and at the hole in the cabin roof out of which the little hawk had fled. There was no sign of her anywhere that I could see.

. . .

I got him right out in my hand with his wings folded properly and I was careful not to startle him. He lay limp in my grasp and I could feel his heart pound under the feathers but he only looked beyond me and up. I saw him look that last look away beyond me into a sky so full of light that I could not follow his gaze. The little breeze flowed over me again, and nearby a mountain aspen shook all its tiny leaves. I suppose I must have had an idea then of what I was going to do, but I never let it come up into consciousness. I just reached over and laid the hawk on the grass. He lay there a long minute without hope, unmoving, his eyes still fixed on that blue vault above him. It must have been that he was already so far away in heart that he never felt the release from my hand. He never even stood. He just lay with his breast against the grass. In the next second after that long minute he was gone. Like a flicker of light, he had vanished with my eyes full on him, but without actually seeing even a premonitory wing beat. He was gone straight into that towering emptiness of light and crystal that my eyes could scarcely bear to penetrate. For another long moment there was silence. I could not see him. The light was too intense. Then from far up somewhere a cry came ringing down. I was young then and had seen little of the world, but when I heard that cry my heart turned over. It was not the cry of the hawk I had captured; for, by shifting my position against the sun, I was now seeing further up. Straight out of the sun's eye, where she must have been soaring restlessly above us for untold hours, hurtled his mate. And from far up, ringing from peak to peak of the summits over us, came a cry of such unutterable and ecstatic joy that it sounds down across the years and tingles among the cups on my quiet breakfast table. I saw them both now. He was rising fast to meet her. They met in a great soaring gyre that turned to a whirling circle and a dance of wings. Once more, just once, their two voices, joined in a harsh wild medley of question and response, struck and echoed against the pinnacles of the valley. Then they were gone forever somewhere into those upper regions beyond the eyes of men.[4]

In this record I wish to fasten upon two things: the kind of uses and treatment of animals registered; and what it is that leads this man (in this instance at least) to repudiate them. I am searching for considerations that will enable us to judge whether this transaction between men and birds has *moral* parameters.

The explicitly registered usage of animals is confinement for human amusement and instruction. "A zoo somewhere abroad needed restocking." The reference to science calls up as well the practice of experimentation on animals; and from here it is a short step by association to their use for the testing of products to assure their non-toxicity for humans.* Finally, it is *conceivable* that the tea-cups on the breakfast table lie side by side with a plate that carries the remains of the smoked and treated carcass of a pig. ("Inconsistencies", answered Imlac, "cannot both be right, but imputed to man they may both be true."[4]) I shall keep, for purposes of brevity, to the matter of confinement.

Hobbes observed more than three centuries ago that the words 'liberty' or 'freedom'

> may be applyed no lesse to Irrationall . . . creatures, than to Rationall. For whatsoever is so tyed, or environed, as it cannot move, but within a certain space, we say it hath not liberty to go further. And so of all living creatures, whilest they are imprisoned, or restrained, with walls, or chayns; [we] say they are not at Liberty, to move in such manner, as without those externall impediments they would.[5]

The physical confinement of any living creature deprives that creature of freedom. Yet concern about freedom, or liberty, has almost always been concern about human freedom, human liberty. Indeed the word 'freedom' is used pre-eminently to refer to a condition of persons considered in respect of their treatment *by other persons*. A man in the grip of a dragon, or entangled by roots, may be able or not to tear free; but when we speak of his freedom, or lack of freedom, we should (unless more is said) be understood to refer to his relation to other men. Thought of freedom enters ordinarily only into our

---

* Which test ordinarily involves the (forced) ingestion of the substance being tested until it is determined at what volume or concentration fifty percent of the test animals *die*.

appreciation of the situation of human beings, in relation to others of their kind. This is implied in the frequently repeated remark that freedom is a political concept. Other animals do not stand in political relations to human kind. They are not included within the *polis*.

Nevertheless, while this last is something we have every reason to believe will not change, the indifference of most human beings to the freedom of beasts is something which must require *justification*. It requires it precisely because, as Warnock points out, we do not consider political or social capacity a requisite for 'moral citizenship' on the part of infants, imbeciles, and people in coma. The involuntary confinement of imbeciles for the delectation of the curious would by every morally sensitive person be not only morally condemned, but apprehended with rage and disgust. But a hawk, as Bentham might put it, is a far more capable and conversable living creature than a human imbecile, and—dare we admit—by *some people* found more easily to be loved.

Now it is, I wish to claim, precisely love which moves the man in the encounter which is our focus to repudiate *the use* of these birds for human purposes, and to return them to their natural *entitlement*. (Where the word 'entitlement' is an expression of just that regard toward the birds which I referred to, and which wrings from one the 'recognition': they ought to be free.) Is this *moral* regard? Is this a 'moral' ought? I want to say it is. And I shall offer two reasons in support of doing so.

The first reason is that if these, and all other animals similarly treated, were to be confined for no purpose—simply confined, and fed automatically by machines, but never viewed or attended to—I believe almost everyone would acknowledge that *this would* be morally condemnable. But secondly, what this shows is that there must be some consideration which justifies—which *morally entitles*—us to confine animals. And of course the answer people will give in respect of zoos is: human amusement and instruction. In the case of the first, I want to claim that no 'quantity' or intensity of human amusement could be sufficient reason to inflict the suffering and deprivation that confinement involves. In respect of the second, the amount of instruction is out of all proportion to the amount of misery, and can be got far more effectively in other, non-depriving, ways.

I hope then to have shown that in one instance at least the claims of morality extend to (and even call for change in) our relations to

non-human life. The further application of this result to other forms
of intercourse with non-human animals I leave to the reader.[6]

III

It remains to say something about the second issue touched upon in
the remarks by Rousseau with which I started; and this will return
me as well to what I said I would try briefly to comment on: whether
we are morally required to give animals *equal* consideration with
humans (rather than *some* consideration, but not the extent of consideration we give the interest and claims of humans).

I will not answer this question here. But I shall try to indicate the
most important thing that will affect our answer. That important
thing (I have already hinted at it) is the character and extent of our
acquaintance-ship with animals; or to borrow Rousseau's language,
the degree of our mutual 'sociability'.

Rousseau sometimes speaks (and the passage I have reproduced is
one such instance) as though compassion and sympathy were innate
responses, in the sense that they are in no way sensitive to, and do not
require for their awakening, social relations with others. (I say
'sometimes speaks', since Rousseau at other moments shows the
profoundest recognition that this is so.) We now know that the
capacity to love *is* deeply sensitive to, perhaps even dependent upon,
a certain kind of social interrelationship with others. 'As our social
life goes, so will our moral sensitivity and understanding', is a
reasonable compression of this fact. (This, if it is a fact, is a psychological dependence, and not to be confused with the philosophical
thesis that our moral judgments are *logically* dependent upon 'social
agreement'.)

But if our moral appreciation of human relationships is sensitive to
our interaction with and knowledge of one another, why should our
moral appreciation of human/non-human relationships not be similarly sensitive? The blighting effect of ignorance on human intercourse is patently obvious to us. But may ignorance not explain a
good deal of the diffidence of most human beings toward other
animals? Contributions to this ignorance are everywhere, and
many-layered. How many people alighting from their automobiles
on the car deck of every British Columbia Ferry, and addressed by
signs which read "NO ANIMALS ABOVE DECK", appreciate

that they ought *together with the crew*, to remain by their vehicles? The tracing out of these connections I must leave to others. But the singular responsibility we have *to attempt* this effort of comprehension, and the nature of what is every moment at stake, confront us in these lines by Blake.

To mercy, pity, peace, and love
All pray in their distress,
And to these virtues of delight,
Return their thankfulness.

For Mercy has a human heart,
Pity a human face;
And Love, the human form divine;
And Peace the human dress.

NOTES

[1] Warnock, *The Object of Morality*, pp. 150–1.

[2] Jeremy Bentham, *The Principles of Morals and Legislation*, Chapter VII, Section IV, Note 1.

[3] Rachels, Op. cit., p. 120.

[4] Loren Eiseley, *The Immense Journey* (New York: Vintage Books, 1959) pp. 186, 188, 188–9, 190–2.

[5] *Leviathan*, Chapter XXI.

[6] For help, and a beginning, here, see S. & R. Godlovitch and J. Harris (eds.), *Animals, Men and Morals* (New York: Grove Press, 1971); Peter Singer, *Animal Liberation* (New York Review and Random House; 1975); and T. Regan and P. Singer (eds.), *Animal Rights and Human Obligation* (Englewood Cliffs: Prentice-Hall, 1976).